Graphic Designer's Guide to

Faster, Better, Easier

Design & Production

About the Author

After graduating from the University of Cincinnati with a degree in Fine Arts, Poppy Evans got her first taste of publishing by functioning as a one-woman production staff—writing, editing and laying out a company newsletter. She has worked as a graphic designer and as a magazine art director for *Screen Printing* and the *American Music Teacher*, the latter a national association magazine that won many awards under her direction for its redesign and its artfully conceived covers.

She returned to writing and editing in 1989 as managing editor of *HOW* magazine. Since leaving *HOW*, she has written many articles that have appeared in graphic arts-related magazines, including *HOW*, *Step-By-Step*, *Publish*, *Single Image* and *Confetti*.

Graphic Designer's Guide to

Faster, Better, Easier

Design & Production

Poppy Evans

NORTH
LIGHT
BOOKS

Cincinnati, Ohio

Disclaimer. Contact information for the companies and organizations included in this book was correct at the time the book went to the printer. Because change occurs quickly and frequently, especially in the computer products industry, some information may have changed subsequent to the book's production. The information in this book is presented in good faith but no warranty is given nor results guaranteed. Since we have no control over physical conditions surrounding the application of techniques and information herein contained, the publisher and author disclaim any liability for results.

Printed and bound in the United States of America.

97   96   95   94   93   5   4   3   2   1

Library of Congress Cataloging-in-Publication Data

Evans, Poppy.
    Graphic designer's guide to faster, better, easier design and production / by Poppy Evans.
        p.   cm.
    Includes index.
    ISBN 0-89134-509-4
    1. Printing, Practical—United States—Handbooks, manuals, etc. 2. Graphic arts—United States—Handbooks, manuals, etc. I. Title.
Z244. E94   1993
686.2'252—dc20   93-21476
                          CIP

Edited by Mary Cropper and Diana Martin
Designed by Brian Roeth
Cover illustration by Brian Roeth

METRIC CONVERSION CHART

TO CONVERT	TO	MULTIPLY BY
Inches	Centimeters	2.54
Centimeters	Inches	0.4
Feet	Centimeters	30.5
Centimeters	Feet	0.03
Yards	Meters	0.9
Meters	Yards	1.1
Sq. Inches	Sq. Centimeters	6.45
Sq. Centimeters	Sq. Inches	0.16
Sq. Feet	Sq. Meters	0.09
Sq. Meters	Sq. Feet	10.8
Sq. Yards	Sq. Meters	0.8
Sq. Meters	Sq. Yards	1.2
Pounds	Kilograms	0.45
Kilograms	Pounds	2.2
Ounces	Grams	28.4
Grams	Ounces	0.04

Dedication

This book is dedicated to my loving parents, Bill and Letha Evans, who have consistently encouraged and supported me in all of my endeavors.

Acknowledgments

Compiling material for a book of this size and putting it into a cohesive, well-organized format requires the help of many individuals. I would first of all like to thank Mary Cropper, my editor at North Light, for proposing a format for this book that greatly aided its organization and my ability to follow through with the necessary information.

I would also like to thank the many designers and graphic arts experts who are quoted throughout this book. In addition to their written contributions, many of them offered ideas that appear in the body of this book, or referred me to other sources of expertise.

The following individuals and organizations also helped in supplying information and visuals: Jim Lenhoff of the Johnston Paper Co., *Screen Printing* magazine, *Signs of the Times* magazine, Polly Pattison, author of *90 Ways to Save Money on Newsletters*, David Doty of *The Page* newsletter, Sam Marshall, Jeff Gray of Print Craft, Inc., Steve Lipson of Lipson Alport & Glass, Continental Plastic Containers, Roger Whitehouse of Whitehouse & Company, Ron Swaboda of Berman Printing, Inc., and Brent Logan of ABC Printing, Inc.

Table of Contents

Introduction

Being a graphic designer can be a wonderful, fun, creative experience. And then there are those days when it seems every client wants a project yesterday and you don't have time to think, much less remember whether you've done the work right. It's even harder when you're a freelancer, because there's no one you can run to and ask if you can't remember a piece of information or an important fact.

Graphic Designer's Guide to Faster, Better, Easier Design and Production gives you quick access to all that often-needed but hard-to-remember information. Every aspect of producing a design is covered. You'll find checklists of steps for designing every kind of printed piece to help you through a new job or that three o'clock in the morning blur when you can't remember your name, much less what you have left to do. You'll find what, where and when details, such as the sizes of stock envelopes available, tips for working with industrial papers, and how to choose the right printing process and special printing effects for your piece.

To make all this information even faster and easier to find, it's organized into a series of lists and checklists. In addition to the index, there's an index of lists by title to help you find the information you need when you need it. To help you find your way around the book, the running heads tell you the first and last list titles on a spread. Cross-references direct you to more in-depth information on a topic of interest. For example, you'll find a list of special techniques that can add punch to your letterhead designs in the chapter on letterhead design, with a cross-reference to detailed explanations of those techniques in the production chapter.

Because design should be fun, the technical information has been broken up with idea starters for different types of design and a collection of fascinating ideas, insights and advice from top designers.

Margo Chase tells how she approaches logo design, Aubrey Balkind offers advice on dealing with clients, and Joe Duffy discusses package design.

I hope you'll learn as much from using this book as I did from writing it. It's been a wonderful refresher course on design and production.

Section 1

The Design Side

Chapter 1

Getting Started

How to Talk to Clients

"Designers need to talk to clients in business terms, then bring a visual solution to it. The solution should be in line with the strategic plan, and that is how it should be communicated.

"A lot of designers will go into a project thinking that the client is interested in design. But talking to a client about design is a dangerous thing to do. They're really interested in communicating their message."

Aubrey Balkind *is the CEO of New York City-based Frankfurt Gips Balkind, the largest independent U.S.-based design agency.*

What Does the Client Want?

Questions to Ask a Client Before Starting Any Project

- (For a new client) Tell me about your business.

- What is the project?

- What is the purpose of the project?

- Who is the audience for this project?

- Who are your major competitors?

- What role does this project play in your firm's overall business strategy?

- What specifications (size, colors, artwork, quantity) do you have in mind?

- Is there a feeling, look or personality you would like this project to have?

- Do you have photographs, artwork or other visuals for me to use?

- Will you provide the copy?

- (If client provides copy) Will the copy be on disk? What kind of computer system and software do you use?

- (If you have to input copy) Will you proof all the copy?

- What is your budget?

- When must the project be completed?

- Do you have any preferred vendors or suppliers of outside services?

- Would you prefer to be billed directly for the printing or other outside services? Or would you prefer to have me handle this for you and charge my usual markup for that service?

Ask Yourself the Following Questions About Each Project

- What is the purpose of this project?

- What is the client's competition doing? How well is it working?

- How can I improve on the result the client got in the past?

- How can I best appeal to the target audience for this project?

- Do I have all the information I need from the client to get started?

- Do I have any other ongoing projects with schedules that will or might conflict with this project's?

- Will I need to hire someone to help complete this project on schedule?

- Will I need to hire a copywriter, photographer or illustrator?

- Will the project budget let me commission photos or artwork?

- What supplies or equipment will I need to purchase that I may not already have on hand?

What Needs to Be Done?

What Will I Need to Do?

Although each project is different, every one goes through similar stages. It's helpful to make a list of what you'll need to do before you start — and to review that list to make sure you haven't forgotten anything. In a typical project you would:

- ❑ Meet with your client.

- ❑ Brainstorm, coming up with ideas.

- ❑ Develop a concept.

- ❑ Rough out thumbnail sketches to work out ideas.

- ❑ Prepare artwork to show the concept to your client.

- ❑ Get client approval of the concept.

- ❑ Develop a schedule for completing the piece.

- ❑ Develop a cost estimate for the piece.

- ❑ Select copywriter, photographer, illustrator and/or typesetter, if needed, and get quotes and schedule confirmations.

- ❑ Send out printing bids.

- ❑ Get approval of prices and schedule.

- ❑ Do rough layouts.

- ❑ Prepare follow-up renderings by traditional or electronic means.

- ❑ Produce comps: This can include in-house typesetting; mocking up calligraphy or hand-lettered type; getting C-prints or computer proofs of artwork and layouts; ordering stats; preparing mock-ups of letterhead or three-dimensional mock-ups of packaging; getting paper dummy made.

❏ Get client approval of comps.

❏ Make any needed revisions.

❏ Set type in-house; create calligraphy or hand-lettered type; scan or stat and create special type. Or get type from typesetter; commission calligraphy or hand-lettering. This stage may include rekeyboarding or disk translating, editing and copyfitting.

❏ Proofread.

❏ Make your revisions and corrections.

❏ Make client revisions and corrections.

❏ Create own illustrations: Diagrams, charts, graphs produced with pen and ink or on the computer. Or choose and modify clip art; scan in art.

❏ Commission/Art direct illustrations or order stock illustrations; commission/art direct photographs or order from stock.

❏ Produce mechanicals: This may include finalizing layouts on the computer and sending for final output from service bureau; pasting up galleys, illustrations, stats; incorporating scans; making acetate and tissue overlays; speccing instructions on mechanicals.

❏ Forward mechanicals to your client for approval.

❏ Make necessary client-requested revisions.

❏ Send out for color separations and/or get revised output from service bureau.

❏ Deliver mechanicals to printer.

❏ Review and approve/change proofs.

❏ Obtain client approval of proofs.

❏ Press approval.

What Will the Client Do?

The role your client plays in a specific project depends on the project, what she wants to do, and what information or material you need to do your design. When and what the client reviews for approval also varies. (Remember that you are entitled to receive the materials you need and to have your design reviewed and approved in a timely manner.) The following are typical materials supplied or activities performed by clients:

- Copy on disk or as manuscript.

- Photographs or illustrations.

- Market research.

- Camera-ready art of existing corporate logo(s).

- Existing promotional and marketing pieces.

- Mailing labels or mailing list(s) on disk to be used in creating mailing labels.

- Review and approve concept.

- Proofread copy that you have rekeyboarded.

- Proofread typeset copy.

- Review and approve rough layouts.

- Review and approve mechanicals.

- Review and approve proofs.

- Pay for printing and outside services such as copywriting (some clients prefer to be billed directly for such costs, and some designers feel that it's better for their cash flow if the client is billed directly).

What Will the Project Cost?

Time Costs

Your time is worth money. Begin any cost estimate for a job by calculating the cost of your time.

1. Divide project into stages and activities; for example, "client meetings," "layout and design." If you will be creating illustrations, don't forget to include time spent on that.

2. Determine how much time each stage will take based on experience with previous jobs; if you suspect the client is fussy, factor in additional time to cover extra rounds of approval and lots of meetings.

▶

3. Multiply each block of hours by your hourly rate, or determine your flat fee or per-page rate, if that's how you'll be charging for this project.

4. Total up all amounts.

5. Check this figure against the budget or budget range you got from the client. If these numbers look high, consider ways that you can spend less time on some areas. Adjust your figures accordingly.

Determine Costs of Materials and Services

1. Determine format: Dimensions, number of pages, types of folds and so on are all part of your printing costs.

2. Establish basic specifications: Number of colors, quantity, paper, proofs, binding, bleeds, and use of halftones or color separations will all affect your production costs.

3. Choose method of print reproduction: What is most cost-effective for the format and basic specifications of the project? Will you need any special processes such as embossing or die-cutting?

4. Determine costs of typesetting: This may include purchasing fonts or ordering type from a type house or commissioning calligraphy or hand-lettered type. (Many designers simply bill costs for in-house typesetting as if it were purchased from a vendor rather than bill separately for time and repro costs.)

5. Get costs for outside copywriting, editing or proofreading if these will not be billed directly to the client by the provider.

6. Get costs for illustrations, whether stock or commissioned.

7. Get costs for photography: This may include stock photography, retouching photos, hiring a photographer, and models or props you supply. (Photographers often arrange for this and include it with their bill.)

8. Estimate the costs of any stats, veloxes or copies: Charge for these even if you're producing them in-house. (You may want to charge for the time needed to scan in and work with artwork as part of your time costs rather than include it with the costs of getting scans output by the service bureau.)

9. Include an amount for miscellaneous materials: This may include Pantone papers, special markers, copies.

10. Get costs for separations, stripping or proofs: In-house production of proofs, separations and other films off the computer, or costs for purchasing these from a service bureau; any stripping charges not assumed by printer.

11. Get printing costs.

Do I Have Everything I Need?

Do I Have All Needed Information, Supplies and Materials?

- Visual reference materials.
- Good supply of basic sketching, comping and pasteup materials.
- Ample disk space on the computer or enough floppies and cartridges.
- Enough toner and paper to make in-house copies and laser prints.
- Enough illustration boards of the right size to complete project.
- Paper samples to test ideas or colors, if needed.
- Any special materials needed to comply with client guidelines: special colors of Pantone markers or paper, for example.
- Sample headlines and copy if you're using an outside copywriter.
- Production schedule.
- Bids and estimates from suppliers and vendors.
- Time sheet to record hours spent on project.

Sample printing bid request form

PRINTING BID REQUEST

Date:

From: _____ To: _____

_____ _____

_____ _____

Phone: _____ Phone: _____

Project Name/Description: _____ Project # _____

Due Date: _____

Printing Specifications

Quantity: _____ Trim Size: _____ Number of Pages: _____

Paper Stock: _____

Number of Sides Printed: _____

Number of Colors

Interior/Side One:

☐ 1 ☐ Black ☐ PMS# _____

☐ 2 ☐ #1 _____ #2 _____

☐ 3 ☐ #1 _____ #2 _____ #3 _____

☐ 4 ☐ Process ☐ Other (specify)

   #1 _____ #2 _____

   #3 _____ #4 _____

☐ 5 4/c + _____

Varnish: _____

Other: _____

Cover/Side Two:

☐ 1 ☐ Black ☐ PMS # _____

☐ 2 ☐ #1 _____ #2 _____

☐ 3 ☐ #1 _____ #2 _____ #3 _____

☐ 4 ☐ Process ☐ Other (specify)

   #1 _____ #2 _____

   #3 _____ #4 _____

☐ 5 4/c + _____

Varnish: _____

Other: _____

Special Printing Requirements

Bleeds: _____ Screens: _____ Reverses: _____

Emboss: _____ Die Cut: _____ Foil Stamp: _____

Thermography: _____ Perforations: _____ Drills: _____

Proofs: ☐ Blueline ☐ Velox ☐ Color Key ☐ Cromalin ☐ Other

Pre-Press

Halftones: _____

Duotones: _____

Tritones: _____

Line Art: _____

4/C Process: _____

Spot Varnish: _____

Other: _____

Finishing/Mailing/Shipping

☐ Saddle Stitch

☐ Side Stitch

☐ Perfect Bind

☐ Other _____

☐ Score

☐ One Fold to _____

☐ Two Folds to _____

☐ Three Folds to _____

☐ Four + Folds to _____

☐ Other _____

☐ Envelope & Label

☐ Label on Cover

☐ Carton Bulk

☐ Polybag & Label

☐ Kraft Wrap & Label

☐ Other _____

Delivery Instructions: _____

Please Return Bid By: _____

Chapter 2

Making Choices—Type

Choosing Type

Points to Remember When Selecting a Typeface

- Match the type to the mood, audience and purpose of your piece. Typefaces have personalities that bring a mood or look to any piece. If the piece goes to investors, make it dignified by using Bookman. If it's for a preschool, use Frutiger to make it playful.

- Consider readability. If readability of the client's copy is the number one objective, you can still select a group of typefaces that satisfies the mood requirement, but make sure there is one in the group that also satisfies the readability requirement. If not, keep looking, or compromise on the mood issue.

- Note copy length. Lines with few words are easy to read at a glance. You can set headlines, headings and other short lines of copy in an ornate or highly stylized typeface, such as Cloister. Long passages of text should be set in a simple typeface. (For suggestions on setting long passages of text in a small space, see Space-Saving Typefaces.)

- Determine optimum type size for final reproduction. The size you select will depend largely on where it will be used—type appropriate to a poster is obviously going to be larger than that for a business card. Size is also a factor when projecting a hierarchy of information. For instance, a reader would be confused if you made the type on a coupon at the bottom of an ad larger than the headline that runs at the top.

- Determine optimum size for special production processes. Ink color will affect a typeface's visibility and size. For instance, white type will always appear larger against a dark background than dark type against white. Blind embossing also has a tendency to visually shrink the size of type.

Type/Font Sources
Sources for Exotic Type

The following type houses are known for their rare and unusual fonts, as well as for having practically every other imaginable typeface on hand:

Ad.Grafic Type

More than 5,000 display typefaces. Normal turnaround time is twenty-four hours.
Located in Santa Ana, California.
Phone: (714)997-5148
Fax: (714)997-5248.

Aldus Type Studio

More than 8,000 headline fonts and 2,000 text fonts. Normal turnaround time is twelve to fourteen hours.
Located in Los Angeles.
Phone: (213)933-7371
Fax: (213)933-8613.

Andresen Typographics

About 7,000 headline fonts and 4,000 text typefaces. Overnight service, with rush service available.
Located in Santa Monica, California.
Phone: (310)452-5521
Fax: (310)452-5521.

Latent Lettering

Approximately 7,000 headline fonts and 2,500 text typefaces. Twelve- to fourteen-hour turnaround, with two-hour rush available.
Located in New York City.
Phone: (212)221-0055
Fax: (212)221-1146.

Lettergraphics International

More than 7,000 typefaces. Normal turnaround time is twenty-four hours or overnight.
Located in Culver City, California.
Phone: (213)870-4828
Fax: (310)202-0990.

LinoTypographers

Approximately 10,000 typefaces, including some that are hot metal. Turnaround time depends on client's request.
Located in Fort Worth, Texas.

Keeping Type Readable

"Word spacing is the single most important aspect contributing to high levels of readability. It should be tight and even. As a guideline, turn the copy upside-down. If you can easily determine one word from another, you have too much word space.

"We read by scanning a line of type and capturing a group of three to four words and then jumping to another group of three to four words. Lines which are easiest to read contain about ten to twelve words—never more than fourteen.

"Graphics and type on 35mm slides should be simple and big. You should be able to read a 35mm slide at arm's length."

Allan Haley, *editorial director of* U&lc *and executive vice president of International Typeface Corp., is a regular contributor to* Step-By-Step, *and has authored several books on using type.*

▶

Phone: (817)332-4070
Fax: (817)429-9780.

M&H Type
Offers hot-metal type, exclusively, with about 500 faces available, many of them vintage. Turnaround time is twenty-four hours.
Located in San Francisco.
Phone: (415)777-0716
Fax: (415)777-2730.

Mastertype
About 10,000 typefaces, half of them specialty fonts. Turnaround time is normally twenty-four hours or overnight.
Located in San Francisco.
Phone: (415)781-8973
Fax: (415)781-7465.

Omnicomp
Approximately 7,000 typefaces, half of them exclusively display. Turnaround time is twenty-four hours or overnight.
Located in San Francisco.
Phone: (415)398-3377
Fax: 415-781-4010.

Phil's Photo, Inc.
Offers a full range of typefaces (approximately 11,000); specializes in display fonts. Normal turnaround time is overnight or twenty-four hours.
Located in Washington, DC.
Phone: (202)328-4144
or out-of-state (800)424-2977
Fax: (800)424-2977.

Photo-Lettering, Inc.
More than 13,000 fonts, including many specialty faces. Turnaround time is normally twelve to twenty-four hours.
Located in New York City.
Phone: (212)490-2345
Fax: (212)682-6052.

Font Sources for Macs and PCs

Adobe Systems Inc.
1585 Charleston Rd.
P.O. Box 7900
Mountain View CA 94039-7900
(800)833-6687
(415)961-4400

Alphabets, Inc.
804 Dempster St.
Evanston IL 60204
(800)326-4083

Bitstream, Inc.
215 First St.
Cambridge MA 02142
(800)522-3668
(617)497-6222

Casady & Greene, Inc.
22734 Portola Dr.
Salinas CA 93908-1119
(800)359-4920
(408)484-9218

Emigre Graphics
4475 "D" St.
Sacramento CA 95819
(800)944-9021
(916)451-4344

Erfort Fenton
P.O. Box 6838
San Jose CA 95150-6838
(408)448-2373

The FontBank, Inc.
2620 Central St.
Evanston IL 60201
(708)328-7370

The Font Company
7850 E. Evans Rd., Suite 111
Scottsdale AZ 85260
(800)442-3668
(Also sells through MasterFont retail centers)

Font Haus
15 Perry Ave., A7
Norwalk CT 06850
(800)942-9110
(203)846-3087

Lasermaster
7156 Shady Oak Rd.
Eden Prairie MN 55344
(612)944-9264

LetterPerfect
6606 Soundview Dr.
Gig Harbor WA 98335
(206)851-5158

Treacyfaces, Inc.
43 Malthy Ave.
West Haven CT 06156
(203)389-7037

Clip Art Alphabet Sources

Dover Publications, Inc.
The #1 clip art alphabet source, Dover currently publishes eighteen books of copyright-free typography. Each volume is classified by style and contains one hundred complete fonts.
Dover Publications, Inc.
31 E. Second St.
Mineola NY 11501-3582.

Art Direction Book Company
This publisher offers several books of alphabets in calligraphic type, various scripts and roman styles.
Art Direction Book Co.
10 E. Thirty-ninth St.
New York NY 10016.

Dynamic Graphics
Offers clip alphabets and digital files of alphabets.
Dynamic Graphics
6000 N. Forest Park Dr.
P.O. Box 1901
Peoria IL 61656-9941
Fax: (309)688-5873
(800)255-8800

Make Your Own Computer Fonts
Font-editing software lets you design your own typeface and use it as a font in the production of text and display type.

- Fontographer, a font-editing program by Altsys Corp., 269 W. Renner Rd., Richardson TX 75080; (212)680-2060.

- Font Studio, a popular font-editing program by Letraset Esselte Pendaflex Corp., 40 Eisenhower Dr., Paramus NJ 07653; (201)845-6100.

- Metamorphosis, by Altsys Corp., converts fonts to Type 1 format so they can be used in font-editing programs. It also converts font characters to outline draw-

ings that can be manipulated in Illustrator. (See Fontographer for address.)

- Multiple Masters lets you create a variety of weights (from ultrathin to ultrabold and whatever falls between) on Adobe fonts that are compatible with the Multiple Masters system. By Adobe, 1098 Alta Ave., Mountain View CA 94039-7900; (800)833-6687.

Low-Cost Way to Create Typefaces
Low-cost transfer or rub-down lettering is an old standby that anyone can use to create print-worthy display type. This lettering application uses two methods: 1) individual letters are rubbed off a dry transfer sheet with a burnisher or 2) printed letters on clear, adhesive-backed film are cut out and lifted off their backing sheet. Sizes range from 6 to 192 points. Letterforms tend to get skewed when rubbing down the smaller sizes. (It's also hard, not to mention tedious, to align text-sized type when trying to rub it down.) Brands include Letraset, Zipatone, Formatt, Geotype and Chartpak. Most brands are available at commercial art supply retail and wholesale outlets. (For other uses of transfer lettering for presentations and comping see chapter 15.)

Using Type

Tips for Reversing Type

- Avoid reversing out typefaces with thin serifs, such as Garamond and Bembo. Chances are pretty good that when your job is at press, thin serif lines will fill in.

- Use heavier typefaces, such as Helvetica Condensed, for reversed out headlines.

- Increase your type size. Reverses tend to visually "shrink" type, so choose a typeface size that is one to two points larger than you would otherwise use.

- Avoid large areas of reverse text. Research has shown that you'll lose 20 per-

OPTIONS FOR TYPE AND LEADING

These options will give you a starting point for finding the right type and leading combinations for your work. Create your own type specimen samples in the faces you use most often to fine-tune these choices to your work. Variations in x-height or characters per pica for a particular face can require adjustments in these figures.

Columns	Type Size	Leading
One	11	13
One	12	14
One	13	15
One	14	16
Two	9	11
Two	10	12
Two	11	13
Two	11	14
Two	12	14
Two	12	15
Two	13	15
Three	8	10
Three	8	11
Three	9	11
Three	10	12
Three	11	13
Three	11	14
Three	12	14
Three	12	15
Four	9	11
Four	10	12
Four	11	13
Four	11	14
Four	12	14
Four	12	15
Four	13	15
Five (double wide text)	9	10
Five (double wide text)	9	11
Five (double wide text)	10	12
Five (double wide text)	11	13
Five (double wide text)	11	14
Five (double wide text)	12	14

cent of your readers if you put a paragraph in reverse.

- Add extra leading and consider increasing letter spacing to boost legibility.

Rules for Using Leading

Standard leading is generally a point or two larger than the size of the typeface. Use extra leading to improve readability when:

- Working with column widths of more than forty characters.

- Using typefaces with a high x-height.
- Using typefaces with a strong vertical thrust.
- Using a sans serif typeface.
- Setting text larger than normal (for example, a typeface normally requiring 2-point leading at 10-point will read better at 14-point with 3-point leading).
- Setting text smaller than normal (for example, a typeface normally requiring 2-point leading at 10-point will read better at 7-point with 3-point leading).

Things to Remember When Working With a Copywriter

- Effective copywriting is clear, strong, exciting and believable. Look for these qualities in your writer's work.

- Assess your reaction to the copy. It should elicit a good feeling from you as a potential customer for the client's products and services.

- Set a firm deadline with your writer and agree upon a price in advance. If the job requires additional writing time because of repeated client alterations, expect to pay more when the project is completed.

- Have a clear understanding of your mutual expectations.

- Determine the copywriter's level of involvement. Will she be involved in meetings and have creative input?

Working With Type in a Layout
Setting Subheads Off From Text

Try each of these solutions alone or in combination.

- Set subheads in boldface or italics.
- Set subheads in all caps.
- Set subheads in a contrasting typeface (e.g., a sans serif with serif text).
- Leave a paragraph break after the text that precedes the subhead.
- Hang the subhead in a scholar margin or alone in a column of a four- or five-column grid. Keep the subhead short, set in upper- and lowercase and

stacked to save space.

- Center the subhead over a column of text.

Ways to Make a Pull Quote Stand Out

Set it bolder, larger, and possibly in a different typeface to set it off from several columns of text.

- Reverse it out from a block of color or black.

- Juxtapose single or double rules horizontally or vertically.

- Print it over a block or tint of your second color.

- Bracket it with a hint of a border.

- Enclose it within oversized quotation marks.

- Begin it with an initial cap.

- End it with the speaker's name.

- Position it in a blank column of a three-column or larger multicolumn grid.

- Center it within a body of text. Leave at least a ¼ inch between the outside border and the text.

- Vary your column length and place the quote in the open portions of each column.

Copyfitting
Copyfitting by Character Counting

To determine approximately how long your original copy will run when typeset:

1. Count the number of characters *and* spaces in the longest line of your original copy. (Or if the copy is short, count all the characters.)

2. Multiply this number by the number of ▶

Subhead layout ideas

Pull quote design ideas

lines in the original copy to determine the number of characters in the copy.

3. Refer to a typeset sample of the typeface you want to use set at the desired line length, and count the characters and spaces in one vertical inch.

4. Divide the number of characters in the original copy by the number of characters in one inch of typeset copy to determine the number of typeset inches your copy will comprise.

Type Tips to Save Space

- Use a condensed version of typeface.
- Reduce horizontal scaling by 10-20 percent.
- Set narrow text columns fully justified rather than ragged right.
- Reduce letter spacing and word spacing slightly.

- Tighten tracking.
- Use a typeface with lowercase characters that are small relative to its uppercase characters.
- Keep leading to a minimum (one or two points).

Space-Saving Typefaces
- Berkeley
- Bernhard Modern
- Bodoni
- Caslon
- Cheltenham
- Futura Condensed
- Futura Light
- Garamond
- Gill Sans
- Goudy Old Style
- Helvetica Condensed
- Korinna
- News Gothic
- Souvenir
- Times Roman
- University Roman

Type Tips to Fill Space
- Use an expanded version of typeface.
- Use a typeface with lowercase characters that are large relative to its uppercase characters.
- Pad lines of type with extra leading.
- Loosen tracking.
- Increase the point size.
- Increase the word and letter spacing.
- Switch to a typeface with a large *x*-height.
- Enlarge headings.
- Put text into sidebar boxes.
- Add dingbats.
- Put information into list format.
- Hang columns from top margin and let "rag" at bottom margin.

Space-Filling Typefaces
- Americana
- Antique Olive
- Bookman
- Century Schoolbook
- Clarendon
- Eurostile Extended
- Franklin Gothic
- Helvetica Regular
- Lubalin Graph
- Memphis
- Optima
- Tiffany
- Trump Medieval

Getting Your Client to Cut Copy
Cutting your own copy is difficult. Asking your client to cut copy that he worked hard to produce (or paid someone else to write) can be like asking him to amputate his right arm. To make cutting copy less painful, point out why the key message or mood of the piece will be diminished if the copy is too long. At the same time, offer him some suggestions. Explain that:

- Copy must be readable. In order to be reader-friendly, the type size must be large enough for people to read without squinting or reaching for their glasses.
- Headlines, illustrations, photos and other elements are attention getters. To reduce them will also reduce the likelihood of capturing a reader's attention.
- Copy can be edited without affecting its meaning. Show your client specific examples of how his copy can be trimmed.
- Only so much copy can fit into any given space. Show your client a dummy of the project, with all the pieces and design in place. Point out where copy literally runs off the dummy.
- Rearticulate how the *approved* design promotes the client's desired image, and how the extra copy affects it.

Chapter 3

Making Choices—Paper

Things to Consider When Choosing Paper

Design Considerations That Affect Paper Choice

- Evaluate the budget. What you or your client can spend on the job will probably have the most impact on what the paper choice will be. If you're designing letterhead for a client with a limited budget, you'll want to come up with a design concept that will work on your printer's "house sheet" rather than on a 100 percent-cotton, fine writing paper. Don't develop a high-gloss cover concept that can only be pulled off on an expensive cast-coated stock if your client can only afford a simple two-color job on the least expensive stock you can find.

- Consider reproduction potential if you're working with photographs or transparencies. If you have great material to work with, such as a large, professionally shot transparency, and you want to reproduce it in detail and in four color, you'll want to go with a premium quality or high-grade coated stock that will give you maximum ink holdout and, ultimately, the greatest clarity. (See Glossary for definition of ink holdout.) When photographic clarity is not a consideration, you can add color and texture to copy-heavy material by selecting an uncoated text or book-weight paper.

- Know the function of the project. Are you designing a book of biblical proportions? If so, go with a lightweight book paper (often referred to as Bible paper). A heavier weight would work better when you want to add some heft (not to mention a rich look) to an annual report. If you're designing a mail piece that will be looked at and pitched, select a lightweight stock that will satisfy the budget needs of the job yet be durable enough to hold up in the mail. Also consider the shelf life of the piece. You will need a sturdier paper for a brochure that the client will use for several months than for a monthly employee newsletter.

- Choose for mood. Conveying an impression through choice of paper is just as important as any other design consideration. Color, texture, the level of gloss (if it's coated), and the tactile quality of a paper all have connotations, just as certain colors do. It's as inappropriate to print a corporate brochure on a flimsy, bright yellow bond, as it would be to print it in fluorescent inks. Any message or mood, whether vintage or modern, friendly or detached, can be enhanced with the right choice of paper.

- Consider quantity, lead time and reproduction method. The quantity of your run will dictate to some degree your best reproduction method and the papers most suitable for it. If your five hundred fliers need to be turned around in a hurry at your local quick print shop, you're limited to papers they can use on their photocopier. However, if you're printing a small quantity of invitations and have a long lead time, you can explore the possibility of running handmade paper or an art paper on a letterpress. If you're involved in a large quantity situation, such as a catalog or other large publication, you'll probably be printing the job on a web press, meaning that you'll be limited to papers that come on rolls.

- Determine the project's size. The format of the job — 8½ × 11-inch sheets for a brochure or large sheets for a 24 × 36-inch poster — is also important. Sheet sizes or the availability of rolls must be considered when planning a design concept.

See chapter 17 for descriptions of and guidelines for different printing methods.

Paper Characteristics That Affect Paper Choice

These nine characteristics determine the quality and price of the paper you buy; keep them in mind when speccing paper for any project:

▶

RECOMMENDED USES FOR UNCOATED PAPERS

Type of Project	Type of Paper	Type of Project	Type of Paper
Annual Reports	Premium Text: 80#, 82#, 85#, 100# Text: 70#, 75#, 80#	**Direct Mail**	#3 Book: 50#, 60#, 70# Groundwood Book: 30#, 32#, 35#, 40#, 45#, 50#
Annual Report Cover	Premium Cover: 65#, 80#, 88#, 100#, 130# Cover: 65#, 80# #1 Cover: 50#, 65#	**Directories**	Groundwood Book: 30#, 32#, 35#, 40#, 45#, 50# #4 or #5 Sulphites: 16#, 20#
Books	#1 Book: 30#, 32#, 35#, 40#, 45#, 50#, 60#, 70# Premium Text: 80#, 100# Text: 70#, 75#, 80#	**Flyers**	#4 or #5 Sulphites: 16#, 20# #1 Book: 40#, 45#, 50#, 60#
Brochures	Premium Text: 80#, 82#, 85#, 100# Text: 70#, 75#, 80# #1 Book: 30#, 32#, 35#, 40#, 45#, 50#, 60#, 70#	**Folders**	Premium Cover: 65#, 80#, 88#, 100#, 130# Cover: 65#, 80# #1 Cover: 50#, 65#
Brochure Covers	Premium Cover: 65#, 80#, 88#, 100#, 130# Cover: 65#, 80# #1 Cover: 50#, 65#	**Invitations**	Premium Cover: 65#, 80#, 88#, 100# Cover: 65#, 80# #1 Cover: 50#, 65#
Calendars	#1 Book: 50#, 60#, 70#	**Letterhead**	100% Cotton: 20#, 24#, 28# 25%-50% Cotton: 20#, 24# #1 Sulphites: 20#, 24#
Catalogs	#1 Book: 30#, 32#, 35#, 40#, 45#, 50#, 60#, 70# #3 Book: 50#, 60#, 70# Supercalendered: 30#, 32#, 33#, 34#, 35#, 36#, 38#, 40# Groundwood Book: 30#, 32#, 35#, 40#, 45#, 50# Specialty Newsprint: 27#, 30#, 32#, 35#, 40#	**Magazines**	Supercalendered: 30#, 32#, 35#, 36#, 38#, 40#
		Newsletters	Premium Text: 70#, 75#, 80# 25%-50% Cotton: 20#, 24# #1 Sulphites: 20#, 24# Text: 70#, 75#, 80#
Catalog Covers	Premium Cover: 65#, 80#, 88#, 100#, 130# Cover: 65#, 80# #1 Cover: 50#, 65#	**Point-of-Purchase/ Table Tents**	Premium Cover: 65#, 80#, 88#, 100#, 130# Cover: 65#, 80# #1 Cover: 50#, 65#

Recycled uncoated papers have not been listed separately in this chart since most standard types of paper (such as text paper) are available as recycleds.

Basis Weight: The weight of a ream of paper after it has been cut to the basic size for its grade. Because paper is sold by the pound, the higher the basis weight, the more expensive the paper—not to mention the extra cost to mail a heavier piece.

Brightness: The amount of light that paper reflects, expressed as a percentage. Used by mills to assign quality classifications.

Bulk: The thickness of paper relative to its basis weight; this affects your paper's opacity and color as well as the thickness of a piece.

Coated vs. Uncoated: Fine printing papers can be broken down into two major categories: coated and uncoated papers. Coated papers generally have better ink holdout (they are less likely to absorb ink and, therefore, can provide better clarity for photographic reproduction).

Color: Produced by the addition of dyes and pigments to pulp. Color may be affected by bulk and finish. The color of the paper affects the printing ink color, especially with lighter tints.

Finish: Something added or done to a paper's surface to alter its appearance, feel and printability. A sheet's surface should have a look and texture that is appropriate for a project and suitable for the method of printing. Surface also affects ink holdout and, therefore, the quality of illustrations and photos, and the readability of type.

Grain: The alignment of fibers in the direction of pulp flow. Grain should run in the direction that allows the printing, folding and binding characteristics you desire; for example, folds in heavy stock are smoother with the grain and stronger against it.

Opacity: The degree to which a paper resists show-through from the other side of the sheet. Opacity increases with basis weight and bulk and can be affected by coatings, colors, chemicals, and ink color and coverage.

Size: Sheets of paper come in standard sizes. Knowing the standard paper sizes will help you choose the sheet and size that will be most efficient for your project and for the press it will run on.

Surfaces and Finishes

When you're choosing a paper, you should also consider its surface and finish (as if you didn't have enough to think about already). The more aware you are of the printing qualities and the look and feel of different sheets, the more likely you are to choose an appropriate paper for the job without lowering quality, breaking the budget or missing deadlines.

Text and bond papers have surface patterns. Uncoated book paper doesn't; its levels of smoothness are determined by the amount of calendering (smoothing the surface by pressing and pulling it through rollers during its manufacture) it receives.

Rough finishes are relatively receptive to ink, allowing it to dry quickly. Smooth finishes have better ink holdout.

Antique finish: Toothy, open-textured paper.

Cast-coated finish: A high-gloss surface achieved by pressing the paper against a hot metal drum while its coating is still wet. Has the most sparkle of all coated papers and costs the most.

Cockle surface: A slightly puckered surface effect that is commonly applied to onionskin and bond papers.

Deckle edge: The feathering that occurs on the untrimmed edges of paper as it is made. It can be left ragged rather than cleanly cut; this look is used on some letterhead and similar applications.

Dull finish: Flat (not glossy) finish on coated paper that is slightly smoother than matte. May also be called suede or velour finish.

Eggshell finish: Simulates the surface (moderately rough) and the color of an eggshell.

English finish: Very smooth finish on uncoated paper.

Felt surface: Paper with a woven pattern on the surface.

▶

> ### Paper Dummies
> Paper mills sometimes make up dummies that show how your piece will work when it's bound or folded from papers you specify. Describe exactly what you want. Give the trim size, the number of pages or panels, the type of binding or folding; specify both interior and cover sheets if you will be using both, as well as pocket height for folders and spine width. If you are going to use more than one interior sheet—perhaps a high-quality printing paper where photos will be reproduced and a recycled stock on other pages—remember to specify both kinds.

RECOMMENDED USES FOR COATED PAPERS

Type of Project	Type of Paper
Annual Reports	Premium Ultra Gloss: 80#, 90#, 100#
Annual Report Covers	Premium Ultra Gloss Cover: 70#, 80# C1S & C2S cast-coated: gloss, .006, .007, .008, .010, .012 Colored cast-coated, metallic & plastic: embossed, gloss or matte, .010, .015 #1 Cover: dull, gloss or matte, 65#, 80#, 100# #3 Cover: dull, gloss or matte, 65#, 80#, 100#
Books	Premium Ultra Gloss: 80#, 90#, 100#
Brochures	Premium Ultra Gloss: 80#, 90#, 100# Premium #1: dull, gloss or embossed, 70#, 80#, 100# #1: dull, gloss or embossed, 70#, 80#, 100# #2: dull, gloss or embossed, 60#, 70#, 80#, 100# #3: dull, gloss or embossed, 60#, 70#, 80#, 100# #3 matte book: 50#, 60#, 70#, 80#, 100#
Brochure Covers	Premium Ultra Gloss Cover: 70#, 80# #1 Cover: dull, gloss or matte, 65#, 80#, 100# C1S & C2S cast-coated: gloss, .006, .007, .008, .010, .012 #3 Cover: dull, gloss or matte, 65#, 80#, 100# Colored cast-coated, metallic & plastic: embossed, gloss or matte, .010, .015
Calendars	Premium Ultra Gloss: 70#, 80#, 90#, 100# Premium #1 or #1: dull, gloss or embossed, 70#, 80#, 100# #2: dull, gloss or embossed, 60#, 70#, 80#, 100# #1 Cover: dull, gloss or matte, 65#, 80#, 100# #3 Cover: dull, gloss or matte, 65#, 80#, 100#

Type of Project	Type of Paper
Catalogs	Premium Ultra Gloss: 70#, 80#, 90#, 100# Premium #1 or #1: dull, gloss or embossed, 70#, 80#, 100# #2: dull, gloss or embossed, 60#, 70#, 80#, 100#
Catalog Covers	Premium Ultra Gloss Cover: 70#, 80# #1 Cover: dull, gloss or matte, 6#, 80#, 100# C1S &C2S cast-coated: gloss, .006, .007, .008, .1010. .012 #3 Cover: dull, gloss or matte, 65#, 80#, 100#
Direct Mail	#3: dull, gloss or embossed, 60#, 70#, 80#, 100# #3 matte book: 50#, 60#, 70#, 80#, 100# #4 free sheet: dull or gloss, 40#, 45#, 50#, 60#, 70# #4 Groundwood: dull or gloss, 40#, 45#, 50#, 60#, 70# #5: gloss, 35#, 40#, 45#, 50#, 60#, 70#
Directories	#4 free sheet: dull or gloss, 40#, 45#, 50#, 60#, 70# #4 groundwood: dull or gloss, 40#, 45#, 50#, 60#, 70# #5: gloss, 35#, 40#, 45#, 50#, 60#, 70#
Folders	Premium Ultra Gloss Cover: 70#, 80# #1 Cover: dull, gloss or matte, 65#, 80#, 100# C1S & C2S cast-coated: gloss, .006, .007, .008, .010, .012 #3 Cover: dull, gloss or matte, 65#, 80#, 100# Colored cast-coated: embossed, gloss or matte, .010, .015
Invitations	Premium Ultra Gloss Cover: 70#, 80# #1 Cover: dull, gloss or matte, 65#, 80#, 100# C1S & C2S cast-coated: gloss, .006, .007, .008, .010, .012 #3 Cover: dull, gloss or matte, 65#, 80#, 100# Colored cast-coated: embossed, gloss or matte, .010, .015

RECOMMENDED USES FOR COATED PAPERS

Type of Project	Type of Paper	Type of Project	Type of Paper
Magazines	Premium Ultra Gloss: 80#, 90#, 100#	Point-of-Purchase/ Table Tents	Premium Ultra Gloss Cover: 70#, 80#
	Premium #1: dull, gloss or embossed, 70#, 80#, 100#		#1 Cover: dull, gloss or matte, 65#, 80#, 100#
	#1: dull, gloss or embossed, 70#, 80#, 100#		C1S & C2S cast-coated: gloss, .006, .007, .008, .010, .012
	#2: dull, gloss or embossed, 60#, 70#, 80#, 100#		#3 Cover: dull, gloss or matte, 65#, 80#, 100#
	#3: dull, gloss or embossed, 60#, 70#, 80#, 100#	Posters	Premium Ultra Gloss: 80#, 90#, 100#
	#3 matte book 50#, 60#, 70#, 80#, 100#		Premium #1: dull, gloss or embossed, 70#, 80#, 100#
	#4 free sheet: dull or gloss, 40#, 45#, 50#, 60#, 70#		#1: dull, gloss or embossed, 70#, 80#, 100#
	#4 groundwood: dull or gloss, 40#, 45#, 50#, 60#, 70#		#2: dull, gloss or embossed, 60#, 70#, 80#, 100#
	#5: gloss, 35#, 40#, 45#, 50#, 60#, 70#		Premium Ultra Gloss Cover: 70#, 80#
Newsletters	Premium Ultra Gloss: 80#, 90#, 100#		#1 Cover: dull, gloss or matte, 65#, 80#, 100#
	Premium #1: dull, gloss or embossed, 70#, 80#, 100#		C1S & C2S cast-coated: gloss, .006, .007, .008, .010, .012
	#1: dull, gloss or embossed, 70#, 80#, 100#		#3 Cover: dull, gloss or matte, 65#, 80#, 100#
	#2: dull, gloss or embossed, 60#, 70#, 80#, 100#		
	#3: dull, gloss or embossed, 60#, 70#, 80#, 100#		
	#3 matte Book: 50#, 60#, 70#, 80#, 100#		

Not many coated papers are currently available with recycled content, but some are. Consult your local paper merchant or paper mill reps for what is available for the kind of paper you want to use.

Gloss finish: Finish on coated paper that reflects light well.

High-bulk finish: A very rough, toothy finish that has undergone very little calendering.

Laid surface: Finish with grids of parallel lines.

Linen surface: Made by embossing paper surface with a linenlike texture.

Lustre finish: Smooth finish on uncoated paper.

Machine finish: Slightly rough finish achieved by calendering paper on the rollers of a papermaking machine.

Matte finish: Flat (not glossy) finish on coated paper.

Satin finish: This can mean either a slightly embossed, fairly smooth finish on text paper or a dull finish on coated paper.

Supercalendered surface: Among the smoothest, glossiest and thinnest stocks.

Vellum finish: Somewhat rough, toothy finish.

Wove finish: Somewhat smooth, slightly patterned finish.

Tips for Printing on Uncoated Papers
- Avoid uncoated paper if achieving showcase-quality reproduction of photos is your main goal.

▶

BOOK

Type of paper———Offset Book
Bright, clean, easy-printing uncoated book. All-purpose sheet for offset or letterpress.

Color and finish———White — Regular Finish (Smooth)

| | | | Per 1000 Sheets | | |
| | | | 500 Shts. | Broken | 500 Shts. |
	Sub	Ctn	Lots	Lots	Lots
Size———8½ × 11	50	5000	6.15		5.90
8½ × 11	60	5000	7.10		6.80
8½ × 11	70	4000	8.30		7.95
8½ × 11	80	3000	9.50		9.10
8½ × 11	100	3000	11.85		11.40
Substance———					
8½ × 14	50	5000	7.80		7.50
8½ × 14	60	5000	9.05		8.70
8½ × 14	70	4000	10.55		10.15
Sheets per carton———					
11 × 17	50	2500	12.30		11.80
11 × 17	60	2500	14.20		13.60
11 × 17	70	2000	16.60		15.90
					———500 sheet price
17½ × 22½ — 41M	50	3000	25.75	33.50	24.70
17½ × 22½ — 50M	60	3000	30.40	39.50	29.20
17½ × 22½ — 58M	70	2000	35.25	45.50	33.85
17½ × 22½ — 66M	80	2000	40.10	52.00	38.50
17½ × 22½ — 83M	100	2000	50.40	65.50	
M Weight———					———Broken lot price
19 × 25 — 50M	50	3000	31.45	40.50	
19 × 25 — 60M	60	2000	36.45	47.00	
19 × 25 — 70M	70	2000	42.55	55.00	
23 × 29 — 70M	50	2000	44.00	57.00	
23 × 29 — 84M	60	1800	51.05	66.00	
23 × 29 — 98M	70	1600	59.55	77.00	
23 × 35 — 85M	50	1500	53.40	69.00	
23 × 35 — 102M	60	1500	61.95	80.50	
23 × 35 — 119M	70	1200	72.30	94.00	
25 × 38 — 100M	50	1600	62.85	81.50	
25 × 38 — 120M	60	1200	72.90	94.50	
25 × 38 — 140M	70	1000	85.05	110.50	
25 × 38 — 160M	80	1000	97.20	126.00	
25 × 38 — 200M	100	800	121.50	158.00	
35 × 45 — 166M	50		104.35	135.00	
35 × 45 — 198M	60		120.30	156.00	
35 × 45 — 232M	70		140.95	182.00	
35 × 45 — 266M	80		161.60	210.00	
35 × 45 — 332M	100		201.70	262.00	

5% Discount for quantities of 500 lbs. or more.

Information in a paper catalog

- Replacing one or more of the process inks with a fluorescent, generally yellow or magenta, will punch up the colors. Fluorescent magenta enhances reds, purples, violets and oranges. Fluorescent yellow brightens reds, oranges, yellows and greens.

- Don't substitute fluorescents if the piece will be exposed to daylight for long periods.

- Consider an undercoat for areas where you want more opaque color coverage; either a white undercoat or a dull varnish will reduce paper absorption.

- Alert your color separator that you are using an uncoated stock, as separations need to be adjusted to reduce dot gain.

- Embossing, debossing and foil stamping work well on uncoated papers.

- Tiny reverse type and delicate serifs can close up when printed on uncoated papers.

- Make the interesting texture of uncoated paper part of your design. Don't cover every inch with ink.

- Allow for extra time at the printer in your schedule; uncoated papers take longer to dry.

Choosing Recycled Papers

- The most environment-friendly papers are those that have the highest percentage of postconsumer waste—paper that has been collected from consumers and made into paper again.

- A No. 1 recycled sheet has characteristics similar to a No. 1 sheet made from virgin pulp.

- Lower grades of recycled paper are still inferior to lower grades made from virgin pulp.

- Press performance of recycled sheets has improved and will continue to do so as demand increases.

- Specks and irregularities are part of a paper's character; the tactile qualities of recycled paper can enhance a design. Work with the character of your sheet.

- Recycled papers work well for processes such as foil-stamping and embossing.

- Waterless offset printing (also called dryography) gives excellent results on recycled paper and, because it uses no water or alcohol, is very environment-friendly. Waterless offset costs about 10 percent more than conventional printing and is gradually becoming more available in the United States. (For more information see page 146.)

How to Read a Paper Swatch Book

Swatch books vary in some respects, depending on the mill and its system for organizing the information within its books. But the basic information is the same. Swatch books contain bound sample sheets, or swatches, from a particular paper line. They also include the following information:

Finishes: Finishes available within a line are usually listed, and sometimes samples are included in the bound swatches. (See pages 21-23 in this chapter for a description of typical finishes.)

Colors: Again, this information could be listed, or it could be charted. But seeing is believing, and because exact color is important in design consideration, most swatch books will include a sample swatch of every standard color in a paper line.

Sizes: Usually represented in a chart or a list, sheet sizes are given so that designers and printers can determine which sheet size will be accommodated by their presses and provide the best cut for a job, with a minimum of wasted paper. Roll sizes (if they are available) for web presses are also given.

Quantities and ordering information: Minimum quantities of paper, availability, and how they are available (reams, rolls, etc.)

Envelopes: Information on matching envelopes and their sizes, as well as minimum quantity and ordering information, is also

Posters on Cardboard

"Villanova commissioned us to come up with a promotional mailer for the fraternity and sorority rush rally. We thought a poster would best serve as a direct-mail piece in this situation.

"Instead of printing the posters on offset paper and mailing them in a tube, we decided to screen print them on corrugated cardboard and mail them out flat. We printed four jewel-tone colors, and because of the relatively small run of 2,000, we were able to save money on the printing, the cost of the mailing tubes, and the handling charges. The finished, 19 × 34-inch poster served double-duty as a poster and an oversized postcard. It also made quite an impact. When the recipients came home, they found a big chunk of cardboard waiting for them under their mailbox, or propped up against their front door. They couldn't miss it."

John Sayles *is principal of Des Moines-based Sayles Graphic Design. He uses industrial papers extensively in his designs.*

EQUIVALENT BASIS WEIGHTS

Equivalents for Book	Book	Bond	Cover
30#	***	12#	16#
35#	***	14#	19#
40#	***	16#	22#
50#	***	20#	27#
55#	***	22#	30#
60#	***	24#	33#
65#	***	26#	36#
70#	***	28#	38#
80#	***	31#	44#
90#	***	35#	50#
100#	***	39#	55#
110#	***	42#	60#
120#	***	47#	65#
Bond/Writing			
12#	30#	***	16#
13#	33#	***	18#
14#	35#	***	19#
16#	40#	***	22#
20#	50#	***	27#
24#	60#	***	33#
28#	70#	***	38#
31#	80#	***	44#
35#	90#	***	50#
40#	102#	***	56#
47#	120#	***	65#
Cover			
25#	46#	18#	***
27#	50#	20#	***
35#	64#	25#	***
40#	73#	29#	***
50#	91#	36#	***
55#	100#	40#	***
60#	110#	43#	***
65#	119#	47#	***
80#	146#	58#	***
90#	164#	65#	***
110#	183#	72#	***

You can't just specify the same weight when changing from one kind of stock to another. This chart gives the equivalent basis weight for commonly used weights of book, bond and cover paper.

often included.

Basis weights: Swatch books list the available weights or thicknesses (measured in calipers) of a paper line. Some books include this information in a chart on their back cover. Basis weights are sometimes listed within a master chart that also lists sheet sizes and colors. Other books may list the weights next to swatch samples in available colors. (See the Equivalent Basis Weights Chart for a comparison of similar weights of bond, book and cover stocks.)

M/Weight: (also written "MWT" and "M Weight") The weight per one thousand sheets and the number of sheets per shipping carton for each size.

The Recommended Uses charts on pages 20-23 describe which kinds of paper are best for different kinds of printed pieces.

Support Your Local Paper Merchant
Paper merchants keep an inventory of blank sheets of different papers, often cut to such sizes as 8½ × 11, 11 × 14 and 12½ × 19 inches. Sample sheets allow you to experiment with papers, test their folding capabilities and make mock-ups.

Printed samples are also available from paper merchants. Some samples are paper mill promotions, while others are pieces produced on the paper. These let you see how a particular sheet responds to various printing processes—they're also a great source of new ideas.

Envelopes—Types and Uses

Envelopes That Match Text/Bond Papers
The following types of envelopes are generally available from printing paper manufacturers in colors and surface finishes to match their text and bond papers. Remember to check mailing costs with the postal service if you're using sizes other than Nos. 9 and 10.

Commercial: Standard envelope for correspondence; used for stationery, mailings.

No. 6¼: 3½ × 6 inches
Monarch (No. 7¾): 3⅞ × 7½ inches
No. 8¾: 3⅜ × 8⅜ inches
No. 9: 3⅞ × 8⅞ inches
No. 10: 4⅛ × 9½ inches
No. 11: 4½ × 10⅜ inches
No. 12: 4¾ × 11 inches
No. 14: 5 × 11½ inches

Window: Name and address show through; used for statements, checks, mailings.
No. 6¼: 3½ × 6 inches
No. 7: 3¾ × 6¾ inches
No. 9: 3⅞ × 8⅞ inches
No. 10: 4⅛ × 9½ inches
No. 11: 4⅛ × 10½ inches

Announcement: Frequently lined with colored paper and may have deckle-edged flaps; more formal than commercial envelopes; used for invitations, announcements, greeting cards.
A-2: 4⅜ × 5¾ inches
A-6: 4¾ × 6½ inches
A-7: 5¼ × 7¼ inches
A-8: 5½ × 8⅛ inches
A-10: 6 × 9½ inches
Slimline (A-Long): 3⅞ × 8⅞ inches

Baronial: Frequently lined with colored paper; more formal than commercial envelopes; used for invitations, announcements, greeting cards.
No. 4: 3⅝ × 5⅛ inches
No. 5: 4⅛ × 5⅝ inches
No. 5½: 4⅜ × 5¾ inches
No. 6: 5 × 6½ inches

Booklet: Open-sided design allows overall printing on envelope; used for annual reports, brochures, sales literature, mailings with inserts.
No. 6⅝: 6 × 9½ inches
No. 6¾: 6½ × 9½ inches
No. 7½: 7½ × 10½ inches
No. 9: 8¾ × 11½ inches
No. 9½: 9 × 12 inches
No. 10: 9½ × 12⅜ inches
No. 13: 10 × 13 inches

Specialty Envelopes

The standard sizes of these envelopes are generally available from paper merchants but do not come in colors and surface finishes to match specific text and bond papers.

Airmail: Lightweight paper with red and blue borders; used for airmail correspondence.
No. 6¼: 3½ × 6 inches
Monarch (No. 7¾): 3⅞ × 7½ inches
No. 8¾: 3⅜ × 8⅜ inches
No. 9: 3⅞ × 8⅞ inches
No. 10: 4⅛ × 9½ inches
No. 11: 4½ × 10⅜ inches
No. 12: 4¾ × 11 inches
No. 14: 5 × 11½ inches

Remittance: large flap allows for printing or coupon; used for statement/return of payment.
No. 6¼: 3½ × 6 inches
No. 6½: 3½ × 6¼ inches
No. 6¾: 3⅝ × 6½ inches

Self-seal: Surfaces seal on contact; used for packing lists and similar applications.
5½ × 4½ inches

Ticket: Used for theater and other tickets.
11⁵⁄₁₆ × 4⁷⁄₁₆ inches

Catalog: Heavyweight paper with heavily gummed flaps; used for catalogs, magazines.
No. 1: 6 × 9 inches
No. 2: 6½ × 10 inches
No. 8: 8¼ × 11¼ inches
No. 13½: 10 × 13 inches
No. 15: 10 × 15 inches

Metal Clasp: Heavyweight paper sealed with a metal clasp; used for catalogs, bulky loose papers.
No. 5: 3⅛ × 5½ inches
No. 35: 5 × 7½ inches
No. 90: 9 × 12 inches
No. 97: 10 × 13 inches
No. 110: 12 × 15½ inches

See also standard sizes of envelopes most commonly used for letterhead on page 60.

Sources of Paper

Major Paper Mills

Contact the following mills for swatch books of their printing papers. Many also

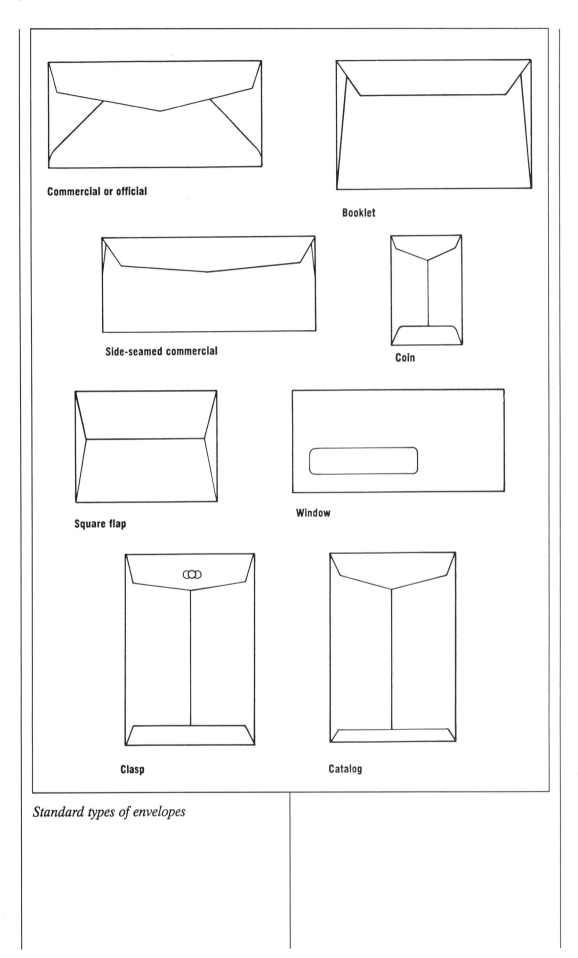

Standard types of envelopes

offer technical guide books and will create comps—utilizing their papers—of folders, boxes, brochures and other items that are custom-made to your specifications.

Ahlstrom Paper Corp. of U.S.
100 Fifth Ave., 9th Fl.
New York NY 10011
(212)337-5524

Appleton Papers, Inc.
825 E. Wisconsin Ave.
P.O. Box 359
Appleton WI 54912
(414)734-9841

Arjo Wiggins
600 W. Puttman Ave.
Greenwich CT 06830
(203)622-4503

Beckett Paper Co.
400 Dayton St.
Hamilton OH 45012
(513)863-5641

Champion International Corp.
1 Champion Plaza
Stamford CT 06921
(800)442-3463

Conservatree
10 Lombard St., Suite 350
San Francisco CA 94111
(415)433-1000

Consolidated Papers, Inc.
231 First Ave., North
Wisconsin Rapids WI 54494
(715)422-3111

Crane & Co., Inc.
30 South St.
Dalton MA 01226
(413)684-2600

Cross Pointe Paper Corp.
1295 Bandana Blvd. N., Suite 335
St. Paul MN 55108
(612)644-3644

Decorated Paper Corp.
Eighth and Erie Sts.
Camden NJ 08102
(609)365-4200

Domtar
P.O. Box 7211
Montreal Quebec H3C 3M2
Canada
(514)848-5400

Eastern Fine Paper, Inc.
P.O. Box 129
Brewer ME 04412
(207)989-7070

Finch
1 Glen St.
Glen Falls NY 12801
(518)793-2541

Fox River Paper Co.
200 E. Washington St.
Appleton WI 54913
(414)733-7341

French Paper Corp.
100 French St.
P.O. Box 398
Niles MI 49120
(616)683-1100

Gilbert Paper Co., a Division of Mead
430 Ahnaip St.
Menasha WI 54952
(414)722-7721

Hammermill Papers
6400 Poplar Ave.
Memphis TN 38197
(901)763-7800

Hopper Paper Co.
P.O. Box 105237
Atlanta GA 30348
(404)521-4000

Howard Paper Mills
354 S. Edwin C. Moses Blvd.
Dayton OH 54407
(513)224-1211
(800)543-5010

International Paper Co.
2 Manhattanville Rd.
Purchase NY 10577
(914)397-1500

James River Corp.
300 Lakeside Dr., 14th Fl.
Oakland CA 94612
(415)874-3400

James River/Premium Papers Group
145 James Way
Southampton PA 18966
(215)364-3900

Kimberly Clark Corp.
P.O. Box 619100
Dallas TX 75261-9100
(214)830-1200

Mead Corp.
Fine Paper Division
Courthouse Plaza, N.E.
Dayton OH 45463
(513)222-6323

Mohawk Paper Mills, Inc.
465 S. Saratoga St.
P.O. Box 497
Cohoes NY 12047
(518)237-1740
(800)843-6455

Monadnock Paper Mills, Inc.
Bennington NH 03342
(603)588-3311

Neenah Paper
1400 Holcomb Bridge Rd.
Roswell GA 30076
(800)338-6077

Patriot Paper
892 River St.
Hyde Park MA 02136
(617)361-3500

Penntech Papers, Inc.
181 Harbor Dr.
Stamford CT 06902
(203)356-1850

Potlatch Corp.
1 Maritime Plaza
P.O. Box 3591
San Francisco CA 94119
(415)576-8800

Simpson Paper Co.
1 Post St.
San Francisco CA 94104
(415)391-8140

Strathmore Paper Co.
S. Broad St.
Westfield MA 01085
(800)423-7313

Ward Paper
North Mill St.,
Merrill WI 54452
(800)365-3413

S.D. Warren Co.
225 Franklin St.
Boston MA 02110
(617)423-7300

Westvaco Corp.
Fine Papers Division
299 Park Ave.
New York NY 10171
(212)688-5000

Weyerhaeuser Paper Co.
P.O. Box 829
Valley Forge PA 19482
(215)251-9220

George Whiting
P.O. Box 28
Menasha WI 54952
(414)722-3351

Recycled/Recyclable Icons
To get the icon that says, "Printed on recycled paper," fax or mail your request to the American Paper Institute, 260 Madison Ave., New York NY 10016; fax: (212)689-2628. After confirming that you have met API standards for recyclability, they'll send you camera-ready copies of the icon.

Sources of Recycled Papers
Recycled papers vary in the amount of preconsumer and postconsumer waste they contain. If you seek paper that is truly recycled, look for those that contain a high content of preconsumer *and* postconsumer waste. Paper mills are constantly trying to increase the waste content of their recycled papers in response to consumer demand. Ask your paper merchant for the current percentages of pre- and postconsumer waste in any recycled paper you are considering.

The papers in the following lists contain at least 10 percent postconsumer waste.

Recycled Uncoated Offset Papers

Cross Point
Genesis
50/50 Recycled
Halopaque
Sycamore Colors

Future Fibres Group
Sav-A-Source

Hammermill
Savings Offset
Savings Opaque

Howard Offset
Patriot

Westvaco
American Eagle Web Offset
Hi-D Bulking Offset
Envelope Wove

Recycled Coated Bond, Text and Cover

Champion
All-Purpose Litho Recycled (bond)
Kromekote (cover)

Conservatree
100 Percent Bond
ESP Gloss
Offset Enamel (cover)
Premium Laid Bond Writing
Premium Rag Bond

Future Fibres Group
Sav-A-Source Premium Cover
Sav-A-Source Quality Cover

Mohawk
50/10 Matte/Gloss

Simpson
EverGreen (cover)

Strathmore
Renewal (bond, text and cover)

Uncoated Bond, Text and Cover

Beckett
Cambric (bond, text and cover; linen finish; sixteen colors bond, twenty colors text, twenty-two colors cover)
Concept (bond, text and cover; several finishes; twelve colors bond, six colors text and cover)
Enhance (bond, text and cover; two finishes; eleven colors bond, fifteen colors text, seventeen colors cover)

Ridge (text and cover, special/fancy finish; six colors text, nine colors cover)
RSVP (text and cover; felt finish; five colors text, nine colors cover)

Champion
Benefit (bond, text and cover; two finishes; two colors bond, seven colors text and cover)

Conservatree
Four Seasons (text and cover)
Premium Rag (bond and cover)

Crane & Co., Inc.
Byron Weston Save a Source (bond and cover; two finishes; three colors)
Cranes Crest Recycled (bond; wove finish; one color)

Cross Pointe
Bellbrook Laid (bond, text and cover; twelve colors)
C.P. Recycled (bond and cover; several finishes; two colors)
Genesis (bond, text and cover; vellum finish; seven colors)
Halopaque (text and cover; satin finish; two colors text, one color cover)
Medallion (text and cover; felt finish; ten colors)
Normandie (bond, text and cover; linen finish; ten colors)
Passport (bond, text and cover; felt finish; nine colors bond, twelve colors text and cover)
Torchglow Opaque (text and cover; smooth finish; fifteen colors)

Domtar
100 Percent Recycled 20/50 (bond, text and cover)
Byronic Recycled (bond, text and cover)
Concerto Recycled (bond, text and cover)

Fox River
Circa '83 (bond, text and cover; two finishes; three colors text, six colors bond and cover)
Circa Select (bond, text and cover; several finishes; five colors bond, eight colors text and cover)
Fox River 100 Percent Recycled Bond/25 Percent Cotton (bond, text and cover)

▶

French Paper Co.
French Rayon (text and cover; smooth finish; five colors)
French Speckletone (text and cover; thirteen colors in antique finish, five colors embossed and flocked)

Future Fibres Group
Sav-A-Source 25 Percent Rag (bond, text and cover)

Gilbert
Esse (bond, text and cover; smooth finish; twenty colors)
Gilbert Recycled (bond and cover; two colors)

Hopper
Proterra (bond, text and cover; several finishes; number of colors varies with finish)
Valorem (text and cover; two finishes; twelve colors)

Howard
Antiqa Parch (bond and cover; wove finish; seven colors)
Capitol Bond (bond; several finishes; two colors)
Crushed Leaf (bond, text and cover; felt finish; ten colors)
Howard Bond (bond; several finishes; eleven colors)
Howard Linen (bond, text and cover; ten colors)
Howard Text and Cover (bond, text and cover)
Permalife (bond, text and cover)

James River
Curtis Linen (bond, text and cover; nine colors bond; fifteen colors text and cover)
Curtis Tuscan Antique (cover; eleven colors)
Curtis Tuscan Terra (text; smooth finish; seven colors)
Graphika! (text and cover; two finishes; eleven colors)
Graphika! 100 (text and cover; vellum finish; five colors)
Retreeve (bond, text and cover; two finishes; seven colors bond, eleven colors text and cover)
Riegel PCW Cover (cover)

Mohawk
Mohawk P/C (text and cover; several finishes; six colors)

Monadnock
Classic Crest (bond, text and cover; wove finish; four colors)
Classic Laid (bond, text and cover; four colors)
Environment (bond, text and cover; two finishes; five colors)

Simpson
EverGreen Script (bond; vellum finish; nine colors)
EverGreen Text (text and cover; vellum finish; thirteen colors)
Gainsborough (bond, text and cover; felt finish; six colors bond, sixteen colors text and cover)
Sundance (text and cover; several finishes; fifteen colors)

Strathmore
Strathmore Bond (several finishes; three colors)

Ward Paper
Cimarron (text and cover; vellum finish; nine colors)

Sources of Special Papers
Small Quantities of Printing Paper

Arvey
Forty locations in major U.S. cities. Call (800)866-6332 for locations.

If It's Paper
A division of Dillard Paper Co., a Southern-based paper merchant, this retail chain includes forty-one stores in North and South Carolina, Virginia, Georgia, Tennessee and Alabama.

Kelly Paper
Twenty-two locations in California, Arizona and Nevada. Call (800)67-KELLY for locations.

Paper and Graphic Supply Centers
Affiliated with Seaman-Patrick; offers retail centers in eleven cities throughout Michigan and Ohio. Call (800)477-0050 for locations.

The Paper Center
Five stores in New England area. Call (800)242-5749 for specific locations.

Paper Plus
Seventy locations in major metropolitan areas in the United States. Check Yellow Pages for locations.

The Paper Shop
Seventeen stores in the Northeast. Call for locations at (215)657-7630.

The Paper Shoppe
Fifteen locations in Canada sell paper cash-and-carry and by the ream. Call (416)736-0484 for locations.

Parsons
Takes phone orders. Call (301)386-4700. Its cash-and-carry retail outlet, The Supply Room, is located in Springfield, Virginia, (703)941-0810.

Press Stock
Thirty-one stores in major metropolitan areas. Call (800)822-6323 for locations.

Specialty Laser Papers

Letraset USA
Paperazzi preprinted, colored papers with marbled, granite metallic and other simulated textures. Available in packages of fifty, one hundred or five hundred sheets. Contact Letraset at 40 Eisenhower Dr., Paramus NJ 07653.

PaperDirect
Mail-order company offering swatch books and catalog. Specializes in preprinted colored and simulated-textured laser printer paper. Overnight deliveries available via Federal Express. Call (800)A-PAPERS for catalog.

Queblo Images
Mail-order company specializing in specialty papers for laser printers. Write for a free catalog: Queblo Images, 131 Heartland Blvd., Brentwood NY 11717.

Handmade Papers

Central Art Supply
Approximately 2,500 kinds of paper in stock from all over the world. Handmade and hand-marbled papers a specialty. Catalog available. Call (212)373-7705.

Dieu Donne Papermill
New York City-based mill makes and sells its own papers. Specializes in archival rag and custom, handmade papers. Call for catalog at (212)226-0573.

Earth Care Paper
Represents "environmentally responsible" mills. Located in Madison, Wisconsin; two-day delivery is made on all orders via UPS. Call (608)223-4000.

The Japanese Paper Place
Carries over two hundred handmade Japanese papers and provides a sample service. Located in Toronto. Cash-and-carry is preferred; minimum ship order is one hundred dollars. Call (416)536-5606.

Kate's Paperie
New York City-based outlet offers sample service. Cash-and-carry or shipping available. Call (212)941-9816 or (212)633-0570.

Magnolia Editions
Oakland, California. Makes and sells its own papers. Call (510)839-5268.

Twin Rocker Paper Mill
Makes a variety of papers in all kinds of sheet sizes, up to as large as 4×8 feet. The mill also makes custom papers and specializes in minimum quantities. Call (317)563-3119.

Sources of Custom Papers
Many paper mills will color match most (if not all) of the papers in their paper lines to your color specifications. When matching colors, mills prefer a swatch of at least 6×6 inches, but most will accommodate any matching request from a customer.

Sources for Unusual Printing Papers
"You can find papers with great printing potential in some pretty unusual places. I once showed my letterpress printer some examples of tissue paper that I had found in Mexico. He went to an art supply store to look for something similar, and came across this Pad-o Palette that is normally used by fine artists to mix oil paints. It's a tablet of heavy tissue paper where each sheet serves as a disposable palette.

"We had a press run of about 2,500 for the job and were able to get the Pad-o Palettes at a reasonable cost from a wholesaler. We tore up the pads and trimmed the sheets to the size we needed for the job. We got the effect of a semi-transparent sheet that we were looking for. Sometimes it helps to look in unusual sources rather than a traditional paper merchant."

Jim Heimann, *of Los Angeles-based Jim Heimann Design, in addition to providing design for clients such as Capital Records, Sony Pictures and Disney, has authored several books and articles on vintage design and frequently speaks on the subject.*

Many mills also do custom flocking, varying the length and density of as well as the color of the fiber to your specifications.

Custom orders on standard items generally take three to six weeks.

Minimum orders are specified by the pound and will vary from 2,250 to 10,000 pounds, depending on the manufacturer. (Consult the chart on the opposite page when translating paper-by-the-pound into sheets.)

The following mills offer custom-matched papers:

Beckett Paper Co.
400 Dayton St.
Hamilton OH 45012
(513)863-5641

Fox River Paper Co.
200 E. Washington St.
Appleton WI 54913
(414)733-7341

French Paper Corp.
P.O. Box 398
Niles MI 49120
(616)683-1100

Gilbert Paper Co.
430 Ahnaip St.
Menasha WI 54952
(414)722-7721

James River Corp.
300 Lakeside Dr., 14th Fl.
Oakland CA 94612
(415)874-3400

Mohawk Paper Mills, Inc.
465 S. Saratoga St.
P.O. Box 497
Cohoes NY 12047
(518)237-1740
(800)441-3408

Strathmore Paper Co.
S. Broad St.
Westfield MA 01085
(800)423-7313

Industrial Papers

Those who frequently use industrial papers cite the following sources of industrial papers. Be aware, however, that industrial papers are likely to challenge your offset printer and may require silkscreen or letterpress printing:

- Paper converters, suppliers and distributors: All of these sources can be found in your local business-to-business directory. Call to check on the availability of chipboard, corrugated cardboard, kraft, butcher and packing paper.

- Paper merchants: In addition to fine printing papers, your local paper merchant will carry newsprint. It's considered to be a printing paper and, as such, isn't handled by converters and suppliers of industrial grades.

- Art supply stores: Small quantities of newsprint (loose sheets and pads), construction and other unusual papers can be found at your local art supply store.

Looks Like Industrial But It's Not
French Paper, in conjunction with Charles Spencer Anderson, has developed a line of printing papers that look and feel like industrial paper. Contact your French Paper merchant for more information about the Dur-O-Tone line, which includes construction, newsprint, butcher, packing and kraft papers.

Sheets Required for a 2,250-lb. Minimum Order

	Basis Weight	Sheet Size 23″x29″	23″x35″	25″x38″	26″x40″	35″x46″
Text (Basis 25"x38")	70#	23,000	19,000	16,100	14,700	9,500
	75#	21,500	17,800	15,000	13,700	8,900
	80#	20,100	16,600	14,100	12,800	8,300
	90#	18,000	14,800	12,500	11,400	7,400
	100#	16,100	13,300	11,300	10,400	6,700
	120#	13,400	11,000	9,400	8,600	5,600
Cover (Basis 20"x26")	50#	17,600	14,500	12,300	11,300	7,300
	60#	14,600	12,100	10,300	9,400	6,100
	65#	13,500	11,200	9,500	8,700	5,600
	70#	12,500	10,400	8,800	8,000	5,200
	75#	11,700	9,700	8,200	7,500	4,900
	80#	11,000	9,100	7,700	7,000	4,500
	90#	9,700	8,100	6,800	6,300	4,000
	100#	8,800	7,300	6,200	5,600	3,700
	130#	6,700	5,600	4,700	4,400	2,800

A minimum order for any custom stock depends on the weight of the sheet.

The number of sheets you need to order to achieve the minimum weight for custom paper varies with the weight of the sheet. This table shows how many sheets you would need to buy in order to meet a minimum order of 2,250 pounds.

Chapter 4

Working With Color

Sources of Information on Color Trends

- The Color Marketing Group is a non-profit association made up of over twelve hundred designers, marketing experts, product developers and others whose business depends on keeping up with color trends. The group sponsors national meetings and workshops and publishes a quarterly newsletter as well as other publications and forecasting tools on color trends. Contact them at: 4001 N. Ninth St., Suite 102, Arlington VA 22203; (703)528-7666.

- The Color Association of the United States (CAUS) is primarily concerned with color for fashion, interior and environmental design. Members include many manufacturers, retailers, designers, architects and stylists. Benefits of membership include the choice of one category of swatched color forecasts for women's, men's or children's wear or interior/home. A monthly newsletter, a color matching service, and access to the CAUS color reference libraries, which contain color swatches dating back to 1915, are also available to members. Contact CAUS at: 409 W. Forty-fourth St., New York NY 10036; (212)582-6884.

Do's and Don'ts of Using Color
DO . . .

- Do use color to draw the viewer's attention to the most important elements in your document.

- Do use color to distinguish among segments of your document—sidebars, introductions, glossaries, and so on—so they stand out.

- Do use a color consistently to link separate elements.

- Do use color to signal section breaks, such as chapter openers, and to further define the format of a publication.

- Do use color as a client identifier. Pick up a firm's logo color and use it frequently in their literature to build and maintain the client's desired image.

- Do try to limit the number of match colors in a document to two plus black—the combination readers remember best. Four distinct colors should be your maximum.

- Do enhance color coding by using the same color on similar shapes, such as boxed headings, spot illustrations or graphic rules. Redundancy attracts attention and makes your message more memorable.

- Do set type larger and bolder when it is specced for a second color. Colored type needs extra size since it contrasts less with white paper than black type does.

- Do compensate for paper color. When selecting a spot color, consider the color of the paper it will print on. A color will look darker on a light background than it does against a dark background.

- Do consider the type of paper your color will run on. Colors look darker on un-coated paper than on coated papers. Remember, too, that unless your inks are opaque, the color of your paper will affect the color of your ink. A brilliant blue will appear dull and subdued if you run it on tan paper.

- Do watch for adequate tonal contrasts. When reversing type out of a background color, check to be sure there is at least a 30 percent difference in tonal value between the type and the background. Use a gray scale to check the value. Pay close attention to a bright background color, which will create the illusion of more contrast than really exists.

DON'T . . .

- Don't use color just because it's available. Decorative color, or color for its own sake, is obvious. Use color to explain, enhance and draw attention to the highlights of your message.

- Don't select a color just because you like it. Make sure the color you choose is compatible with the mood of your message and suitable to your audience.

▶

Color Trends for the '90s

"Remember that taste in color undergoes constant change. Grabbing someone's attention depends on being cognizant of what palette is likely to be appealing to American consumers at a given point in time.

"For example, during the 1980s, black was a pivotal color. Forecasters generally agree that the 1990s will see an increasing predominance of white. All shades [of other colors] will move, accordingly, to softer, lighter and clearer variations.

"Red, white and blue were also popular colors in the '80s. In the [early] '90s we have already experienced a shift of interest to greens, yellows and oranges."

Margaret Walch is associate director of The Color Association of the U.S., an organization made up of professionals who make color forecasts.

- Don't overwhelm your layout by using bright colors, such as lime green or purple, on a bold headline or as a tint behind a large block of text. Big, bold areas need pale, subtle tones. Save bright colors for small areas of your composition.

- Don't use many different colors. For one thing, you risk gaudiness. Select a minimum number of colors and use them consistently, particularly when color coding a series of documents or a number of pages within a single document.

- Don't use bright colors, such as fuschia or orange, for text. They tend to exhaust the eye and discourage reading beyond the first sentence or two.

- Don't print low-contrast black-and-white photos "as is." Add contrast, and so vitality, by turning them into duotones (adding a second color such as blue to the black) or a tritone (adding two colors such as blue and gray to the black). Two dark colors and one light color are usually used for a tritone.

- Don't combine colors—for example, printing red on blue or yellow on purple—without considering their hues and values. Colors printed in pure, 100 percent hues and with close (50 percent or higher) values are likely to vibrate visually and lessen readability. To avoid this, weaken the intensity of one of the hues to lower its value. This will ease the visual dissonance.

Guidelines for Adding Color to Colored Paper

To ensure that your match or process colors will look good on the colored paper you've selected, follow these guidelines.

- Underprint opaque white on uncoated paper. Run at least one layer of opaque white ink to flatten the fiber and to provide an undercoat for a brilliant color that might otherwise wash out. Underprinting is time consuming and expensive. It may also give a mottled texture to photographic images. Ask your printer if underprinting has a place in your project.

- Enhance a transparent ink. Add opaque white to transparent inks to increase their opacity, preserve their color, and prevent show-through of background color.

- Use a varnish. Apply an aqueous varnish to your paper for your color. (See page 46 for more information.)

- Consider using metallic, rather than transparent, inks. Metallic inks are more opaque than transparent inks and create the most contrast on colored stocks. Use them alone or in combination with transparent inks.

- Use foil stamping. When printing on an uncoated stock, use foil stamping to get true reflectivity. You may still get an attractive effect from a metallic ink, but it will be subtler than you'll get with foil.

- To avoid surprises, ask your printer for an ink drawdown.

- Avoid running fine line art or small text copy on dark stock. The paper color will overwhelm these subtle, printed areas.

- Choose a paper with good ink holdout.

- Substitute fluorescent inks. If you expect process colors to flatten out on your chosen stock, substitute fluorescent inks for the standard magenta, cyan or yellow to brighten color dramatically.

- Double bump a transparent ink (applying two hits of the ink when printing) to enhance a color's value on colored paper. Dry trapping (printing the second application after the first has dried) takes longer, but it generally produces better results.

- Don't use a line screen higher than 150 when applying colored ink to uncoated paper. Finer screens plug up and cause loss of detail.

- Consider taking advantage of thermography's opacity so your printed ink will hold its own on colored paper.

- Consider silk-screen printing or engraving for small runs. These processes offer more opaque color coverage.

COMBINATIONS FOR ONE INK COLOR ON PAPER

Paper	Ink Color
Ivory	Ochre Purple Dark Brown Process Blue (Cyan) Warm Gray
Tan/Oatmeal	Black Dark Brown Dark Gray Process Blue (Cyan) Orange Metallic Copper Medium Green
Light Gray	Dark Burgundy Light Teal Royal Blue Avocado Dark Teal Purple Dark Gray
Blue Gray	Metallic Copper Dark Burgundy Royal Blue Magenta Light Teal Purple Metallic Silver
Violet	Royal Blue Magenta Dark Purple Metallic Silver Black
Peach	Black Orange Dark Olive Mustard Metallic Silver
Pale Pink	Warm Red Metallic Silver Dark Olive Black Light Aqua
Burgundy	Black Metallic Gold Metallic Silver Light Magenta Dark Gray
Yellow	Black Emerald Green Orange Dark Blue Bright Red Rust Dark Brown

Ideas for combining one ink color with a paper color

Working With Pastel Ink Colors

Pastel match colors have been available for only a few years, and as a result, designers are always learning something new about working with them. These tips will help ensure success for your pastel venture.

- Choose pastel inks (match colors) over four-color process blends or tints. Pastel ink colors usually offer better coverage, stronger, richer color and sharper edges than pastels created through four-color process blends or tints of solid colors.

- Include a nonyellowing varnish in your print run. Some pastels, such as light blues and grays, can fade and yellow. If this poses a problem for your project, discuss the varnish additive with your printer.

- Consider adding a pastel ink color to lightly tint a clear varnish.

- Use lightfast pastel ink for posters and packaging or for annual reports that need to retain their impact long term.

- Pastel inks are highly transparent and can be affected by subtle tints in a paper that appears to be white. The desired color can often be obtained by blending color on press and making needed modifications at that time.

- Have your printer do a test run. Pastel ink's transparency may allow your paper color to show through. A test run will let the printer adjust the color for the paper, if needed.

Getting Color Ideas From Fine Art

"You can pick up color combinations from paintings. In fact, fine art is one of the best sources for creative use of color. Fine artists come up with amazing combinations of colors that a commercial designer would never think of combining.

We were working on a project for Swatch once, designing an apparel product called 'Bora Bora.' We felt Gaugin captured the feeling we wanted to project in the colors he used in his paintings of the tropics. We took a cab to the Metropolitan Museum of Art to see his paintings and we discussed them with the client while we were there."

Maruchi Santana *is vice president and creative director of Parham Santana, a New York City-based design firm that specializes in designing for products targeted at the youth market.*

TWO AND THREE INK COLOR COMBINATIONS

Here are some ideas for two-color and three-color combinations plus some options for paper colors to get you started. The ink color combinations will work on white paper as well as the color given.

Color 1	Color 2	Color 3	Paper
Black	Ochre	Process Blue (Cyan)	Ivory
Black	Purple	Warm Gray	Ivory
Black	Magenta	Warm Red	Ivory
Dark Brown	Avocado	Dark Orange	Tan/Oatmeal
Black	Warm Red	Metallic Silver	Tan/Oatmeal
Black	Orange	Medium Green	Tan/Oatmeal
Blue	Orange	Metallic Copper	Tan/Oatmeal
Dark Gray	Warm Red	Metallic Silver	Tan/Oatmeal
Blue	Warm Red	Metallic Gold	Tan/Oatmeal
Burgundy	Metallic Copper	Avocado	Light Gray
Burgundy	Magenta	Royal Blue	Light Gray
Burgundy	Metallic Copper	Light Teal	Light Gray
Dark Teal	Metallic Copper	Light Teal	Light Gray
Burgundy	Metallic Copper	Royal Blue	Light Gray
Dark Purple	Magenta	Light Teal	Blue Gray
Dark Purple	Purple	Royal Blue	Blue Gray
Dark Purple	Metallic Copper	Light Teal	Blue Gray
Dark Teal	Metallic Copper	Light Teal	Blue Gray
Dark Teal	Magenta	Royal Blue	Blue Gray
Dark Purple	Purple	Royal Blue	Violet
Dark Teal	Purple	Light Teal	Violet
Burgundy	Metallic Silver	Light Teal	Violet
Burgundy	Metallic Silver	Royal Blue	Violet
Black	Dark Peach	Metallic Silver	Peach
Dark Olive	Mustard	Dark Peach	Peach
Dark Olive	Orange	Metallic Silver	Peach
Dark Peach	Tan	Blue	Peach
Aqua	Lavendar	Dusty Rose	Pink
Black	Orange	Warm Red	Pink
Aqua	Lavendar	Metallic Silver	Pink
Slate Blue	Silver Pink	Warm Red	Pink
Black	Metallic Gold	Light Magenta	Burgundy
Black	Metallic Silver	Gray	Burgundy
Royal Blue	Metallic Gold	Light Magenta	Burgundy
Black	Dark Green	Warm Red	Yellow
Dark Blue	Orange	Bright Red	Yellow
Dark Blue	Orange	Turquoise	Yellow
Dark Brown	Green	Orange	Yellow
Dark Green	Apricot	Avocado	White
Charcoal	Bright Red	Camel	White
Black	Dark Orange	Hot Pink	White
Navy Blue	Magenta	Metallic Silver	White
Dark Green	Dark Orange	Camel	White
Black	Bright Red	Hot Pink	White
Navy Blue	Bright Red	Metallic Silver	White
Charcoal	Apricot	Avocado	White
Sage Green	Apricot	Camel	White

Chapter 5

Working With Illustrations and Photographs

Illustrations

Illustration Specialists and What They Do

There are several basic categories of commercial illustration. All have varying applications in advertising, marketing, editorial/publishing and specialty markets.

Medical: This market is highly specialized, and illustrators who do this type of work usually do nothing else. Many have special training and/or a knowledge of science that helps them understand and render anatomy and other biological subjects accurately. Medical illustrations are used in advertising, such as pharmaceutical sales brochures and ads in medical journals; in promotional or informative literature, such as pamphlets explaining surgical procedures; in mainstream advertising; and in editorial applications in magazines, journals and textbooks.

Fashion: This is another highly specialized area, and practitioners rarely branch into other areas. Fashion illustration has print applications in magazine and newspaper advertising, catalogs, direct mail, signage, books and posters.

Cartoon/caricature: Cartoonists are a group of specialists who hone their unique and individual styles. Their work is used mostly in editorial illustration, book publishing, direct mail, print ads and promotional literature. Other uses include storyboarding for broadcast media and textbooks.

Realistic: Used to depict events, people and objects (historical, current or futuristic), realistic illustration includes the specialized fields of architectural and mechanical illustration, where products and structures must be rendered before they are manufactured or built. This specialty is used in educational and sales brochures to give an enhanced impression of a product or setting. It also has many editorial applications in magazines, children's books, book cover design, textbooks, posters, print and outdoor advertising. This kind of illustration is used to diagram parts, procedures, products, and so on for instructional forms, manuals and other diagrammatic applications.

Conceptual: Abstract and looser illustrations are created with the primary purpose of arresting a reader or viewer's attention or when exaggeration and dramatic effect are needed to depict a mood or an impression. These illustrations are also used to create an effect of impressionistic fantasy or the surreal. Although its primary application is editorial—to draw the reader's attention to or illustrate a magazine article, for example—this specialty is also used in children's books, record jacket design, book jacket and cover design, posters, and print and outdoor advertising.

Where to Find an Illustrator

Talent Directories of Professional Organizations

Most professional organizations publish a talent directory, and many major cities have local chapters. Groups that list members include:

- Art directors' clubs
- Ad clubs

American Institute of Graphic Artists
1059 Third Ave.
New York NY 10021
(212)752-0813

Association of Medical Illustrators
1819 Peachtree St., N.E., #560
Atlanta GA 30309
(404)350-7900

Graphic Artists Guild
11 W. Twentieth St., 8th Fl.
New York NY 10011
(212)463-7730

Society of Illustrators
128 E. Sixty-third St.
New York NY 10010
(212)8328-2560

SPAR (Society of Photographer and Artist Reps)
1123 Broadway
New York NY 20020
(212)822-1415

National Directories of Creative Talent

Listed below are some of the largest and best-known resource books for illustrators and photographers. The *WorkBook* also includes an alphabetical listing of over one hundred local, specialty and national talent directories.

American Showcase
915 Broadway, 14th Fl.
New York NY 10010
(212)673-6600

The Creative Black Book
The Creative Illustration Book
115 Fifth Ave., 3rd Fl.
New York NY 10003
(212)254-2330
(310)858-0013
(312)944-5115

RSVP
P.O. Box 314
Brooklyn NY 11205
(718)857-9267

The WorkBook
940 N. Highland Ave.
Los Angeles CA 90038
(213)856-0008
(800)547-2688
(212)674-1919

Stock Illustration Agencies

Culver Pictures
(historical)
150 W. Twenty-second St., Suite 300
New York NY 10011
(212)645-1672

Image Bank
111 Fifth Ave.
New York NY 10021
(212)529-6700

The Stock Illustration Source
20 Waterside Plaza
New York NY 10010
(212)679-8070

Stockworks
445 Overland Ave.
Culver City CA 90232
(213)204-1774

Sources of Art for the Budget Conscious

Government agencies will frequently furnish, free of charge, anything they've published. You can, for example, get illustrations from the Folger Shakespeare Library. Phone the agency that published the piece you're interested in to learn where to address your written request.

Books that have passed into the public domain or old advertisements often include good period illustrations. Local newspapers, historical societies and colleges or universities may also be able to supply you with artwork.

Sources of Clip Art Books and Services

The Art Director's Library
10 E. Thirty-ninth St.
New York NY 10016
(212)889-6500
Clip art books of vintage illustrations, old engravings and composites; the illustrations of Ron Yablon; design elements and quaint cuts.

Art Plus Repro Resource
P.O. Box 1149
Orange Park FL 32067-1149
(904)269-5139
Subscription service. Focuses on illustrations suitable for newsletters and bulletins; many pieces with religious or educational themes, also holidays, seasonal.

Clipper Dynamic Graphics
6000 N. Forest Park Dr.
P.O. Box 1901
Peoria IL 61656
(309)688-8800; fax: (309)688-5873
(800)255-8800
Offers yearly subscriptions to the *Clipper*, a volume of clip art issued monthly. Provides file binders, layout ideas and timely seasonal art.

Dover Publications, Inc.
31 E. Second St.

▶

Mineola NY 11501
(516)294-7000
Dover offers over one hundred books that depict anything and everything—silhouettes, vintage art, Victorian cuts, reproductions of old Sears Roebuck and Montgomery Ward catalogs, clip art alphabets, trademarks and symbols.

Editor's Choice Clip Art
500 S. Salinas, 6th Fl.
Syracuse NY 13202
(315)472-4555
Subscription service targeted to major corporations that publish employee newsletters. Serious and humorous editorial illustration, graphics, etc.

Graphic Source Clip Art Library
Graphic Products Corporation
1480 S. Wolf Rd.
Wheeling IL 60090-6514
(708)537-9300
Offers over sixty books in many styles on a variety of subjects. Each book contains at least one hundred illustrations. The company sells most of its books through art supply stores, but orders of twenty-five dollars or more are accepted.

Health Care PR Graphics
500 S. Salinas, 6th Fl.
Syracuse NY 13202
(315)472-4555
Subscription service targeted to hospitals and other health care organizations. Offers line illustration, spot drawings, graphics, cartoons related to health care, hospitals, etc.

Metro Creative Graphics, Inc.
33 W. Thirty-fourth St.
New York NY 10001
(212)947-1500
Subscription service. Categories include all themes associated with retail sales, classifieds, promotion and advertising. Also offers some computer-generated art for Macintosh desktop publishing.

North Light Books
1507 Dana Ave.
Cincinnati OH 45207

(800)289-0963, (513)531-2690
Offers twelve books covering the following subject areas: holidays, animals, food and drink, sports, men and women. Also: abstract and geometric patterns, graphic textures and patterns, and borders and spot illustrations. Also publishes *Pictograms and Typefaces of the World* and *Trademarks and Symbols of the World*.

Digital Clip Art Sources

Adobe Illustrator Collector's Edition
P.O. Box 7900
Mountain View CA 94039-7900
(800)344-8335

Artagenix
Devonian International Software Co.
P.O. Box 2351
Montclair CA 91763
(714)621-0973

ArtClips
Tactic Software
13615 South Dixie Hwy., Suite 118
Miami FL 33176
(305)378-4110

Artmaker Company
500 N. Claremont Blvd.
Claremont CA 91711
(714)626-8065

ArtRoom/Digi-Art
Image Club Graphics, Inc.
1902 Eleventh St., S.E.
Calgary Alberta T2G 3G2
Canada
(800)661-9410

Arts & Letters
5926 Midway Rd.
Dallas TX 75244
(214)661-8960

ClickArt EPS Illustrations
T/Maker Co.
1390 Villa St.
Mountain View CA 94041
(415)962-0195

Clip Art for Ministry
The Church Art Works

875 High St., N.E.
Salem OR 97301
(503)370-9377

Clip Art Libraries
Stephen & Associates
5205 Kearny Villa Way, Suite 104
San Diego CA 92123
(619)591-5624

Clip Charts
MacroMind, Inc.
410 Townsend Ave., Suite 408
San Francisco CA 94107
(415)442-0200

Cliptures
Dream Maker Software
4020 Paige St.
Los Angeles CA 90031
(213)221-6436

Designer ClipArt
Micrografx, Inc.
1303 Arapaho Rd.
Richardson TX 75081
(800)272-3729

Digiclips
U-Design, Inc.
201 Ann St.
Hartford CT 06102
(203)278-3648

Dynamic Graphics
Electronic Clipper
6000 N. Forest Park Dr.
Peoria IL 61656-9941
(800)255-8800

Flash Graphics
P.O. Box 1950
Sausolito CA 94965
(415)331-7700

Illustrated Art Backgrounds
ARTfactory
414 Tennessee Plaza, Suite A
Redlands CA 92373
(714)793-7346

Images with Impact
3G Graphics
11310 N.E. 124th St., Suite 6155
Kirkland WA 98034
(206)823-8198

Metro ImageBase Electronic Art
18723 Ventura Blvd., Suite 210
Tarzana CA 91256
(800)525-1552

Moonlight Art Works
Hired Hand Design
3608 Faust Ave.
Long Beach CA 90808
(213)429-2936

Picture Fonts
% Fonthaus
15 Perry Ave., A7
Norwalk CT 06850
(800)942-9110

PS Portfolio, Spellbinder Art Library
Lexisoft, Inc.
P.O. Box 5000
Davis CA 95617-5000
(916)758-3630

TextArt
Stone Design Corp.
2425 Teodoro, N.W.
Albuquerque NM 87107
(505)345-4800

Totem Graphics
5109-A Capitol Blvd.
Tumwater WA 98501
(206)352-1851

Vivid Impressions
Casady & Greene, Inc.
26080 Carmel Rancho Blvd., Suite 202
Carmel CA 93923
(800)359-4920

Works of Art
Springboard Software
7808 Creekridge Cir.
Minneapolis MN 55435
(612)944-3915

Sources of Made Art and Found Art
These techniques are fast, easy and cheap. Use these techniques to produce editorial illustrations, spot illustrations, background imagery or texture in borders. Use the resulting image or texture as reflect art.

• Photocopy a flat object. Leaves, buttons,

▶

doilies, paper clips, coins, etc. all reproduce very nicely on a photocopier.

- Photocopy a texture. Crumpled paper, patterned or heavily textured fabric such as lace, burlap or terry cloth, gift wrap patterns and wood make great background textures when copied. "Degenerate" a texture by making copies of copies.

- Make a rubbing. Place newsprint or drawing paper directly over a flat but sculpted object (for instance, a coin) and rub back and forth over it with a soft pencil or crayon.

- Make a collage of photocopied images. Use a photocopier to reduce or enlarge photographs and clip art images. You can superimpose a head from one figure onto another, place people into settings of your choice, and so on. Experiment — you can come up with some great images by combining all of the techniques mentioned above. Make a photocopy of the final collage.

- Use a flat bed scanner to reproduce found objects that will fit the dimensions of your scanner. You can get some interesting distortions by shifting the grid while scanning.

- The International Society of Copier Artists publishes a quarterly book of copier art submitted by its members. To join the ISCA call: (212)662-5533, or write them at: 800 West End Ave., New York NY 10025.

Ways to Use Tints and Varnish as Art

- Run a series of images or a pattern in a screen tint of a color or colored varnish.

- Overprint a photograph with type in clear gloss varnish. Remember that it won't always be visible.

- Run a texture in a screen tint of a color or a tinted varnish for a subtle background effect.

- For a really subtle effect, run an illustration, pattern or texture in a clear gloss varnish on matte stock or in a matte varnish on glossy stock.

- Use a tinted varnish to reproduce a delicate portrait.

- Run an illustration, pattern or texture in a slightly different shade of colored ink on similarly colored stock.

- Lay a grid over a map by printing the grid lines in spot dull varnish.

- Create transparent callout lines with gloss or dull varnish.

Photographs

Photo Repro Options

Reproducing a black-and-white or color photo in print typically requires screening it into a group of dots. Various effects can be achieved, depending on the type of screen used and how the screened image is combined with color:

Black-and-White Simple Line Conversion: This method eliminates gray tones from a black-and-white photo so you can use it as line art.

Black-and-White With Line Conversion Screens: Dots are screened to create textural effects, such as waves or diagonal lines or concentric circles. This method can also create a mezzotint effect.

Posterization: This technique makes a photo posterlike. A high-contrast (strong blacks and sharp whites with distinct tonal areas) line shot is made from continuous-tone copy; four shots are made with various degrees of under- and overexposure and then reassembled.

Duotone: A duotone is a black-and-white halftone that is printed in two colors, one of which is usually black. The process uses two screen angles and two exposures. The photo can be screened for highlights and shadows or for tonal range and midtones.

Tritone: This technique reproduces a continuous-tone, black-and-white photo with three halftone negatives, each shot to emphasize different tonal values of the original. Usually printed with two screens of black and one of a dark or neutral color to give additional depth to a black-and-white photo.

Quadratone: Continuous-tone, black-and-white photos are reproduced using four halftone negatives, each shot to emphasize different tonal values of the original. Usually printed with two screens of black and two of gray to give additional depth to a black-and-white photo.

Silhouette: In this process, the separator eliminates a photo's background, leaving only the subject. This is often done when the background is distracting.

Vignette: The vignette technique lets you modify the framing of a photo. You can frame it with a shape, such as an oval, or within a textured edge, such as a fade.

Sources of Stock Photography

For your convenience in finding specialized or unusual subjects, agencies whose collections have a specific focus have been listed separately by type of image, such as historical photos, animal photos, science photos, etc. after the listing of agencies with large, diverse collections.

Large Collections With Many Subject Areas

The following stock agencies have at least 300,000 photos on file:

Adstock Photos
Phoenix AZ
(602)277-5903

Peter Arnold, Inc.
New York NY
(212)481-1190, (800)289-7468

Black Star Publishing Co.
New York NY
(212)679-3288

Comstock
New York NY
(212)353-8600, (800)225-2727

FPG International
New York NY
(212)777-4210

Four By Five
New York NY
(212)633-0200, (800)828-4545

Globe Photos, Inc.
New York NY
(212)689-1340

The Image Bank
New York NY
(212)529-6700

Harold M. Lambert Studios, Inc.
Philadelphia PA
(215)224-1400

MI Stock
Seattle WA
(800)248-8116

Jay Maisel
New York NY
(212)431-5013

Nawrocki Stock Photos
Chicago IL
(312)427-8625, (800)356-3066

Pacific Stock
Honolulu HI
(808)922-0975, (800)321-3239

Douglas Peebles Photography
Kailua HI
(808)254-1082

Photo Researchers, Inc.
New York NY
(212)758-3420

Photobank
Irvine CA
(714)250-4480

The PhotoFile
San Francisco CA
(415)397-3040

The Picture Cube
Boston MA
(617)367-1532

H. Armstrong Roberts
Philadelphia PA
(215)386-6300, (800)786-6300

Sharpshooters, Inc.
Miami FL
(305)666-1266

▶

Southern Stock Photos
Ft. Lauderdale FL
(305)486-7117

Tom Stack and Associates
Colorado Springs CO
(719)570-1000

Stock Editions, Inc.
Studio City CA
(800)445-4495

Stock Imagery, Inc.
Denver CO
(303)592-2090, (800)288-3686

The Stock Market
New York NY
(212)684-7878

Tony Stone Images
Los Angeles CA
(213)938-1700

Tony Stone Worldwide
Chicago IL
(312)787-7880

Streano/Havens
Anacortes WA
(206)293-4525

SuperStock International
New York NY
(212)633-0708

Third Coast Stock Source
Milwaukee WI
(414)765-9442

Uniphoto, Inc.
New York NY
(212)627-4060

Visuals Unlimited
East Swanzey NH
(603)352-6436

Westlight
Los Angeles CA
(310)820-7077, (800)872-7872

Woodfin Camp and Associates, Inc.
New York NY
(212)381-6900

Zephyr Pictures
Del Mar CA
(619)755-1200, (800)537-3794

Animals/Nature/Earth Science Photos

Allstock, Inc.
Seattle WA
(206)622-6262, (800)248-8116

Animals Animals/Earth Scenes
Chatham NY
(518)392-5500

Animals, Animals Enterprises
New York NY
(212)925-2110

Earth Images
Bainbridge Island WA
(206)842-7793

Ellis Wildlife Collection
Brooklyn NY
(718)243-2250

Grant Heilman Photography, Inc.
Lititz PA
(717)626-0296

Hunt Institute for Botanical Documentation
Pittsburgh PA
(412)268-2434

Terraphotographics/BPS
Moss Beach CA
(415)726-6244

Art/Architecture Photos

Art on File
Seattle WA
(206)322-2638

Art Resource
New York NY
(212)505-8700

ESTO
Mamaroneck NY
(914)698-4060

Fashion/Human Interest/Celebrities Photos

Fashions in Stock
East Elmhurst NY
(718)721-1373, (800)873-7862

Life Picture Sales
New York NY
(212)522-4800

Magnum Photos
New York NY
(212)966-9200

Mega Productions, Inc.
Los Angeles CA
(213)462-6342

Movie Star News
New York NY
(212)620-8160

Visions Photo Agency, Inc.
New York NY
(212)255-4047

Medical/Science and Technology Photos

Custom Medical Stock Photo
Chicago IL
(312)248-3200, (800)373-2677

Fundamental Photographs
New York NY
(212)473-5770

Medichrome
New York NY
(212)679-8480

Photri-Photo Research
Alexandria VA
(703)836-4438, (800)544-0385

Nostalgia/Historical Photos

The Bettman Archives/Bettman Newsphotos
New York NY
(212)777-6200

Culver Pictures, Inc.
New York NY
(212)645-1672

Historical Pictures Service, Inc.
Chicago IL
(312)733-3239; (800)543-5250

Library of Congress Prints and Photographs Division
Washington DC
(202)707-6394

Observer
Bellmore NY
(516)679-9888

Seascapes, Hunting, Boating Photos

Jordan Conrad Imagery Unlimited
Alameda CA
(415)769-9766

Mountain Stock Photography and Film
Tahoe City CA
(916)583-6646

Sports Photos

All Sport Photography USA, Inc.
Santa Monica CA
(310)395-2955

Duomo Photography, Inc.
New York NY
(212)243-1150

Focus on Sports, Inc.
New York NY
(212)661-6860

Long Photography
Los Angeles CA
(213)888-9944

National Baseball Library
Cooperstown NY
(607)547-9988

Transportation Photos

Jordan Conrad Imagery Unlimited
Alameda CA
(510)769-9766

Cindy Lewis
Sherman Oaks CA
(818)788-8877

Budget Sources of Photos

National Archives and Records Services: Close to 5.5 million photos; most predate World War II. All types of subject matter relative to American life — immigrants, city and rural settings, military, industrial subjects, portraits of famous Americans, and so on. Delivery

▶

can take eight to ten weeks. Charges are $5.25 for an 8 × 10 inch black-and-white print of any work on file. Contact: Still Picture Branch, National Archives and Records, Room 18N, Washington DC 20408; (202)523-3236.

Library of Congress: Over twelve million images, dating back to around 1800, that depict all aspects of American life. Library holdings include etchings and illustrations as well as photos. Charges are $7.00 each for 8 × 10-inch black-and-white prints. Contact: Prints and Photographs Division, Library of Congress, Washington DC 20540; (202)707-6394.

National Park Service: Scenic and wildlife shots from national parks; also shots of monuments and battlegrounds. *Lends* color transparencies and black-and-white prints at no charge for most usage situations. Contact: National Park Service, 1849 C St. NW, Washington DC 20240; (202)208-7394.

NASA: Shots of earth from space, space shuttle liftoffs and landings, past space missions, moon landings, and more. Contact: NASA, 400 Maryland Ave. SW, Rm. 6035, Washington DC 20546; (202)358-1900.

Chambers of Commerce: Will generally lend slides and transparencies of local subjects for a nominal fee or at no charge.

State and Local Boards of Tourism: Good sources of geographic, metropolitan or landmark photos.

Universities: Campus life, buildings and grounds, academic or research subject matter. Some may have a collection of historical or local culture subjects.

Trade Associations: Photos related to specific businesses or industries.

Finding a Photographer
Photo Specialties
Photographers have specialties, just as il-lustrators do. Some can do great studio shots but may fall short on location. Your objective should be to find a photographer appropriate for the project's budget, message, overall look and purpose. Here are some photographic specialty areas:

- Advertising
- Catalog
- Editorial
- Events
- Fashion
- Food
- Journalism
- Portraiture
- Product
- Promotion
- Travel

How to Find a Photographer
Check the following to locate photographers:

- National talent directories listed on page 43 for well-known photographers and those in larger cities.
- State or city talent directories for local photographers. Check at area chapters of the professional organizations listed below.
- Photographers' representatives and agencies.
- Yellow Pages.
- Recommendations from others.
- Area ad agencies and design studios.
- Schools with courses in photography.
- Credits attached to published photos.

Professional Photography Organizations
Advertising Photographers of America
27 W. Twentieth St., #601
New York NY 10011
(212)807-0399

American Society of Media Photographers
419 Park Ave., South

New York NY 10016
(212)889-9144

Picture Agency Council of America
222 Dexter Ave., North
Seattle WA 98109
(206)622-6262

Professional Photographers of America
1090 Executive Way
Des Plains IL 60018
(708)299-8161

Professional Women Photographers
17 W. Seventeenth St.
New York NY 10011
(212)255-9678

Graphics That Add Punch to a Piece

Ways to Use Graphic Elements

- Use a border to frame the live area of a page, or an entire spread.

- Separate an ad from the rest of the material on a page with a border.

- Group several visuals and their captions by placing a border around them.

- Surround the message area of a letterhead with a border.

- Place a background texture or tint behind a visual and related copy to show the reader that these two elements belong together.

- Overprint type on a screened-back appropriate photo to have an effective, textural background for your copy.

- Drop type out of a ramp of gradated color.

- Set off a sidebar or pull quote with a tint box.

- Box a pull quote to separate it from surrounding text. Experiment with boxes with unusual shapes or edges such as scrollwork.

- Make reader response coupons with boxes made up of dashed lines.

- Tie together all the pieces of a stationery system by using the same background in each piece.

- Separate columns of type with vertical rules.

- Emphasize a headline or a subhead by running a rule beneath it.

- Mark off sections of information in the financial section of an annual report with a double rule under the totals.

Borders, Backgrounds and Textures

Borders and rules: These separate elements, such as text from text, visuals from text, or ads from editorial matter. They can also be purely decorative. You can purchase them as transfers in a variety of sizes, ranging from narrow (hairline and 1/2-point) to wide (18-points and higher, depending on manufacturer). Stylistic treatments and strips of multiple rules are also available. Manufacturers include Formatt, ChartPak and Letraset, as well as traditional and digital clip art sources (see pages 43-45 earlier in this chapter). You can create rules from hairline up to 12-points wide and create frames (borders) around elements.

Backgrounds and textures: Textural effects can be purchased as transfers in black and white and can be used as background for type and images, screened back as a halftone tint, or run in a second color. They come in a variety of abstract patterns and simulations of textures, such as stipled and crosshatched. Manufacturers include Formatt, ChartPak and Letraset. Full-color, realistic background representations can be obtained from Backgrounds for Advertising, Los Angeles CA, (213)820-7077, or New York NY, (212)685-3870. You can also scann found objects with a pattern or texture to create original textures.

Charts and Graphs

Line charts: Show the relationships between data plotted on a line. Typical examples are time lines and calendars where events are marked on a horizontal axis that reads chronologically from left to right.

Matrix charts: Show relationships between data plotted on two axes. They can show a

▶

scattering of points or provide specific information, such as the mileage between cities.

Bar charts: Show length, area or volume data on a bar or column. Variations include radial bars, where all bars begin at a common center; deviation or two-directional bars, where bars are set against a single value line (frequently zero with negative values emanating to the left, and positive to the right); divided bars that contain subdivisions within each column; and range or floating bars, where bars don't emanate from a single value line.

Pie charts and sector charts: Show segments of information as parts, typically percentages, of the whole.

Line graphs: Plot points on a graph with two axes to indicate a trend. A downward direction generally indicates decline, and an upward direction indicates improvement.

Flow charts: Use geometric shapes and arrows to show the sequence of, or relationships between, processes.

Three-dimensional graphs: Use three axes to plot information that has two common factors and one variable.

Sources of Typographic Ornaments, Woodcut Ornaments and Dingbats

- *1,000 Quaint Cuts*, Andrew Tuer (ed.), Art Direction Book Co.

- *Design Elements 1, 2, 3 & 4*, Richard Hora and Mies Hora, Art Direction Book Co.

- Adobe Experts Sets include typographic ornaments. Current sets available are Adobe Caslon, Adobe Garamond, Adobe Minion and Adobe Utopia. Call Adobe Systems, at: (800)344-8335.

- Adobe has two collections of woodtype ornaments. Call Adobe Systems, at: (800)344-8335.

- Fontshop has a set of ornaments in their font package Woodtype 1 for both Mac and PC. A set of Granjon Ornaments is also available for Mac. Call Fontshop at: (800)463-6687.

- The Lanston Type Library has several sets of ornaments: Fleuron Units; Suite of Fleurons; Fleurons, Folio One; and Vine Leaves, Folio One. These fonts are distributed by Precision Type; call: (800)248-3668.

- The Linotype Type Library has two packages, Woodtype Ornaments 1 and 2, that have ornaments from a variety of woodtypes such as Ironwood and Birch. Call Linotype at: (800)633-1900.

- *Borders, Frames and Decorative Motifs from the 1862 Derriey Typographic Catalog*, Charles Derriey, Dover Books.

- *Alphabets and Ornaments*, Ernst Lehner, Dover Books.

- *Pictorial Archive of Printer's Ornaments from the Renaissance to the 20th Century*, Carol Belanger Grafton (ed.), Dover Books.

- *The Enschede Catalog of Typographic Borders and Ornaments: An Unabridged Reprint of the Classic 1891 Edition*, Joh. Enschede and Sons, Dover Books.

- *Exotic Alphabets and Ornaments*, William Rowe, Dover Books.

- Monotype offers Columbus, an Expert Set with ornaments. Call (800)666-6893.

Chapter 6

If You Are Working on Logos

Get Your Viewer Involved in the Logo
"A successful mark often requires visual completion by the audience it addresses. Viewers express acceptance of a mark more readily when they are allowed to participate by mentally finishing the design. A corporate image should be allowed to romance its viewer. Allow your mark to convey its primary story, but at the same time enclose alternative symbology that will unfold over a period of time.

"This may sound rather high-minded, but it all boils down to this: We develop a sense of ownership when we feel like we understand the inner secrets and true intent of a creative endeavor."

Bill Gardner *is principal and co-founder of the Wichita, Kansas-based design firm, Gardner+ Greteman, a multi-faceted design firm that has won many awards and specializes in image development, corporate communication and packaging.*

When Designing a Logo, Remember:

- Keep it classic looking. It can be a trend-setting design by today's standards, but you'll be doing your client a disservice if it looks dated a few years down the road.

- Make it flexible. It should be easily reproducible and legible in all sizes, from 4-point type to billboard blow-ups.

- Make sure it's adaptable. It must be useful in black-and-white as well as color applications.

- Know that it's unique. Uniqueness within your client's industry means that the logo is instantly recognizable and not easily confused with a competitor's logo.

- Give it universal meaning. A logo should have a clear, positive connotation in other countries or languages if your client will be marketing outside the English-speaking market.

- Think positively. Avoid any negative connotations in a logo.

- Use a baseline. Research shows that clients and consumers usually respond more favorably to a logo that is grounded with a baseline.

- Design simply. Intricate logo designs are usually less memorable and harder to reproduce than strong, simple designs.

- Be direct. Avoid ambivalent or foggy notions of what needs to be conveyed.

- Consider its compatibility. Keep in mind the overall identity system the logo is a part of. How will it look on brochures? How will it work with accompanying typography on a variety of materials?

- Avoid using only the company's initials in the logo. Initial names and identities work well only when a company has built equity in the entire name.

- Use figurative or descriptive symbols rather than abstract ones to help convey a unique or especially attractive aspect of a company's personality.

- Abstract symbols, although appropriate for some clients, can be more difficult to interpret than figurative ones and often become generic through overuse by many companies. Chase Manhattan's octagonal symbol has been copied so many times that it's now a cliché.

- Identify any key, successful elements of a client's existing symbol and incorporate them into your new design. You don't have to retain any such element exactly as it is; your design can reflect or reinterpret that element in a new way. A circular shape could become an oval or even irregularly shaped. It could become part of the typographic design if the company's name has the letter *O*.

- Try to link the elements of a name and symbol-based logo so they are not easily separated. Clients can and often will split name and symbol apart, using each separately and inappropriately.

- Design with budget in mind. Don't create a six-color logo for a client whose budget allows only for a one-color quick printing.

- Symbolic logos work well for companies whose names suggest a shape or figure, such as Bell Telephone or Shell Oil.

- Express the ordinary in an extraordinary way. Inject humor into a design or reinvent a classic symbol. A caterer could be represented by a flying covered dish rather than a stationary one. It could ride on a wagon or roller skates or become a minivan ready to roll.

Ten Questions to Ask Your Client When Developing a Visual Identity

Zeroing in on the right logo for a client boils down to understanding what the firm's identity is. You don't need to psychoanalyze your client, but you will need to ask a series of probing questions:

1. Why has the company decided to have a new logo designed? Have there been any changes that have brought about this need?

2. What is the company's history? How long has it been in business? Has it

changed much over time?

3. What are its products and services and where are they marketed? How large is it? Are there several divisions?

4. How does the company market its products and services?

5. How is the company perceived by its market? What evidence supports that impression?

6. How accurate are the market's perceptions? Where are they inaccurate? How does management want the company to be seen? What direction will it take in the future?

7. What is management's current vision of the company? Does the current logo support management's vision? Is it distinct from competitors?

8. What are the company's specific communication objectives? How does—or doesn't—the current logo meet them?

9. How does the company fulfill its current design needs? Through an agency or studio or using in-house designers?

10. How will the new logo be used by vendors and/or staff?

Types of Logos

While there are many possible variations in logo design, there are only three main types of logos.

Descriptive: This logo uses an image to depict or suggest the firm's name or business. Because these are so specific, they work best when conveying an image of a single product line or the character of a company or organization. They are never appropriate for large corporations with a diverse line of products or services.

Abstract: This is a nonliteral and nonfigurative design. As such, it doesn't convey an immediate association with a product or service. Abstracts work well for diversified corporations and conglomerate businesses, although they can be used for any client wanting to convey a "corporate" look.

Typographic: The company's name or initials are graphically represented. Typographic logos are commonly referred to as logotypes. Descriptive names such as Ford Motor Company verbally identify a company's business and are often appropriate to include in a logo for new businesses. Initials are often used in designing a logotype for a company with a long-standing reputation, such as GE for General Electric.

Logo Variations

One-color or black and white: For clients on a limited budget, maintaining a one-color approach (typically black and white) is usually a priority. In this situation, create a design with strong graphics that aren't dependent on color for interpretation. Consider adding color by using colored paper.

Halftone: When literal depiction of an image is important, yet the budget restricts your design to one color, halftone logos are an option. You can also explore other vehicles for reproducing your image, including silhouetted, stippled and linear versions. Applications of "screened-back" halftones include subordinate graphics that work in concert with, but secondary to, typography or other graphics.

Two-color: Adding a second color adds the distinction of a "signature" color to a company, further differentiating it from its competitors. In an overall identity strategy, it can help to unify literature, products and other communication vehicles. This approach is often appropriate when a company wants to convey a conservative, corporate look on a moderate budget. However, a two-color logo printed on colored stock can also be used to convey a more designerly, festive look.

Three- or four-color: Using more than two colors can be appropriate for descriptive logos where a combination of colors is important to a literal depiction of an image, as well as for logos that will be used frequently in four-color, high-budget applications. When designing for packaging, retail, entertainment and dining establishments, consider all color possibilities

Logo Pros and Cons
"Finally, the best logo projects are the ones you're happy with, but don't exactly know why. We've found that often the best litmus test for a mark is what our parents see in it, and how it looks in the Yellow Pages."

Forrest and ***Valerie Richardson*** are principals of the husband-and-wife design team Richardson or Richardson, a Phoenix-based, multi-discipline design firm well-known for its award-winning logo designs.

▶

for maximum visual impact and communication effectiveness.

Production Techniques

Logos look especially distinctive when they are handled with special printing or finishing techniques.

- Foil stamping a logo offers several options. Metallic foil imparts a glitzy look that can be particularly effective when played against a rustic industrial paper surface. On a smooth vellum, it can convey pure class—the look of flawless, glossy black against pristine white, for instance. The rich look of a gold foil stamp against deep burgundy, navy or dark-colored text paper is classic.

- A blind emboss makes a subtle statement. It conveys a sense of refinement and understatement—a classic touch that is frequently used to convey the look of a corporate "stamp."

- A printed emboss "pops." Combine embossing with printed ink to enhance the three-dimensional effect and make a symbol jump off the page.

- Thermography creates a raised, rough surface with a visual and tactile effect. It imitates engraving but is faster and costs less. Options include flat or metallic ink, or tinted or clear varnish.

- Clear spot varnish makes a design sparkle; it makes colors more brilliant and photos sharper.

- Rubber stamping is a low-cost option for creating innovative, one-of-a-kind designs of type, logos or visuals. Premade stamps offer outstanding illustration imagery and quality.

- Die-cutting is an affordable, unique way to present a logo. Die-cuts, which cut into and remove small areas of paper, can be made into special shapes. Consider a die-cut that lets a background color show through.

See pages 148-150 for a detailed explanation of some of the different techniques.

Ways to Manipulate Type for Logos

- Make the name conform to an image. Initials and letterforms can easily be made to flow into the shape of, or a suggestion of, an image, particularly using computer drawing programs. (See description below.)

- Incorporate an object into a letterform. Suggest a firm's business focus by making the white space within a letterform conform to an image shape.

- Use an object to suggest a letterform. Just make sure the object's shape is similar to that of the letter it's replacing.

- Illustrate a name or letterform with a linear treatment. Lines can be used to suggest motion, perspective, and the shading of an object.

- Illustrate a name or letterform in 3-D or relief. This can be particularly effective when trying to convey a solid look.

Typestyling Programs

Typestyling programs have been especially designed for manipulating type and creating special typographic effects. These programs generally provide more accessible tools and greater ease in manipulating type than do standard drawing programs. At the time of this writing, TypeStyler by Broderbund Software, Inc., and LetraStudio by LetraSet Esselte Pendaflex Corp. are the two premier typestyling programs, providing many of the features available in drawing programs plus additional options.

Chapter 7

If You Are Working on Letterheads

Elements of Letterhead Design

Steps in Designing a Letterhead

❏ Get to know your client. The letterhead must project your client's personality. Make sure the letterhead design is consistent with marketing and communication goals and the image your client desires.

❏ Determine correspondence needs. Will there be other communication vehicles, such as press releases, memo forms and so forth?

❏ Determine quantity requirements to meet each correspondence need.

❏ Determine the client's budget. What production method, colors and papers will best achieve the desired image and communication goals within the budget?

❏ Check out the competition. What colors, paper and layouts are competitors using? Should your design fit in or contrast with their looks?

❏ Develop the logo design if you are creating one as part of the design. Make sketches of the logo on various components of the stationery system to see how well it will work at any size, on any component, including business cards, envelopes, mailing labels, forms, etc.

❏ Establish a prominent position for your client's logo, logotype or other representational image within the letterhead layout. Let the logo and other graphic elements determine the design. A client's logo and communication needs may automatically impose some limitations on your letterhead layout.

❏ Arrange copy—company name, address, phone number, etc.—so the most important information is most prominent.

❏ Design with correspondence in mind. There should be plenty of room for the message. Mount a typed letter on acetate and superimpose it on your layout to determine how well the letterhead design will work. Learn what fonts are most commonly used in the client's correspondence; that way your design can complement the way the message will actually look.

❏ Consider using graphic elements such as shapes, boxes, rules or triangles as indicators for placement of the salutation and body of a letter.

❏ Develop initial concepts. Work up rough sketches for the layout of each component of the system.

❏ Show roughs to the client and determine the two or three best ideas, then refine them.

❏ Choose the paper if you don't already have something in mind. The paper is an integral part of the letterhead; it shouldn't be chosen as an afterthought. The color, look and feel of a paper help create a look and an image for a client. Also consider whether you will use the same paper for all components of the system or different papers for different applications, such as a glossy, coated cover stock for a business card.

❏ Determine if special production techniques will be needed to execute your design. For example, embossing is expensive, but it adds a subtle, extra dimension to a quality letterhead. Foil stamping makes a strong color statement, while metallic and pearlized foils add sheen. Thermography can give your letterhead the look of engraving at lower cost.

❏ Prepare comps for presentation to the client. Show the design applied to all the core components. Make it look as real as possible; get paper samples, type a letter on the stationery sheet and address an envelope.

❏ Refine the chosen idea and get final client approval.

When Designing a Letterhead, Remember:

• Make letterhead design consistent with the look of the company's other literature and business materials.

• The top third of the letterhead is the

first glimpse the letter's recipient will see, so keep in mind how the design will look when the letter is folded.

- Letterhead is meant to be written on. Don't make your design so big that it leaves no room for writing or so noticeable that it distracts from the message.

- Any tint or imagery in the message must be light enough not to interfere with the legibility of the message.

- Create a design that complies with postal regulations for positioning of information.

- Select paper and a production method that will run through your client's copiers and laser printers.

- Be sure it's appropriate for typed correspondence. Some textured papers don't take impressions from typewriters or printers well, leaving broken type. If your client uses a roll-fed computer printer, have the letterhead printed on continuous roll paper.

- Make sure your client's equipment can print on embossed paper before you incorporate an emboss into the design.

- Die-cuts can also present problems if your client's printers or other equipment needs to grip the paper where a die-cut has been made.

- Make sure the paper and production method you've chosen are compatible with your design objectives. For example, a quick-print shop can't run a bleed design on 8½ × 11-inch sheets of paper. A job like this is best run on a larger press that can accommodate the trim required for a bleed.

- Make sure the quantity and production method you've chosen are compatible with one another. For instance, it wouldn't be cost effective to pay the prep charges on a multicolor letterhead for a quantity of less than five thousand.

See chapter 3 for more information on paper. See chapter 17 for additional discussions of various printing methods and processes.

Typical Components of a Stationery System

- Letterhead sheet

- Specialized correspondence vehicles such as press release letterhead, memo and fax forms

- Several types of envelopes beyond the standard No. 10, such as business reply envelopes, No. 9 enclosure envelopes and window envelopes

- Mailing labels

- Business cards

- Business forms such as purchase orders, invoices, etc.

Layout Options

Here are some ideas on where to put logos and other letterhead information:

- Logo and company name centered at the top with address and other information at bottom. This format works well with symmetrical logos.

- Logo centered at top, company name and address centered at bottom. This format also works well with symmetrical logos, particularly those with a strong horizontal thrust.

- Logo and company name in the upper left-hand corner, other information stacked directly beneath it, or in the bottom left-hand corner. This format works well if there's lots of information to include, such as company branches with addresses and phone numbers.

- Logo in upper-right corner, company name and other information stacked beneath. This works well with asymmetrical logos, particularly those with a thrust of movement that will direct the viewer's eye to the left.

- Logo and company name in the upper-right corner, other information stacked in the upper- and/or lower-left corner. This works when it's necessary to offset logo placement in the upper right and there is enough information to include on the left to counterbalance strong right-hand emphasis.

An Inside-Out Approach to Letterhead

"Printed correspondence materials always have two sides, and don't forget it. The back of a letterhead, business card or the inside of an envelope should be looked at as fields where a corporate image can be further played out.

"Consider the integration of corporate colors or textures in these areas. Think about the transparency of the materials you will be printing on. Could a reversed-out image on the back of the materials become an effective "ghost" image on the face of a letterhead or envelope? Envelopes are easily converted after you've printed on their interior side. This unexpected burst of color within an envelope adds visual mileage to the correspondence package."

***Bill Gardner** is principal and co-founder of the Wichita, Kansas-based design firm, Gardner + Greteman, a multifaceted design firm that has won many awards and specializes in image development, corporate communication and packaging.*

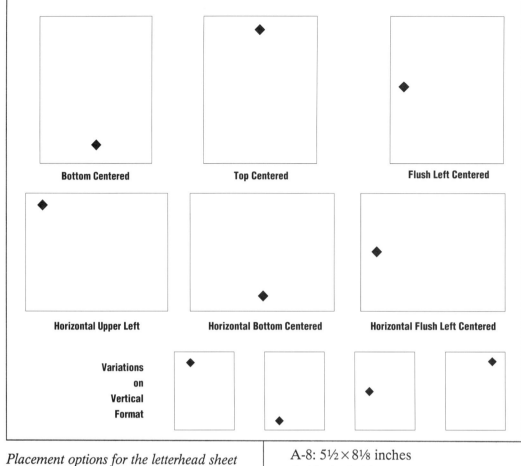

Bottom Centered   Top Centered   Flush Left Centered

Horizontal Upper Left   Horizontal Bottom Centered   Horizontal Flush Left Centered

Variations on Vertical Format

Placement options for the letterhead sheet

Standard Sizes for Items in a Stationery System

Letterhead
Regular letterhead: 8½ × 11 inches
Monarch letterhead: 7¼ × 10½ inches

Regular Business Envelopes With/Without Windows
Monarch: 3⅞ × 7½ inches
No. 10: 4⅛ × 9½ inches
No. 10 with single or dual windows:
(same dimensions as above)

Return or Business Reply Envelopes With/Without Windows
(All fit inside a No. 10)
No. 9: 3⅞ × 8⅞ inches
No. 8¾: 3⅜ × 8⅜ inches
No. 7: 3¾ × 6¾ inches

Announcement Style Envelopes
A-2: 4⅜ × 5¾ inches
A-6: 4¾ × 6½ inches
A-7: 5¼ × 7¼ inches
A-8: 5½ × 8⅛ inches
A-10: 6 × 9½ inches
Slimline (A-Long): 3⅞ × 8⅞ inches

Remittance Envelopes
No. 6¼: 3½ × 6 inches
No. 6½: 3½ × 6¼ inches
No. 6¾: 3⅝ × 6½ inches

Baronial Style Envelopes
No. 4: 3⅝ × 5⅛ inches
No. 5: 4⅛ × 5⅝ inches

Booklet Envelopes
No. 6½: 6 × 9 inches
No. 9½: 9 × 12 inches
No. 13: 10 × 13 inches

Business Cards
Standard is 3½ × 2 inches

Press releases
8½ × 11 inches

Invoices, purchase orders and packing lists
8½ × 7 inches (fits into a No. 10 envelope when folded in half)

Statements and invoices

8½ × 11, 8½ × 8¾, 8½ × 8½ inches (fits into a return envelope when folded)

Labels

Pressure-sensitive mailing labels: 3⅞ × 2⅞ inches and 3⅞ × 2¾ inches

For more information on different types of envelopes available, especially specialty envelopes, see pages 26-27.

Ideal Papers and Weights for Letterhead

Bond and writing papers are commonly used for business correspondence. They have lighter basis weights than text and book papers. Because they are uncoated, they handle easily and have enough "tooth" and absorbency to reproduce copier and laser-printed type as well as a penned note. When choosing a paper consider the following:

- Letterhead papers generally come in 20, 22, 24 and 28 lb. weights. This weight range takes up less bulk and weight in mailings and facilitates easy handling by copiers and laser printers. The best weight for any project depends on the statement the company wants to make and how the sheet will be used. A heavier sheet gives a letterhead a substantial feel and an air of importance. A lighter sheet costs less to mail.

- How a letterhead feels conveys a message. A recycled paper with a fibrous texture and flocking says "honest, natural, environmentally friendly." Patterns such as smooth, laid, linen, vellum, cockle and wove each have their own personality. Finish and texture also affect printing. If you're doing a sheet with a halftone logo, for example, a smooth finish gives better results.

- Better letterheads are often produced on paper with a cotton content, because cotton gives a sheet strength, durability and a prestigious appearance. Many kinds of writing papers are made of 25-100 percent cotton. There are even a few recycled papers that are still partly made of cotton. Crane's Crest R is 100 percent cotton even though it is 50 percent recy-

cled; C.P. Recycled, Fox River, Gilbert Recycled, Curtis Linen and Environment, among others, are 25 percent cotton.

- You don't have to choose between speccing an attractive paper and being environmentally friendly. Many writing papers and bonds are now made from recycled papers. (See pages 30-31 for a list of papers that use at least 10 percent postconsumer waste.)

- Business cards can be printed on Bristol ▶

Options for folding business cards

board or on coated or uncoated cover paper to match the text or bond paper that is being used.

- Grain-long paper (where the grain runs the vertical length of the sheet) feels crisper than grain-short paper (where the grain runs across the sheet) and works better in photocopiers and printers.

- When planning full-bleed coverage of a sheet with a tint, choose a bright white sheet with a blue undertone. Neenah Classic Crest is frequently used beneath full-bleed coverage on a letterhead sheet or envelope.

- For a nitty-gritty or industrial look, consider industrial papers or the new French Speckletone Kraft, a printing paper with the look of kraft paper. A letterhead printed on real industrial paper must be letterpressed or silkscreened. Speckletone Kraft can be used on an offset press.

- New papers are being developed all the time. ESSE from Gilbert was developed with designers in mind in a collaboration between Joel Fuller, Robin Rickabaugh and Gilbert. The paper was seen in a number of stationery systems, including that of Pinkhaus (not surprisingly), soon after it was launched.

Guidelines for Envelope Conversions

Have envelopes converted (folded and glued) after the graphics have been printed if your design includes:

- Four-color process. Four-color printing equipment generally won't accept finished (prefolded) envelopes.

- Engraving, foil-stamping or embossing. If these techniques were applied to finished envelopes, the image would appear on both the front and the back of the envelope. However, finished (prefolded) envelopes can be used for thermography; the flap and face can be printed at the same time.

- Tight register of two or more colors. Fin-

Custom Papers

Clients may want you to match their letterhead paper to their product or use a color that is unique to their identity but can't be matched to the standard colors produced by paper manufacturers. You can solve your problem with a custom paper if your client will pay for a large enough quantity. You can also order a special size, weight or finish. Custom papers solve problems with unusual, specialized production needs such as specific fold or strength requirements. Many mills will produce specific color combinations of flocking and base sheets.

Many paper mills will also color match most (if not all) of the papers and envelopes in their paper lines (listed in their swatch book) to your color specifications. You can often order a discontinued color. Minimum orders are calculated by the pound and depend on the basis weight of the paper, but some mills will produce a custom order for as few as seven thousand sheets. (See pages 33-34 for a list of mills that produce custom papers.)

Remember to adjust your production schedule to allow time for the custom paper to be produced. Turnaround time depends on the type of order. If you want a special size or color of a standard paper, allow about three to six weeks to get it. Papers made to a specific strength or other production requirements can take three to six months. Private watermarks take roughly six to eight weeks from the time the design is approved. (See pages 64-65 for more on private watermarks, and pages 26-27 for more information on common envelope sizes available.)

ished envelopes move too much for tight registration when run through a press.

- Printing a solid color, tint, type or a graphic on the inside of the envelope. Be careful not to print a dark color that will show through to the outside of the envelope.

- A bleed over a folded seam. The color will be uneven where the thickness changes. Prepare the mechanical so that the image prints ⅛ inch beyond any fold.

- Full-bleed coverage (ink covers entire visible front and/or back). The printed image must extend ⅛ inch beyond the die-cut edge of the envelope.

Printing Techniques That Add Pizzazz

Here are some special techniques that can add distinction to your letterhead design:

Die-cutting: Because die-cutting is not commonly used for letterhead, it can make a memorable impression. Die-cutting can be used to cut a shape into the letterhead sheet or to change the shape of the sheet itself. It can add dimension by cutting out the panes of a logo that incorporates a window frame. It can also create a scalloped edge or rounded corners on the letterhead sheet or business card.

Mechanical die-cutting should be done on heavyweight papers. Laser die-cutting works best on lighter weight papers. Intricate designs should be produced by laser die-cutting, not mechanical. Remember to avoid making cuts that will get in the way of a typed message or prevent the paper from feeding easily into a copier or typewriter. The cost of a die-cut from a standard die is equivalent to the cost of adding an additional color of ink. Custom dies generally cost around seventy-five to one hundred dollars.

Embossing: Embossing adds dimensionality, creating a logo that can be felt (it actually invites touch) as well as seen. An emboss can be either single- or multilevel. Debossing, in which the image is pressed below the paper surface, is less common in letterhead design, but it can also add a spe-

cial dimension to your design.

When combined with ink, embossing can further enhance dimensionality in a logo or image. The emboss can even be registered to a process color print. Embossing and foil stamping are a natural combination that creates a powerful visual impact through dimension, color and sheen. If the letterhead will be used in a laser printer, no more than a medium-height embossed image can be used.

A blind emboss (an emboss that is not combined with ink or foil stamping and not registered with an image) of a logo yields a subtle, three-dimensional effect by sculpting an image in relief on paper. The image is subtly defined without the visibility that an inked image would have.

Heavier sheets (20 to 24 lb.) take embossing well, but cotton content and other factors have an impact on how well a paper embosses. It's best to consult your paper merchant or printer for recommendations. Custom dies for simple embossing generally start in the one-hundred dollar range.

Foil-stamping: This is the process of applying high-gloss, opaque and metallic color to a logo or other image at relatively small expense (usually fifty to two hundred dollars for a die). You can achieve a glitzy effect in gold, silver and other metallic colors or high-gloss color with far more opacity than is possible with offset ink. Foil comes in a clear gloss that gives the effect of spot varnish; it can also be used to create marble and wood grain effects. Even holographic foils are available.

Foils can be combined with embossing to give a logo or other image both color and dimension. Foils can also be stamped over each other. Pastel and light tints work best when the paper color is a close complement to the foil, such as in light-colored and earthtone papers.

Some paper colors—brown, orange and yellow—can be discolored by the heat involved in the process. Foils tend to spread; they should be confined to isolated, moderately sized image areas and avoided for all except large, bold areas of type. Foil stamping should be used on rigid, 20 to 24 lb. writing papers.

Engraving: Engraving produces a slightly raised impression where ink is applied. It reproduces halftones, fine lines and extremely small type with great precision and conveys a sense of prestige. Glossy and dull engraving inks can match any color. Lighter weight papers don't hold up to the stress exerted by the press, but heavier writing papers (20 to 24 lbs.) work well with this printing method. If the letterhead will be used in a laser printer or a photocopier, the engraver must use special heat-resistant inks.

The cost of creating a plate makes engraving impractical for short-run, one-shot situations. However, the engraving plate is a one-time expense. If you have a large run—printing a thousand each of an engraved letterhead sheet, envelope and business card—or plan for the artwork to be reused with only minor changes, such as a change in address or phone number, it can impart a sense of quality at not too much expense.

Thermography: An inexpensive way to duplicate the look of engraving, thermography creates a raised, opaque impression with a high sheen. Virtually any offset ink can be matched, and thermographic powder can be combined with a metallic ink or with a tinted or clear varnish. Thermography works well with die-cutting.

Thermography works best on 20 lb. or heavier stock and with linear art and type; it's not appropriate for halftones. Avoid broad areas of color, which tend to get mottled. Thermography is not always appropriate for stationery that may be laser printed or photocopied. Check with your thermographer before committing to this technique.

Split fountain printing: Split fountain involves dividing a single ink fountain on an offset press into sections so that more than one color can be run from it. This substantially reduces the cost of multicolor printing; for example, a two-color job costs no

more than one color, a four-color job no more than two colors. If the ink roller is not split when the fountain is, the inks will blend on press, producing a gradated color. This gradated, rainbow effect can create vibrant, colorful images or soft, subtle graphic effects.

For further information on these techniques and other printing and finishing methods, see chapter 17.

Custom Papers

Clients may want you to match their letterhead paper to their product or use a color that is unique to their identity but can't be matched to the standard colors produced by paper manufacturers. You can solve your problem with a custom paper if your client will pay for a large enough quantity. You can also order a special size, weight or finish. Custom papers solve problems with unusual, specialized production needs such as specific

---

Watermarks
Getting a Private Watermark

1. Tell your local paper distributor that you would like to have a private watermark created for you or your client and what kind of paper you want to use.

2. Establish the order quantity.

3. Prepare the black-and-white line art you would like to use for the watermark. This can be a symbol—perhaps the client's logo—a shape, a typographic element, or a figurative design such as a bird, flower or animal. This will be submitted to the mill by the distributor for a sketch. Allow approximately two weeks to receive your sketch.

4. Approve the sketch. The mill orders the dandy roll that will be used to make the actual watermark and paper.

5. The mill schedules production.

6. Six to eight weeks after you approve the sketch, the paper is ready for shipment to the printer, the client or wherever you want it sent.

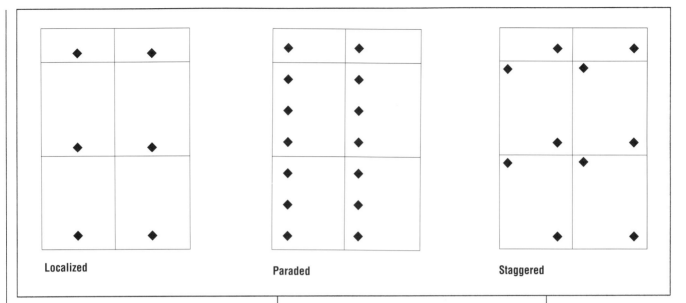

Localized   Paraded   Staggered

Watermark placement options

Guidelines for Ordering a Private Watermark

- The letterhead should be printed with the watermark right side up and reading forward. For example, if you have a figurative symbol for a watermark, it should be facing the right edge of the paper.

- Minimum quantities, based on pounds of paper purchased, vary greatly from mill to mill. As a general rule, however, you should plan an order of at least ten thousand 8½ × 11-inch sheets if you want a custom-watermarked letterhead.

- Pricing policies vary widely, depending on the mill. Some mills tack on a surcharge for smaller quantities. Cost also depends on the complexity of your design. Most mills need to see the imprint you intend to watermark before they can quote on a job.

- Keep watermarked images simple. Complex designs are totally lost with the subtle handling of a watermark.

- Most mills prefer that you prepare artwork for a watermark as black-and-white line art at the actual size it will appear on the paper, although they can work from a line negative. Designate placement on sheet as localized or random, single, staggered or paraded, and include a sketch to verify placement.

Some Sources for Watermarks

Mills that produce uncoated papers and particularly those that specialize in bonds and writing papers will do custom watermarks. The following mills are able to handle smaller quantities of custom-watermarked papers:

Fox River Paper Co.
200 E. Washington St.
Appleton WI 54913
(414)733-7341

Gilbert Paper
430 Ahnaip St.
Menasha WI 54952
(414)722-7721

James River Corp.
300 Lakeside Dr., 14th Fl.
Oakland CA 94612
(415)874-3400

Simpson Paper Co.
1 Post St.
San Francisco CA 94119
(415)391-8140

Chapter 8

If You Are Working on Identity Systems

The Elements of Identity Design

Steps in Designing an Identity

❏ Talk to your client. Query the firm's executives to determine its position in the industry, marketing objectives and corporate needs as well as why the firm needs a new identity.

❏ Discuss collateral materials. Find out exactly what types of collateral materials are to be incorporated into the client's identity package.

❏ Determine the short-range budget. What is the client's immediate budget for the initial designs, mechanicals, signage, etc.

❏ Determine the client's long-range budget. What is the client's long-range budget plan, and which of your identity concepts must accommodate reprints and new applications as they develop?

❏ Assess your client's in-house design and production capabilities. How much of its current and future identity needs can be handled in-house?

❏ Do a design audit. Inventory your client's current identity system.

❏ Check out the competition. Research and collect samples of what your client's competitors are doing.

❏ Brainstorm and develop image/identity ideas.

❏ Inform client of design audit findings. Discuss and agree on the client's image and the direction the development of a new identity strategy will take. Determine what should be conveyed in a new logo design.

❏ Develop initial logo concepts. Render sketches to show typical applications for basic needs, such as letterhead and key client collaterals.

❏ Evaluate and refine an identity strategy. How will the visual theme and image be applied to the various printed materials? How can the application and production processes be unified to save time and money?

❏ Present your proposal. Come up with a proposed schedule and budget for implementing design on all applications you deem pertinent to the client's visual communication needs, including business materials, advertising, signage and packaging.

❏ If the client accepts and agrees to your proposal, develop sketches, mechanicals and so on according to the schedule and overall plan for identity development.

See pages 134-135 for a typical production schedule for developing an identity.

Things to Remember About Identity Design

• Use a classic, timeless approach in identity design. You'll be doing your client a disservice if it looks dated a few years down the road.

• Make an identity unique so it will not be easily confused with a competitor's.

• Make a design universal. Your design must have universal meaning if your client will be represented outside the English-speaking market.

• Plan a coherent strategy. Create a familial look among the various identity pieces and ensure that their projected image matches your client's desires.

• Provide color guidelines. If color is used in a variety of applications, such as uniforms, signage and packaging, make sure it's used consistently.

• Make the identity appropriate. Identity should be more than a pretty or strong design. It should be appropriate to the client and congruent with a client's overall image, public relations efforts and marketing strategy.

• Don't make the logo overcomplicated. Intricate logo designs are usually less memorable and harder to reproduce than strong, simple designs.

• Know typical client preferences. Logo designs that are grounded with a suggested baseline are usually preferred by clients.

• Make the logo versatile. The logo should

Concepting an Identity Program
"Identity programs are best attacked by thinking through the challenge rather than designing through it. Often, we will force ourselves to write out hundreds of words that could express the client's product or service. As these words are generated, they are connected to other words until a huge list is realized. From this list we talk and brainstorm, eventually settling on possible directions to take. Only then do we begin to think visually."
Forrest *and* ***Valerie Richardson*** *are principals of the husband-and-wife design team Richardson or Richardson, a Phoenix-based, multidisciplined design firm that is known for award-winning logos and identity systems.*

▶

Design Corporate Identity for the Future

"Done right, a C.I. program is the design solution that reflects the heart and soul of a company. To visually communicate the spirit and personality of your client in a consistent and exciting manner, you have to think of the future of the client, and design for it. We've tried to develop a methodology for bringing every environmental, visual and promotional aspect of our client, and its activities, into a consistent, harmonious visual expression that communicates not only the corporate purpose and direction, but also its promise."

Walter Landor, *founder and chairman of Landor Associates, has created corporate package and service industry identities for Coca-Cola, Levi's, GE, McDonald's, British Air, GM's Saturn, and the 1996 Atlanta Olympic Centennial mark.*

work effectively in color applications, as well as black and white.

- Make the logo readable. It should work effectively (be legible as well as recognizable) from a range of distances, whether it fits into the corner of a business-card or fills the side of a truck.

Collateral Materials

Applications in Identity Systems
Common Applications in an Identity System

Coordinating a company's identity means designing logo applications and maintaining a consistent look for a number of materials, including:

- Letterhead (may include variations for corporate, division, departmental, plus second sheet applications)
- Envelopes, mailing labels
- Business cards
- Memos, press releases, or other specialized correspondence needs
- Business forms such as purchase orders, invoices, shipping forms
- Signs and signage systems
- Catalogs
- Newsletters
- Certificates
- Product packaging, labels, etc.
- Exhibition materials
- Marketing aids such as matches, pens, etc.
- Vehicles such as delivery trucks and railway cars
- Uniforms and other articles of clothing

Special Applications in Identity Systems for Restaurants
- Menus
- Tableware such as napkins, china, etc.
- Employee identification materials and uniforms
- Training materials
- Take-out containers

Special Applications in Identity Systems for Retail Operations
- Price tags
- Hang tags
- Clothing labels
- Catalogs
- Gift boxes and shopping bags
- Display systems
- Print ads

Special Applications in Identity Systems for Lodging and Real Estate
- Keys
- Linens
- Guest registers
- Amenities
- Flags or banners
- Names tags or badges
- Uniforms
- Promotional materials
- See items under Restaurants also

Special Applications in Identity Systems for Nonprofit or Special Interest Groups
- Posters
- Fund-raising materials

Guidelines for Producing Collateral Applications
Options for Identity Coordinated Clothing
- Silkscreening (also called screen printing)
- Embroidery
- Custom manufacturing from a uniform supply company
- Sublimation transfers (heat set on fabric)
- Airbrush (small quantities only)
- Custom manufacturing from a linen supply service

Guidelines for Working With Multiple Suppliers
- At a minimum, block out all applications before the first one goes to the printer.

▶

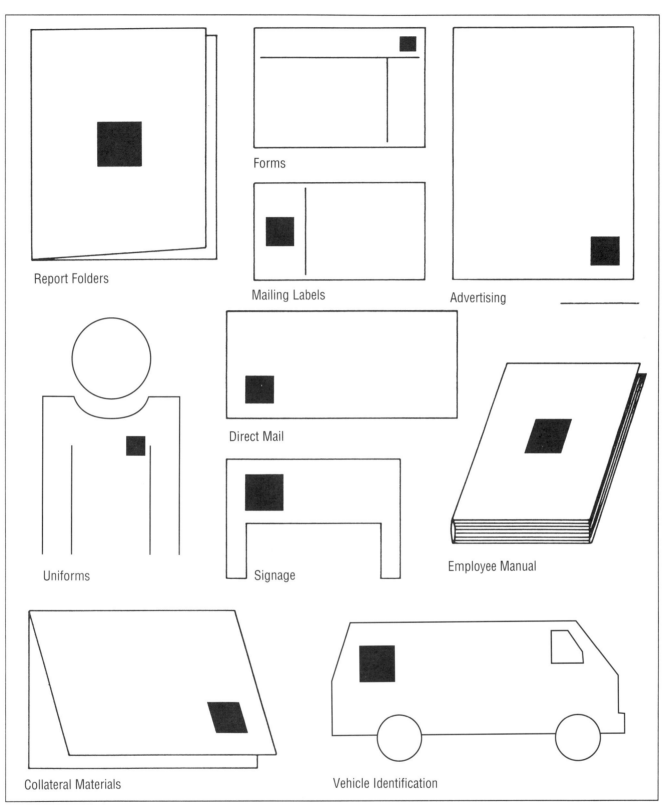

Report Folders

Forms

Mailing Labels

Advertising

Uniforms

Direct Mail

Signage

Employee Manual

Collateral Materials

Vehicle Identification

Types of collateral that may be part of an identity system

Classic Design for Corporate Identity
"It's not a matter of talent, research, or cutting-edge graphics. As the designer, you have to develop an ability to put yourself in your client's position and develop what I would call an informed intuition, *to see the design problem from the client, consumer and marketplace perspectives. If your client is working within the complexities of a global environment, find those common denominators of visual response that read globally, but also reflect cultural values. In this way you can avoid the risk of developing a homogenized international design."*
Walter Landor, *founder and chairman of Landor Associates, has created corporate package and service industry identities for Coca-Cola, Levi's, GE, McDonald's, British Air, GM's Saturn, and the 1996 Atlanta Olympic Centennial mark.*

This lets you catch any problems with color and layout when they're most easily corrected.

- Prepare a detailed, carefully conceived identity manual with specifications for each application.

- Establish the deadline(s) for implementation with the client. Determine how much of the new program will be implemented immediately and what parts will occur gradually.

- Work out production schedules with each supplier based on the timetable for the launch and implementation. Peg all work to either the application that will take longest to produce or an application to which others must be color matched.

- Use a color matching system that provides swatches. Make it clear to each supplier that this swatch must be matched as closely as possible. You may not always get a perfect match due to differences in production methods, but do encourage suppliers to try. If exact color matching is important, you may need to modify your color palette.

- Pad schedules whenever possible to allow for problems such as difficulties in color matching or the receipt of materials.

- When possible, subject to budget or time constraints, use the same supplier for several applications or work with suppliers who are located close together. This makes coordination among the suppliers easier and will help to reduce your time out of the office to supervise their work.

- Check regularly on how the work is progressing at each supplier. If the business form printer needs a sample of the letterhead to use for matching printer color, a delay in printing the letterhead or in getting a sample to the business form printer can throw off the production schedule. Don't assume things are proceeding smoothly solely because no one has told you they aren't.

Guidelines for Signage

Some of the easiest and most common fabrication processes and the materials most suitable for each are described here:

Screen printing (silkscreening): This option offers design flexibility. The colors are practically limitless, and the technique offers the advantage of printing practically any sized image precisely and repetitively, if necessary. Camera-ready art or a computer-generated negative can easily be used for a silkscreen stencil. Suitable surfaces include metal, paper, wood, plastics, glass, ceramics and fabric. Applications include interior and exterior signs where mass production and a wide range of graphic effects and color are needed. Subsurface printing (printing the opposite side of clear plastic in reverse) makes this technique especially useful when signs need to be vandal resistant. Typical uses include rest room and directional signs, exhibit and display signage.

Sandblasting: This technique creates a relief (raised) effect on your sign. A stencil made of adhesive paper, tape or a rubber solution is placed against the sign surface to protect surface areas against the abrasive effect of the sand. The sandblasting leaves the protected areas smooth and raised and the exposed areas rough textured and recessed. Camera-ready art or computer-generated negatives can be used to make stencils. Suitable materials include metal, plastics, wood, glass, brick, concrete and stone. Sandblasting is appropriate for one-time or limited applications where color isn't a factor and a strong sense of dimensionality is needed. It is often used to project a sense of permanence, such as sandblasting a company's name in granite over the entrance of a building.

Photoetching metal: Suitable for small and intricate design elements, this process employs an acid bath that eats away the surface of the metal. A film positive is made from camera-ready art and produces letterforms and images in shallow, negative relief. These etched out areas are frequently filled in with enamel paint. It is used on metal in many institutional applications to project a sense of permanence and is frequently used on dedication plaques and museum and hospital signs.

Hand-lettering: One-of-a-kind signs on glass, vans and so on are often most practically handpainted with sign paints and primers specially suited for each surface. Sign painting is typically contracted through a commercial sign painter. Many of these "masters" specialize in gold leaf techniques and know the ins and outs of working on all kinds of surfaces.

Adhesive film: This ultrathin vinyl with a self-adhesive backing is cut into letters and shapes that can then be applied to any smooth surface. Film is available in a limited number of opaque and translucent colors. Standard typefaces in a variety of sizes are available, or camera-ready art can serve as a template for a CAD/CAM cutter to produce the vinyl pieces that will be affixed to the final sign. Suitable surfaces include all kinds of metal, plastics, glass and ceramics. Computerization has made it widely available in recent years to anyone seeking inexpensive signage.

Decals: Lettering or an image on a decal is printed right-reading on the face-side of adhesive vinyl film. This is a practical approach when mass-producing images for trucks and so forth. Produced by large screen printing shops, decals can be made up to eight feet tall.

Sources of Business Forms

Business forms in duplicate, triplicate and quadruplicate copies can be purchased as carboned and carbonless blanks in various sizes from sources where you can usually purchase fine printing papers.

- Small quantities of blank forms can be purchased from most paper and office supply merchants that sell small quantities of fine printing papers. Consult the listing of sources for small quantities of paper for a merchant in your location.

- Business forms can usually be purchased

from your local distributor of fine printing papers.

- Direct-mail orders usually require minimum orders of one hundred.

The Identity Manual

What Goes in a Simple Identity Manual?

- Introduction, with information on how to use the manual.

- Table of contents.

- Logo treatment: guidelines for color applications, use of graphic elements, reverse and screened applications and compatible typography.

- Letterhead: a diagram and description of proper logo placement and variations for departments and divisions, paper, ink and typography choices.

- Business forms and cards: a diagram and description of proper logo placement, paper, ink and typography choices for memo forms, press releases, fax forms, etc.

- Mailing labels and envelopes: a diagram and description of proper logo placement, paper, ink and typography choices for envelopes and mailing labels.

- Typing guidelines and reordering information for all stationery, forms and labels.

What Goes in a Complex Identity Manual?

In addition to the above, more complex identity manuals for large corporations may include:

- An introductory message from the CEO or other company official.

- Corporate logo colors.

- Logo applications for divisions and subsidiaries.

- Corporate literature: annual and quarterly reports, brochures, newsletters.

- Marketing needs: catalogs, merchandising aids, direct-mail pieces, point-of-purchase displays, tags and labels, exhibits, etc.

- Packaging guidelines: color, layout, logo and typographic applications for all packaging needs including product packaging, cartons, bags, gift boxes, etc.

- Signage guidelines: color, layout, logo and typographic applications, construction materials, illumination and installation methods for all interior and exterior signage needs.

- Transportation-related guidelines: for vans, trucks and other service vehicles, corporate airplanes, and including parking lot stickers.

- Miscellaneous uses: uniforms, labels and tags, employee name tags or pins, stickers, T-shirts.

- Guidelines for ensuring color consistency on all of the above.

Chapter 9

If You Are Working on Brochures

Brochures

Steps in Designing a Brochure

❑ Meet with your client.

❑ Determine the brochure's purpose. Is it to sell, inform or educate? What is the primary sales message?

❑ Identify the brochure's audience. Is it a wide range or a select group of people?

❑ Determine the brochure's strategy. Will it appeal to the reader's emotions or be purely utilitarian?

❑ Establish the brochure's environment. Will it be competing for attention with other brochures or will it have a captive audience?

❑ Get brochure specs from your client, including budget and quantity. Use the budget to plan any missing specs such as maximum page count, size and number of colors.

❑ Get all client-supplied copy or begin work with your copywriter. If your client is supplying all the artwork, get that, too. Determine whether the brochure will be visually or verbally driven.

❑ Establish the hierarchy of information. Determine what information needs emphasis and what doesn't. Determine heads and subheads.

❑ Organize information—copy and visuals—in a rough layout. Give prominence to the most important items. Plan for ease of eye movement and a logical sequence of information.

❑ Do a number of thumbnails to explore different formats and arrangements of information. Should it be a folded brochure or a booklet with cover and inside pages? What type of fold will work best? (See the diagram showing a variety of options for folding a brochure on page 80.)

❑ Explore cover and front panel options. Since it is the first thing a reader sees, the cover or front panel must communicate quickly. It should compel the reader to investigate further.

❑ Select one or two formats for further exploration. How can you fit all the elements into a reasonable number of pages and still have pleasing-looking layouts? How many pages can you have in the brochure and still fit within the budget?

❑ If the piece is to be mailed, establish whether the piece will be a self-mailer or sent in an envelope. Determine kind and placement of any response vehicle. Will information need to be arranged around having part or all of the back panel torn off and returned?

❑ Choose a flexible grid. Determine if elements will best fit in a one-, two-, three- or four-column format. If the brochure is large, and information is varied, decide whether or not a two-column grid will be broken down into four columns. On a multipanel brochure, establish sinks, hanglines, and vertical spacing.

❑ Explore typographic treatments. Estimate copy length based on different typefaces. What face(s) give you the look you want and still help fit the copy into the space available for it?

❑ Determine the color treatment. Plan visuals. Will there be graphic elements, photos, illustrations, clip art? Will photos be black and white, duotones, tritones or full color? Will there be line art or continuous tone illustrations? What medium or style is best for illustrations?

❑ Determine what kinds of paper are appropriate and what printing method and other production procedures are necessary to achieve the desired effect.

❑ Prepare comps to present your idea(s) to the client. Get a paper sample of the stock you want to use and show how it will look folded. Show cover stock and inside pages. Output or have type set in the actual face you want to use. Mockup visuals that will be commissioned; show samples of work that illustrate the photographic or illustration style that would suit this material. Have sample copy for the client to review.

❑ Present proposal to client. Include costs and timing for photo shoots, commissioning illustrations, copywriting or arranging for other outside services.

❑ Make refinements and adjustments to get final approval of proposal.

❑ Commission photographs or illustrations. Begin search for visuals and prepare graphic elements, charts and diagrams, borders or backgrounds you will create. Copywriter prepares copy. If the client is supplying the copy, final copy must be written and forwarded to you.

❑ Have copy typeset. Edit and if needed, proofread it. If a copywriter is supplying the copy, have the client read and sign off on it. The client should read and proofread any client-supplied copy again. Make necessary revisions and changes. It's cheaper to make client changes now than in the mechanicals.

❑ Finalize layouts. Check copyfitting, estimating spaces for visuals.

❑ Art direct illustrations or photography. Have client approve any product shots. Many clients have stringent requirements for how products must be shown, including interpretation and appearance as well as correct package color. Depending on your relationship with the client, you may want to have illustrations and photography approved as you go rather than when the whole project is almost complete.

❑ Prepare mechanicals. You may want to put together a dummy to help the client visualize how the piece will look.

❑ Review mechanicals with client. Make required revisions or changes and have the client approve them.

❑ Deliver mechanicals to printer.

For more information on folding and binding see pages 79-81.

When Designing a Brochure, Remember:

- Catch the audience's attention. Cover design is especially important.

- Keep marketing objectives in mind. Get your client's sales message across.

- Support the client's image with concept and appearance. Give the brochure a mood or feeling that suits that image.

- Support the brochure's message with concept and appearance. It's not enough to project a favorable, consistent image for the client; the mood or feeling has to support the message.

- Tie in with related literature if appropriate. The design should be consistent with the look of other company literature.

- Design within the target budget.

- Maintain visual unity. Margins and typefaces for heads, subheads and text should be consistent. Repeat graphic elements and treat photos and illustrations consistently to carry out a theme.

- Display reader response information prominently.

- Choose an easy-to-mail format if that's how the brochure will be distributed. You may want to keep page count to a minimum and use a self-cover on a multipage brochure that will be mailed.

- Choose a format that fits the organization of the material. For example, if the copy should be read in a definite, tight sequence, use an accordion fold so there's no chance that the brochure will be read in the wrong order.

- Determine the relationship between the cover and the interior. If you want the cover to attract attention and serve as an introduction or teaser for the brochure, choose a cover stock that contrasts with the interior paper, then leave the inside covers blank. If you want the reader's attention to flow from the cover into the brochure without pause, a self-covered brochure or one with a closely coordinated cover paper that is printed on the inside covers would be a better choice.

- Use a binding appropriate for the weight and size of the brochure. Saddle stitch-

▶

ing is less expensive than perfect binding, but your brochure may have enough pages or weigh enough that you'll need perfect binding.

- Plan the sequence and flow of information to reflect how people read—from left to right and top to bottom.

- Find natural breaks in the information and separate it onto panels carefully. Don't split heads or put the head on one panel and the copy on the next.

- Some element must dominate. You can't make every element in a brochure big and bold.

- Plan white space carefully. Clients may want to pack so much information into a tiny brochure that it seems impossible to leave white space. Remember that one or two large areas of white space are more effective than several tiny spots.

- Leave white space between columns to accommodate folding inaccuracies.

- On heavier stock score lines where folds occur so that the creased paper won't crack or show stress from the bend. Score the outside of the fold.

- If your brochure will be mailed, make a dummy for each of the papers you are considering for the job and weigh each dummy on a postage meter to see what the mailing charges would be.

- If copy dominates the brochure, break it up. If you don't have good visuals to work with, you can still use large initial caps, tint boxes, reversed type or pull quotes to open up the page.

- Leave plenty of space on the back panel for mailing information if the brochure is a self-mailer.

Elements of a Well-Designed Front Panel or Cover

- A brochure cover must communicate quickly. It must attract attention, convey a message and make the viewer want to find out more.

- A dominant visual grabs the viewer's at-

tention and can be used to communicate the message of the brochure.

- Keep the design and message simple.

- Keep copy to a minimum. A teaser or short title is more likely to be read and comprehended at a glance.

- Relating copy to the key visual reinforces both and amplifies the message.

- Create a strong association with a brand or the corporate image—use the company logo or the product's colors.

- Contrast attracts attention. Put a light-colored visual on a dark cover or dark, bold type on a light cover.

- Texture adds interest to a cover. Choose a cover stock with an interesting texture, emboss a design on the cover or foil stamp the type.

Cover Options With Uncoated Stock

The following options will give your brochure a dynamic look with limited color on uncoated stock (for best results with many of these approaches, use a premium cover paper with a basis weight of 60 to 100 lbs.):

- Letterpress, foil stamp or screen print on industrial paper for an interesting textural effect.

- Foil stamping, or pastel leafing, foil stamping with embossing, or blind embossing yields a rich effect on dark-colored uncoated cover stock.

- Printing and selectively overlapping two or three transparent offset inks on a colored cover yields a subtle, rich effect.

- Gloss varnishing an image or series of images on dark-colored cover stock creates a subtle background that won't compete with type or other cover graphics.

- A subtle visual effect can also be achieved by printing an image in black on dark gray or by using dark, silvery shades of metallic ink on dark stock.

- Turn a black-and-white photo into a duotone or tritone, using black and a second color such as brown, tan, red, blue or green. Print on textured white, light-colored, or subtly flocked cover stock.

- Print type and/or graphics in one or two colors on fluorescent cover stock for an eye-catching statement.

- For high-contrast, black-and-white images on darker cover stock, print one or two undercoats of opaque white, then overprint in black.

- Chipboard and corrugated cardboard make excellent covers if you want a natural, honest or simple look. These industrial papers are also much less expensive than traditional printing papers. Chipboard and corrugated cardboard must be printed on a letterpress or silkscreened. You can also print type and a graphic on a pressure-sensitive paper and apply the "label" to the cover.

Cover Options With Coated Stock

Cast-coated, premium ultragloss and Nos. 1, 2 or 3 grade coated cover stocks with a basis weight of 60-100 lbs. are commonly used for most of these techniques:

- When representing a product or scenery, crisp reproduction of four-color photography is best accomplished on coated cover. Work from a large transparency (4×5-inch or 8×10-inch) and select a fine screen (150 to 200 lines per inch) for separation.

- Use glossy varnish to play up photographs against a dull-coated stock.

- Use dull varnish on the areas surrounding photos to play them up on high-gloss, coated stock.

- Eliminate a press run altogether by foil stamping and embossing type and graphics on colored stock.

- Convey a very rich, elegant look using colored metallic inks.

Combinations of Text and Cover Papers

There are so many papers to choose from that it's hard to know where to begin. Here are some suggestions to help you get started.

Slick papers are the premium, high-gloss, cast-coated text and cover weight stocks; they're only available in white and have a basis weight of 60-100 lbs. Popular papers include James River's King James Cast Coat, Champion Kromekote, Alstrom Master Art Gloss and Westvaco Inspiration. These papers project an image of high quality, elegance and richness and reproduce areas of color and photographs beautifully. They have been staples of annual report production because of these qualities, but few are available as recycled papers. (If you feel strongly about using recycled paper, ask your local paper merchant what recycled stocks are available; you may also need to approach mill reps for information.)

Smooth papers are both the premium and No. 1 grade matte-finished, coated text and cover weight stocks and the smooth-finished, uncoated text and cover weight stocks. They're available in whites and ivory and have a basis weight of 60-100 lbs. These aren't as shiny as the slick papers but have a slightly softer, warmer look. They allow good reproduction of colors and photographs. Popular papers include Potlatch Karma, Simpson Kashmir and Strathmore Renewal. Premium coated grades are not often available as recycled paper, but many uncoated, smooth-finished text and cover stocks are.

Soft papers include all heavily textured uncoated papers, including those with flocking. Choose text and premium-grade text with a basis weight of 65-100 lbs. for a high-quality look. Use No. 1 grade book papers with a basis weight of 30-70 lbs. for more budget-conscious brochures and catalogs. Translucent papers, such as vellum, may be used for fly sheets and similar purposes. Uncoated papers are available in text, writing and cover weights in both white and colors and in a wide variety of finishes, including linen, laid, smooth, cockle and felt. Most lines include at least some recycled papers. You can reproduce photographs and color well on uncoated

▶

papers, but you will not get optimum results with either. The texture of the paper that gives each sheet its unique character has imperfections and irregularities that can interfere with color reproduction. An undercoat of dull varnish or opaque white may be used to improve reproduction. Popular papers include James River's Curtis Flannel, Gilbert Oxford, Gilbert ESSE, French Speckletone, Beckett Cambric, Strathmore Americana, Simpson Sundance, Hopper Chambray, Neenah Classic Linen and Mohawk Molino.

Slick Cover With Slick Interior. Project a high-tech, youthful, extremely sophisticated or deluxe look with a spectacular full-color image on the cover followed by more glossy images inside.

Slick Cover With Soft Interior. Use white papers for both interior and cover with black-and-white printing throughout for a look of understated elegance or for stark emotional impact. Powerful black-and-white photos printed as duotones or tritones with more than one black or with added silver will heighten the effect. The sparing use of a second color adds variety and emphasis.

Slick Cover With Smooth Interior. Use a great full-color photograph printed with showcase quality printing on high-gloss cover stock. The smooth finish of the interior paper lets you continue using high-quality four-color images throughout, whether illustrations or photographs. Running a gloss varnish over full-color photography on the interior pages gives extra impact to the photographs while leaving a soft, nonglare paper behind the copy for easier reading.

Soft Cover With Slick Interior. A richly colored and/or flocked, heavily textured cover paper creates an exciting contrast to the glossy-looking interior with beautiful type and photographs. Emboss or foil stamp the cover for even more impact.

Soft Cover With Smooth Interior. Use a cover stock in a soft, warm color with em-

bossing and a low-key duotone or black-and-white photograph. Carry this look throughout the interior with a smooth-finished, uncoated paper. Choose line art, woodcut-style illustrations, black-and-white photographs, duotones or tritones — all of which reproduce well on this stock — for a simple, earthy or period look.

Soft Cover With Soft Interior. Create a warm, casual look with off-white or colored papers for cover and interior. Keep cover and interior graphics simple and typography strong for a unified statement.

Papers for Folded Brochures

Work on your paper selection early when you're designing a folded brochure. The type and number of folds you want play a major role in determining what paper will work best. Some stocks are too heavy to be folded and scored effectively. If there are more than three or four panels, the piece will be difficult to fold at all — much less correctly — by the time the final fold is made. How much the piece will weigh is another concern.

Weight and foldability must be balanced against sturdiness, especially if the brochure will be handled extensively by the recipient. A price list that tears or becomes hard to read won't be used for long. And of course, you must consider reproduction requirements. Full-color visuals require a smooth-finished or glossy stock for best reproduction.

The best way to choose paper for a folded brochure is to choose several papers that suit your reproduction requirements and then have a paper dummy made of each. This will let you see how each paper performs when folded to your specifications. You can also take dummies to the post office in their envelopes and have them weighed to determine your mailing costs.

How to Handle Business Reply Cards and Coupons

- Make the tear-out easy for the reader. If you can afford to do it, consider perforating the card or coupon.

- Highest response occurs when the coupon or business reply card is positioned in the lower right-hand corner of a page.

- Set off the coupon or business reply card from the rest of the page by enclosing it in a border or using a dotted line to indicate where it should be clipped or torn.

- Leave room for the reader to comfortably write in necessary information.

Folding Options

Although binding equipment can handle many sophisticated types of folds, check with your shop to see what its machines can handle. Here are some of the most common folds:

Accordion Fold: Paper folded in parallel several times in alternating directions; the result resembles the bellows of an accordion. Helpful in presenting information that must be read sequentially.

Barrel Fold: Also called a roll fold or a wraparound fold. A series of parallel folds is made in the same direction so that each fold wraps around the previous one. Each panel, going from the outermost to the innermost panel, is slightly smaller than the previous one.

Broadsheet: Also called a broadside. The paper is printed on both sides and then folded horizontally. It may then have one or more parallel folds to create more pages. (See illustrations of twelve-page and sixteen-page broadsheets on page 80.)

French Fold: The paper is printed on only one side and then folded twice with the folds at right angles to each other to form an uncut, four-page brochure.

Gatefold: A page wider than the page size of the brochure is folded to form a flap to match the page size. It can be made with two flaps that fold back to reveal an area three or four times the size of the other pages. Gatefolds are used for large illustrations, maps or textual material that needs the extra space.

Short Fold: The paper is not folded corner to corner; the edge of one sheet extends beyond the edge of the other. This allows a border to show.

Single Fold: The paper is folded once, either horizontally and vertically. The simplest and least expensive way to create a four-page brochure is to print two pages on each side and then have a single, vertical fold.

How to Avoid Problems When Scoring and Folding

- Use paper coated on one side.

- Plan the printing of the piece so that the folds run in the direction of the paper's grain.

- Run the paper *grain long* on press (with the grain of the paper parallel to the width of the press cylinder) to promote less cracking when scoring and folding.

- Score wherever there is to be a fold. Letterpress scoring is particularly effective in guarding against cracks on cast-coated papers.

Binding Options

Mechanical Binding: Metal or plastic rolls, clasps, prongs, screw posts or rings are used to hold pages together. Plastic binding, also called comb binding, is available in diameters from 3/16 to 2 inches thick. Product names are Spiral, Wire-O and Sure-lox. Comb binding is the best option when the pages need to lie flat when a brochure or book is opened. This can also be a very quick and inexpensive way to bind a small quantity of booklets or brochures.

Perfect Bound: Sheets are roughened and then attached to the cover by glue to form a spine. Frequently used for magazines and catalogs, and information on the spine is helpful for referencing.

Saddle Stitching: Folded sheets are stapled down the gutter and through the cover. Ap-

▶

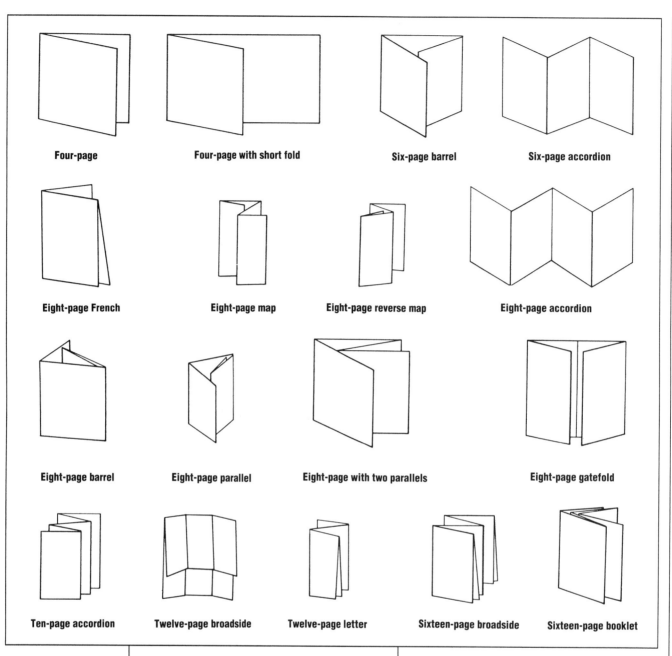

Four-page   **Four-page with short fold**   **Six-page barrel**   **Six-page accordion**

Eight-page French   **Eight-page map**   **Eight-page reverse map**   **Eight-page accordion**

Eight-page barrel   **Eight-page parallel**   **Eight-page with two parallels**   **Eight-page gatefold**

Ten-page accordion   **Twelve-page broadside**   **Twelve-page letter**   **Sixteen-page broadside**   **Sixteen-page booklet**

Folding options

propriate for smaller publications and quick turnaround projects. Saddle stitching can generally be used for brochures, catalogs and booklets that are up to eight pages long of 60 or 70 lb. paper.

Side Stitching: The signatures are stacked and a wire stitch (staple) is pushed through ⅓-in. in from and parallel to the spine. The cover is glued to the back, covering the stitches. Brochures up to 1½ inches thick can be side stitched, but publications thicker than ½ inch may look and feel cumbersome.

Smyth Sewing: The pages of each signature are sewn together. Then all the signatures are sewn together to form the whole book. This is a very strong binding and allows the book to open and lie fairly flat.

Pocket Folders
Printing Fewer Than Five Hundred

- A cost-effective way to print small quantities of pocket folders is to purchase unprinted, preassembled two-pocket folders from a local paper merchant.

- Obtain folders at quick-print shops, photocopy shops, and outlets with no minimum quantity; choose a standard

Type of Binding	Applications	Visual
Saddle Stitching	thin brochures, newsletters, catalogs	
Side Stitching	magazines, catalogs, frequently used publications	
Spiral Bound	notebooks, calendars, parts listings, brochures that must lie flat or that have pages that fold out	
Plastic Comb	presentation packets, brochures	
Wire Comb/ Wire-O	training manuals, brochures, calendars, menus	
Loose Leaf	sales catalogs, price lists, newsletters or other publications retained for reference as a set	
Perfect Bound	magazines, brochures, annual reports, large catalogs	

Binding options

cast-coated, or dull-finished cover stock.

- Given enough lead time, some paper merchants will assemble other types of cover stocks into folders.

- Graphics can be applied by printing crack-and-peel labels (in glossy or dull-coat finish, to match the folder) trimmed to a designated size. Crack-and-peel labels adhere tightly to coated stock, making label edges virtually undetectable.

- Screen printing and foil stamping are cost-effective alternatives to offset printing.

- If you or your client assemble the folders rather than having the printer or binder do it, costs drop considerably. Have the printer score the folders and ship them flat. For simple gluing get two-sided tape with a release liner.

Printing Five Hundred or More
- When you want a custom-printed, large run of 9 × 12-inch, two-pocket folders, the cutting die required for this size and type of folder is fairly common.

- Folders are printed flat, then converted after printing.

- Virtually any type of cover stock available to your printer can be used in a custom-designed folder.

- Four-color process printing, full-bleed coverage, protective varnishes, and a variety of finishing techniques are all feasible because these techniques can be applied before conversion.

- Most local print shops equipped to handle four-color and specialty runs can handle a pocket folder run.

Cover Options for Folders
Folders can be made from heavy, uncoated, coated or cast-coated cover weight stocks. Some of the following printing techniques may work better on one type of stock than another. Consult your printer or paper merchant.

- Offset, four-color process or color-matching system printing of type and graphics.

- Screen printing.

- Embossing; since the embossed element will leave a reversed impression on the inside, place the emboss on the lower portion of the cover and plan a pocket inside to cover it.

- Foil stamping.

- Holography.

- Printed pressure-sensitive labels.

- Gold stickers, which can be used as medallions and combined with other processes; they're very inexpensive.

When Designing Folders, Remember:
- The pockets must be big enough to hold the planned inserts but not so big that the inserts slide around in them.

- A single-scored pocket (scored and folded over once) is easy to glue and can ship flat, but it cannot hold an insert bigger than 3/8 inch. For larger inserts you must go to two pockets or a box (scored and then folded over twice so it stands away from the folder) or a gusseted pocket (scored and folded over three times with the middle fold tucked inside the other two).

- Make a full-sized dummy to work out exact dimensions and folds.

- Show a diagram of your design to the printer at an early stage so the piece can be printed on the most cost-effective sheet. When laid out flat, flaps and glue tabs can present quite a challenge to efficient imposition. The more complex the design, the more difficult it is to print cost effectively.

- Consider varnishing the covers of any piece that will be handled extensively to reduce fingerprints, spots and damage.

- Weight is critical. Too light a paper makes a folder flimsy and cheap looking; a paper that's too heavy may be stiff and may not lie flat when folded.

- Check the blueline against your mechanical and artwork. Check a proof of any embossing, stamping or die-cutting.

- Don't design elements to print in scored and folded over areas; breaking and cracking may occur.

Catalogs, Magazines and Other Large Publications

When Designing Large Publications

- Determine whether the visuals or the copy will be the dominant element. If photographs will be of poor quality, it's best to keep them small.

- Establish the best size and format for the project. What page count best fits the budget and the amount of material? Will it be large format to attract attention, small enough to mail easily, or a standard size? Most magazines use a format of 8½ × 11 inches, while some are 9 × 12 inches or tabloid size for impact, and others are as small as 6 × 9 inches for easy, inexpensive mailing.

- Determine the audience. A magazine for teenagers will make use of splashy graphics, trendy styles and bright colors. A catalog targeted to conservative or elderly consumers will have a conservative look and large, easily read type.

- Determine the overall mood of the publication. What tone will the editorial copy have? What photography or illustration styles are most appropriate?

- Determine whether a catalog will be primarily functional or entertaining.

- For a magazine, learn what regular features will appear and establish a design for them. Determine the client's choice for a balance between editorial and advertising content. Remember that this can change if more advertising pages are sold unexpectedly.

- Use type, graphic elements, color(s) and/or column grid consistently to maintain continuity from one page to the next.

- If only some of the material within a publication will need to be in four col-

ors, plan to print a limited number of four-color signatures. Print the rest in black or black plus a second color.

- Find out if your printer prefers mechanicals "one-up" (one page per board) to facilitate ganging several pages on one piece of film.

- Check to see if your publication is being jogged (aligned) to the head or to the foot and find out how much head and/ or foot trim the printer will take.

- If your publication has a spine, find out what the spine size will be before producing a mechanical for your cover.

- Check to see if your printer handles presorting, bagging and mailing. If this is handled in-house, can you save postage money by having the mailing ganged with another?

Steps in Producing a Catalog

- Establish the budget and size of print run with your client.

- Obtain copy and photographs or at least an estimate of the number of photos to be included and an approximate word count for each entry. Learn if there will be editorial copy and roughly how much space should be allotted to it.

- Choose a format that enhances product shots and makes it easy to associate product copy with visuals. Use a grid to provide consistency from one page to the next.

- Establish how many products will be shown per page and how much space will be devoted to visuals and copy.

- Work up rough layouts.

- Determine how product shots will be handled, which ones will be in four colors, and what size photos or transparencies will be used.

- Finalize specs. Determine size, page count and color imposition. Select a page count that is divisible by 16 or 32 for the most cost-effective printing.

- Choose papers, printing and binding.

- Submit specs to at least three printers for quotes.

For more details on producing a catalog, see the sample catalog production schedule on pages 135-136.

Preparing a Catalog Printing Bid

Be sure to include the following information when soliciting a bid from a printer:

- Job name.

- Type of job or unit: catalog, envelope, etc.

- Quantity of print run.

- Dimensions of finished, printed piece after binding but before folding.

- Size of finished piece after it is folded; for example, 8½ × 5½ inches or "to fit a No. 10 envelope."

- Number of pages.

- Number of colors and whether four-color process and/or match colors, plus varnish (if any).

- Bleeds, their pages and specific edges.

- Paper name, surface (coated or uncoated), finish, and basis weight or caliper (thickness). Include swatches of paper samples.

- Special finishing, such as embossing, foil stamping or varnish.

- In-line personalization for mail-order blanks or the back cover. Find out if the printer can handle computer tapes or affix labels.

- Finishing and binding. Specify binding method, perforating and die-cutting.

- Types and quantity of proofs needed.

- Packing/shipping. Specify cartons, skids, shipping or delivery method and final destination(s) for printed pieces.

- Delivery date: when all materials must be at their destination(s).

Catalog Formats

Although a catalog can theoretically be any trim size and number of pages, most catalogs are trimmed to either 8½ × 11 inches or a 5½ × 8½ inches for cost-efficient printing and mailing. Some high-end catalogs are printed with a 9 × 12-inch trim size, while a few others are 11 × 17 inches with few pages to help them stand out in the mail.

Guidelines for Papers for Catalogs and Magazines

- Choose papers that work well on a web press; the large-volume printing of magazines and catalogs generally requires a web press. (See page 145 for more information on web offset printing.)

- Choose a paper that suits the reproduction requirements of your publication.

- Choose a paper that reflects the audience for and image of the publication. The high gloss and snap of a premium paper projects a look of prestige, an important factor in conveying the right image for a magazine or catalog that targets an elite audience.

- Products with more utilitarian appeal (or product photos that lack pizzazz) don't need expensive paper. In fact, trade magazines, catalogs with limited four-color reproductions, and those promoting utilitarian products can usually suffice with grades 3, 4 and 5 coated stock and uncoated book weight stock.

- Choose paper that deemphasizes less-than-perfect photos, which usually look shabbier on expensive stock. Premium papers tend to emphasize any flaws in a poorly shot photo or transparency.

- Consider lightweight papers for the interior if the catalog has many pages. You'll lose some opacity but a lot of mailing weight.

- Opt for a varnish on the cover of a high-end catalog, especially if it's printed with full-bleed coverage of an ink. This will keep the cover looking fresh longer.

- Remember that higher grade papers are always more expensive than lower grades, but there is a real difference in quality. Coated stocks are graded by opacity, whiteness and printability in grades from ultrapremium and premium (the highest) followed by grades 1, 2, 3, 4 and 5. Grades 4 and 5 are also likely to contain some groundwood.

For more information on the types, grades and finishes of paper, see chapter 3.

How to Manage Lots of Photos

- Label the back of each photo with the name of your firm and phone number, so that if any photo gets misplaced, it can be readily identified.

- Code each photo for the page it will appear on. For instance, code all photos on a particular page with that page number, and then assign a letter of the alphabet. Even if you are using FPO prints to show where each photo will go, coding will help to keep photos organized and be a backup means of assuring that each photo is stripped into its assigned spot.

- Tape a pasteboard tag to the bottom of each photo, transparency or illustration, identifying the job, percentage of the reduction or enlargement, and coded position on the mechanical. Have these tags printed in large batches with boxes or lines for the information.

Annual Reports

Steps in Producing an Annual Report

- ❑ Determine amount of copy, visuals and budget.

- ❑ Develop a concept and format appropriate to client's image and budget.

- ❑ Determine specs, including size, approximate page count and number of colors.

- ❑ Acquire or commission photographs of the corporate headquarters, CEO, other company officials, and so on, as needed.

- ❑ Make a dummy with paper choices to determine what mailing charges will be.

- ❑ Obtain and have typeset all copy except the financial data (the financials usually need at least a slightly different treatment because they are in table, chart or graph form).

- ❑ Obtain financial data and have typeset; create information graphics.

- ❑ Refine format and layout with budget considerations and corporate input in mind. Come up with final page count.

When Designing an Annual Report, Remember:

- Project the corporate image and mood throughout the design.

- Take advantage of white space. Use it to help organize charts and isolate information that you want to direct the reader's attention to. Large areas of white space convey a sense of quality.

- Use color and consistent treatment of type and graphic elements to provide continuity from one page to the next. This is especially important when connecting table-heavy pages of financial information with photography and non-financial information in the front and back of the report.

- You may be dealing with officials who are not accustomed to visualizing design concepts or a printed piece in the works. Make clear presentations.

- Make sure that existing photos are free of any copyright restrictions and credited to their source.

What Goes Into an Annual Report
Required Financial Information

The Securities and Exchange Commission (SEC) has governed that the following audited financial statements must be included in all annual reports:

- Consolidated balance sheets (for the past two years)

- Consolidated statements of income

▶

(for the past three years)

- Consolidated statements of changes in financial position (for the past three years)
- Consolidated statements of shareholders' equity or footnote disclosure (for the past three years)
- Notes to consolidated financial statements
- Report of independent public accountants

Optional Financial Information
- Gross profit
- Net sales
- Net income or loss
- Income or loss before extraordinary items and cumulative effect of any change in accounting policies
- Per share data based upon such income or loss
- Any disagreements on accounting and financial disclosures

Editorial and Other Copy
- Annual message from the CEO or letter to stockholders
- Information on company progress
- Sales projections
- Income statement; earnings per share
- Training programs; production achievements
- Corporate goals
- Promotions
- New facilities and equipment
- Information on international operations
- Five-to-ten year financial summary

Chapter 10

If You Are Working on Newsletters

The Basics of Newsletter Design

Steps for Designing a Newsletter

❑ Discuss the client's goals and the audience for the newsletter. Will it be a marketing tool or a way to inform employees about company news and social events?

❑ Establish the client's per-issue budget. Base your design on the client's budgetary needs and make production considerations based on what your budget dictates.

❑ Learn how many issues there will be per year and what quantity will be distributed each time. The tight turnaround time on a weekly newsletter distributed to salespeople or in-house employees dictates extremely simple production and printing. A monthly or quarterly newsletter can have a longer production cycle that would let you use some color and photos.

❑ Determine which production and printing methods are best for your distribution quantity. If the quantity is over one thousand, offset printing is more cost effective than a copy shop or quick printer.

❑ Establish a production schedule and win the client's agreement to it. If possible, arrange to supply the copy yourself or get it from a professional copywriter. Heavily pad your production schedule if the client will be supplying copy and visuals; this minimizes your hassles if the client doesn't deliver materials on time.

❑ Choose the format based on the content, design considerations, budget and production issues. Will there be much or little copy? How many and what quality visuals will you have to work with? Do you need to keep the page count low to reduce mailing costs? Does the newsletter need to be oversized to stand out in a stack of mail? Can the client afford a slick newsletter with a glossy cover and saddle stitching?

❑ Choose the grid based on the format, budget, production issues and other design considerations. Take into account

who will be producing each issue. If you are not only designing but managing the production, you can experiment with complex grids and layouts. If you are designing a template that the client will use to produce each issue, take into account the client's production skills. Someone inexperienced with production will turn out more attractive newsletters when they can work with simple layouts.

❑ Establish the major publication elements that each issue will have. Be sure that you've covered every possible situation. What will you need to use beyond heads and body copy to organize the information and make it attractive and easy to read? Will there be visuals or information graphics that need captions? Will subheads be used as teaser copy to lure the reader into articles?

❑ Begin your typographic design with the nameplate, that will set the tone for the whole newsletter. Find the typographic treatment or combination of type and visuals that will convey the tone and personality of the newsletter. Start with thumbnail sketches and then work the best ones up as more detailed renderings.

❑ When you've arrived at the right design for the nameplate, develop your typographic strategy for the other primary publication elements. This should be related in some way to the nameplate design. Explore many combinations of typefaces, styles and sizes. Look for combinations that will give your newsletter a unified look without being boring.

❑ Take your two or three best type designs and explore how they work with various graphic elements. How do they work with the content of photos or with different types of line art? How can you make best use of a second color if your budget allows it? What can you do with rules, boxes or borders?

❑ Prepare fairly detailed roughs of the best two or three designs with your type and visuals.

❏ If you don't already have a paper in mind, choose one now. Ask your paper merchant for samples printed on papers you like that have similar artwork or production considerations to yours. Get a paper dummy made up with the approximate number of pages your newsletter will have. Have it weighed at the post office to determine your mailing costs.

❏ Refine your designs with your paper and mailing requirements in mind. Remember to leave at least a third of the back page of a self-mailing newsletter for the mailing area.

❏ Prepare comps to show your client. If a mailing permit is needed, the process of obtaining one should begin now.

❏ Present your proposal. Show your comps and review the production schedule. If you are designing a template for the client to use, describe optimal word counts, article lengths and visual sizes. Help the client visualize how the piece will be produced. Work with the client to select the best idea for refinement.

❏ Make any client-requested revisions.

When Designing a Newsletter, Remember:

- Convey an image that is appropriate to the client's image and that of the newsletter's recipients.

- Unify the different elements of a newsletter with consistent color and graphic treatment.

- Consider how much illustration or photography the client can afford and what quality it will be.

- Make sure your newsletter design is appropriate to what you will be working with. If your client will be furnishing lots of great photos, come up with a format that makes the most of them. If your client's newsletter will be text heavy, come up with a design solution that adds visual interest through creative typography.

- Consider *all* the elements that will go into the newsletter, including ads if they are part of it.

- Make sure your design is compatible with the client's production capabilities, turnaround and budgetary needs. For instance, if your client will be composing copy on the computer and needs quick turnaround, your newsletter design should be one that can be quickly laid out and produced on the computer.

- If the final typesetting will be done on a 300 dpi laser printer, pick fonts that look good at that low resolution. Run some test proofs if you're not sure how a particular face will look. Check for such problems as type that looks too light, serifs that break up or disappear altogether, or bowls and counters that fill in.

- Can your client afford two colors? If not for each run, can the client afford to have a second color printed, in advance, on a year's supply of newsletters on nameplate, sidebar tints, etc.?

- Can your client afford a slick image, coated stock or expensive display faces from a type house?

- Remember to leave adequate white space, no matter how much copy and artwork your client wants to include.

- Keep in mind that a paper that is too light may not have the opacity to prevent printing on the opposite side from showing through—particularly if you're working with large areas of solid color.

- Give your client budgetary options. Before you lock in on a design strategy, break down costs on printing and production options by coming up with a cost per copy. Add up all charges for typesetting, photography, miscellaneous expenses and postage, then divide by the total number of copies printed.

Managing the Cost of Services for Your Publication

- Write down the cost of all services and supplies. Identify the value of staff time, in-house services and donations. Learn the true, full costs of production, then set a budget. Use expense figures to project outlays of time and money.

Copy: From Client to Computer

"We generate copy on a job by keying in copy, feeding it into our computers from what a client has furnished us on modem or disk, or by using an OCR scanner. It doesn't matter whether your client keyed it in, or you did—getting it right is always a shared responsibility, and as the designer, you look bad if there's an error in the copy.

"We're always looking to reduce the number of passes involved when it comes to proofreading, and approving copy. We are currently refining our ability to receive faxes with our Macs and translate that copy, using OCR technology, into an editable word processing document."

Mike Zender *is founder and principal of Zender Associates, an award-winning, Cincinnati-based design studio.*

▶

- Shop for services. Write specifications for every job, then get quotes for any job you think will cost more than a modest amount.

- Work from your budget, not from supplier's fees. Stay in control by letting designers and other service people know how much you have to spend. Good professionals are problem solvers. It's their job to know about sources of supplies, new technologies and creative approaches.

- Consider long-term contracts. Build specifications for services and supplies around yearly periods or longer. Take advantage of savings from long-range planning, quantity buying, and the secured income that contracts give your suppliers.

- If the date your readers receive their newsletter is not critical, ask your printer if you can go on press during a slow period of the month in exchange for lower prices.

- Mail bulk rate instead of first class to save 33 percent. Nonprofit organizations in the United States qualify for even deeper discounts.

- Avoid paying yearly permit fees by using the services of a mail house that already has a permit.

Tips courtesy of newsletter design and production expert Polly Pattison, author of the pamphlet "90 Ways to Save Money on Newsletters."

Money-Saving Tips for Newsletter Design and Production

- Avoid bleeds. Pictures or art designed to run off the page require extra paper and cost more to print.

- Avoid tight registration. Stylish design elements such as rules around photos sometimes require extra care in printing.

- Design for self-mailing. Save the cost of envelopes by building in an address panel on the back page.

- Use veloxes (halftone positives). Most suppliers who make PMTs or Copy-proofs can also make veloxes. Paste veloxes directly onto the mechanical to be shot for printing along with type and art. (Caution: The quality of printed photos is not as good as when using halftone negatives.)

- Use clip art. The variety is so huge and the quality so good that it can often be used instead of hiring an illustrator. If you have established a good relationship with a printer, you may be able to use clip art from his archives.

- Set standing heads once. Make a supply of PMTs to use for each issue, then keep originals in your files.

Tips courtesy of newsletter design and production expert Polly Pattison, author of the pamphlet "90 Ways to Save Money on Newsletters."

Common Formats for Newsletter Design

- 5½ × 8 inches, four pages, printed on the front and back of a 8½ × 11-inch sheet

- 8½ × 11 inches, four pages, printed on the front and back of a 11 × 17-inch sheet

- 8½ × 11 inches, four pages, printed on the front and back of a 11 × 17-inch sheet, folded in half for self-mailing with address panel occupying half of the back page

- 8½ × 11 inches, eight pages, saddle stitched, self-cover

- 8½ × 11 inches, eight pages, saddle stitched, self-cover, folded in half for self-mailing with address panel occupying half of the back page

- 8½ × 11 inches, sixteen, thirty-two or forty-eight pages, with separate cover, mailed in envelope or polybag

- 11 × 15 inches (newsprint), four or eight pages, folded in half for self-mailing with address panel occupying half of the back page

- 11 × 15 inches (newsprint), four or more pages, folded in thirds for self-mailing with address panel occupying one-third of the back page

- 11 × 17 inches, four pages printed on the

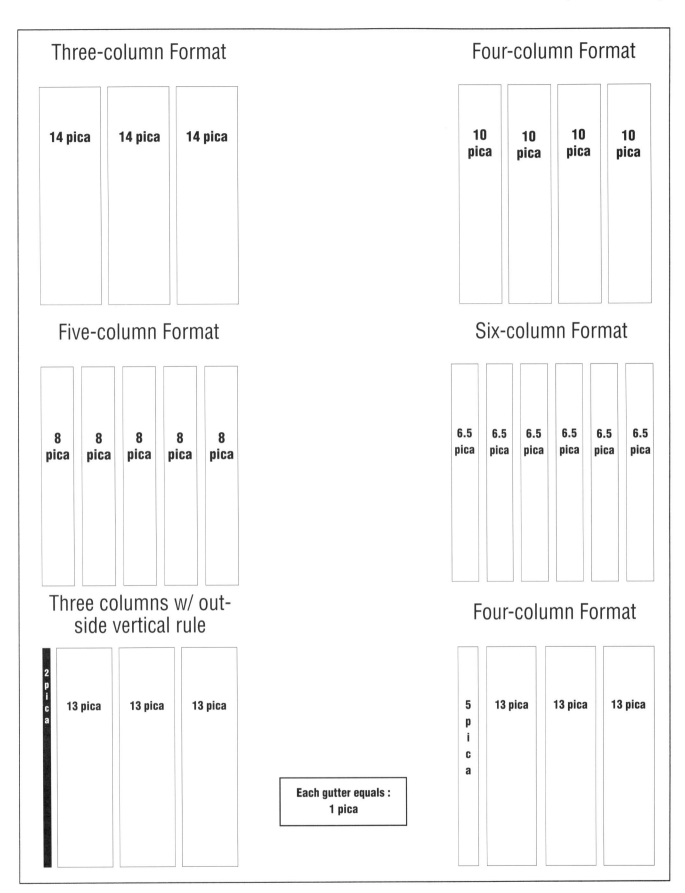

Three-column Format

14 pica 14 pica 14 pica

Four-column Format

10 pica 10 pica 10 pica 10 pica

Five-column Format

8 pica 8 pica 8 pica 8 pica 8 pica

Six-column Format

6.5 pica 6.5 pica 6.5 pica 6.5 pica 6.5 pica 6.5 pica

Three columns w/ outside vertical rule

2 pica 13 pica 13 pica 13 pica

Four-column Format

5 pica 13 pica 13 pica 13 pica

Each gutter equals : 1 pica

Sample newsletter grids

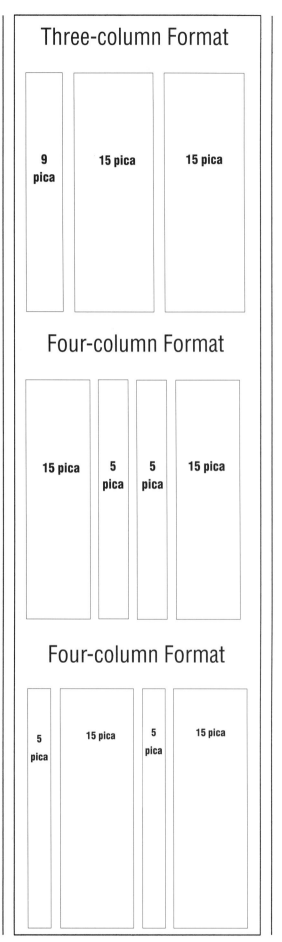

Three-column Format

9 pica | 15 pica | 15 pica

Four-column Format

15 pica | 5 pica | 5 pica | 15 pica

Four-column Format

5 pica | 15 pica | 5 pica | 15 pica

front and back of a 22 × 34-inch sheet

- 11 × 17 inches, four pages printed on the front and back of a single 22 × 34-inch sheet, folded in half for self-mailing with address panel occupying one-quarter to one-half of the back page

- 11 × 17 inches, eight or sixteen pages, self-cover, saddle stitched, folded in half for self-mailing with address panel occupying one-quarter to one-half of the back page

The Essential Parts of a Newsletter

Address Panel: area reserved for mailing label.

Alley: white space between two columns (called a gutter in most page layout programs).

Body Copy: main body of text.

Byline: author identification, usually placed at the beginning of an article if short—"By Jane Doe"—or at the end, especially if it contains a brief biography of the author.

Caption: copy that describes a photo, illustration or chart.

Deck: external subhead that appears immediately below the headline to help explain the content of the story.

Department Heading: standing head above regular columns or features or on regular pages of a publication.

Filler: story, cartoon or clip art used to fill an area short on copy.

Folio: page number.

Footer: information such as newsletter title and page number that appears on the bottom of every inside page.

Gutter: blank space between inner edge of two pages, where fold or binding exists.

Header: copy that recurs at the top of every inside page, usually the newsletter title or subtitle, issue, date and the page number.

Headline or Head: the article's title, which should invite readers into the copy that follows.

Indicia: postal permit imprint used in place of a stamp.

Jumpline: the notice to readers that an article continues on another page, often written as "Cont. on page 4."

Kicker: secondary headline on the line above the main headline.

Mailing Area: space reserved on back cover of self-mailing newsletters for mailing information: mailing label, return address, postal permit, address correction request. Teasers (brief message intended to lure readers into the publication) may also appear but should be placed so they won't interfere with postal service equipment.

Masthead: the listing of staff, address, subscription information, copyright notice and ISSN (if the newsletter has one); generally placed on the second page.

Nameplate: the newsletter title with accompanying graphics such as a company or organization's logo; there may also be a subtitle or motto that tells something about the company or organization's purpose (also called a banner or, incorrectly, the masthead).

Pull Quote: pulled from within the story and used to catch the reader's attention (also called breakout, callout or blurb).

Sidebar: an article that supplements a longer article with related information or sidelights.

Subhead: a secondary head that breaks up

long articles and provides an opportunity for skimmers to learn what's in an article.

Table of Contents: a listing with page numbers of the articles in a newsletter; can include teaser copy or visuals to encourage readers to explore the whole issue.

What's an ISSN?

ISSN is the abbreviation for International Standard Serial Number. These are assigned by the Library of Congress to magazines, newsletters and other serial publications such as scholarly journals on request. An ISSN is used to ensure efficient ordering and accurate cataloging or inventory control of serial publications by libraries, booksellers and newsdealers.

What to Include in the Masthead

- Name of the publication
- Name of publisher
- Frequency of publication
- Publisher's address and phone number
- Staff (editor, art director, etc.)
- Mission statement
- Copyright notice: © 19XX by (name of sponsoring organization)
- Information on submitting articles (optional)
- Date of issue
- Volume and issue number, if that's how you keep track of it
- Cost, if any
- ISSN if you have one

Required Mailing Information for Self-Mailers

- Indicia in upper right-hand corner of mailing area with mailing permit number, name of organization and post office of mailing origin.
- Return address in upper left-hand corner of mailing area.

Nameplate or Masthead?

That thing—the name flying on the top of the first page of your newsletter. Is it a logo? Is it a masthead? Is it a banner?

According to a survey conducted by newsletter expert Polly Pattison, most professionals in publication, editing and design call it a nameplate or a logo. (The dictionary defines *masthead* as the staff credit box inside the publication. Don't feel dumb. It came as a surprise to me to finally learn this after eight years of working as a magazine art director and managing editor.)

▶

- Address panel for affixing label or typing recipient's name and address.

- Add "Address Correction Requested" above the address area at least two or three times a year. This will help to keep the subscriber list up-to-date.

See pages 119-121 for more information on postal regulations.

Tips for Mailing Labels

- Speed up production of mailing labels for large mailings (five thousand pieces or more) with computer-generated mailing labels. Common brands are Cheshire and Kirk-Rudy (both cut-and-glue labels that are affixed to the address panel on a special machine) and Avery (pressure-sensitive labels with self-adhesive backs under a protective strip).

- Computer-operated label printers are now available for desktop publishers. These simplify and speed production of labels from your computerized mailing lists.

- Try to standardize the number of lines in each address that will be printed on a mailing label. This helps ensure that they'll print properly.

- Convert as many zip codes as possible to Zip + 4; print addresses on the mailing labels this way to simplify sorting and to reduce mailing costs.

- Postal regulations for bulk mail are very strict. Verify that your address labels and address panel meet those regulations well in advance of trying to mail. Failure to do so can be expensive and time-consuming.

DATES

Lorem ipsum dolor sit amet, consectetuer adipiscing elit, sed diam nonummy nibh euismod tincidunt ut laoreet dolore magna aliquam erat volupat. Ut wisi enim ad minim veniam, quis nostrud exerci tation ullamcorper suscipit lobortis nisl ut aliquip ex ea commodo consequat. Duis autem vel eum iriure dolor in hendrerit in vulputate velit esse molestie consequat, vel illum dolore eu feugiat nulla facilisis at vero eros et accumsan et iusto odio dignissim qui blandit praesent luptatum zzril delenit augue duis dolore te feugait nulla facilisi. Lorem ipsum dolor sit amet, consectetuer adipiscing elit, sed diam nonummy nibh euismod tincidunt ut laoreet dolore magna aliquam erat volupat. Ut wisi enim ad minim veniam, quis nostrud exerci tation ullamcorper suscipit lobortis nisl ut aliquip ex ea commodo consequat.

Duis autem vel eum iriure dolor in hendrerit in vulputate velit esse molestie consequat, vel illum dolore eu feugiat nulla facilisis at vero eros et accumsan et iusto odio dignissim qui blandit praesent luptatum zzril delenit augue duis dolore te feugait nulla facilisi. Nam liber tempor cum soluta nobis eleifend option congue nihil imperdiet doming id quod mazim placerat facer possim assum. Lorem ipsum dolor sit amet, consectetuer adipiscing elit, sed diam nonummy nibh euismod tincidunt ut laoreet dolore magna aliquam erat volupat. Ut wisi enim ad minim veniam, quis nostrud exerci tation ullamcorper suscipit lobortis nisl ut aliquip ex ea commodo consequat. Duis autem vel eum iriure dolor in hendrerit in vulputate velit esse molestie consequat, vel illum dolore eu feugiat nulla facilisis at vero eros et accumsan et iusto odio dignissim qui blandit praesent luptatum zzril delenit augue duis dolore te feugait nulla facilisi.

Ut wisi enim ad minim veniam, quis nostrud exerci tation ullamcorper suscipit lobortis nisl ut aliquip ex ea commodo consequat. Duis autem vel eum iriure dolor in hendrerit in vulputate velit esse molestie consequat, vel illum dolore eu feugiat nulla facilisis at vero eros et accumsan et iusto odio dignissim qui blandit praesent luptatum zzril delenit augue duis dolore te feugait nulla facilisi.

Lorem ipsum dolor sit amet, consectetuer adipiscing elit, sed diam nonummy nibh euismod tincidunt ut laoreet dolore magna aliquam erat volupat. Ut wisi enim ad minim veniam, quis nostrud exerci tation ullamcorper suscipit lobortis nisl ut aliquip ex ea commodo consequat.

Autem vel eum iriure dolor in hendrerit in vulputate velit esse molestie consequat, vel illum dolore eu feugiat nulla facilisis at vero eros et accumsan et iusto odio dignissim qui blandit praesent luptatum zzril delenit augue duis dolore te feugait nulla facilisi.

minim veniam, quis nostrud exerci tation ullamcorper sus-

INFO 1993

Nonummy nibh euismod tincidunt ut laoreet dolore magna aliquam erat volutpat.

- Ut wisi enim ad minim

- veniam, quis nostrud exerci tation ullamcorper suscipit lobortis nisl ut

- aliquip ex ea commodo consequat. Duis autem vel eum iriure dolor in hendrerit in vulputate velit esse molestieconsequat, vel illum dolore

En feugiat nulla facilisis at vero eros et accumsan et iusto odio dignissim qui blandit

Praesent luptatum zzril delenit augue duis dolore te feugait nulla facilisi. Lorem ipsum dolor sit amet, consectetuer adipiscing elit, sed

Piam nonummy nibh euismod tincidunt ut laoreet dolore

NEXT ISSUE

Valiquam erat volutpat.
Ut wisi enim ad minim veniam, quis nostrud
Exerci tation ullamcorper suscipit lobortis nisl ut
Aliquip ex ea commodo consequa

Lorem ipsum dolor sit amet, consectetuer

adipiscing elit, sed diam nonummy nibh euismod tincidunt ut laoreet dolore magna aliquam erat volutpat.

Ut wisi enim ad minim veniam, quis
nostrud exerci tation ullamcorper suscipit lobortis nisl ut aliquip ex ea commodo consequat. Duis autem vel eum iriure dolor in hendrerit in vulputate velit esse molestie consequat, vel illum dolore eu feugiat nulla facilisis at vero eros et accumsan et iusto odio dignissim qui blandit praesent luptatum zzril delenit augue duis dolore te feugait nulla facilisi.

Lorem ipsum dolor sit amet, consectetuer adipiscing elit, sed diam nonummy nibh euismod

aliquam erat volutpat. Ut wisi enim ad minim veniam, quis nostrud exerci tation ullamcorper suscipit lobortis nisl ut aliquip ex ea commodo consequat.

Duis autem hendrerit in
vulputate velit esse molestie

consequat, vel illum dolore eu feugiat nulla facilisis at vero eros et accumsan et iusto odio dignissim qui blandit praesent

luptatum zzril delenit augue duis dolore te feugait nulla facilisi. Nam liber tempor

possim assum. Lorem ipsum dolor sit

Sample masthead

When Choosing Papers, Remember:

- Light-colored papers offer better legibility than dark ones. They also tend to be less expensive.

- A bright white works well for a clean, technical look. Consider an off-white or ivory for reducing glare and conveying a friendly, informal look.

- Heavy bonds and lightweight book and text papers with a smooth texture work best for newsletters on an 8½ × 11-inch or larger format. Basis weight should fall somewhere within the range of 30 to 70 lbs. Some 24 lb. bond papers with high opacity will do.

- Heavily textured, uncoated papers give newsletters a lot of character, but they can cause reproduction problems. Work with your printer to get the best results.

- Recycled papers can be used quite effectively for newsletters. They're available in a variety of whites, colors and finishes. Work with your printer to get the best reproduction with any uncoated paper.

- Newsprint has the right combination of high opacity and light basis weight to make it appropriate for low-budget newsletters. Avoid the lower grades, however; they tend to yellow and have very poor print quality.

- The smooth surface of coated stock makes it an ideal surface for optimum resolution of photos and fine type; however, coated stock requires printing on an offset press and is not appropriate for short-run jobs that are more economically printed on a photocopier.

- Consider weight and bulk when choosing a paper; those characteristics affect your mailing costs.

Printing Options for Newsletters

You have to consider a number of factors when choosing the right printing option for your newsletter. Think about what you want to do and then look for the best method for achieving that goal. Remember to consider all the factors before making a final decision. You may need to print only five hundred copies of your newsletter, which would make photocopying a viable option. However, you may also want good reproduction of photographs or the option of using a second color. A copy shop does neither of these well.

How Many Copies?

- If you need to print five hundred copies or less, use photocopying.

- If you need to print five hundred to one thousand copies, use a quick printer.

- If you need to print more than one thousand copies, use offset printing. Use sheetfed offset for runs of one thousand to twenty thousand press sheets (one copy of a newsletter may take more than one press sheet). Consider web offset printing for runs of over twenty thousand press sheets.

What Is Your Format?

- An 8½ × 11-inch format can be run anywhere. Copy shops and quick printers generally only stock cut sheets in 8½ × 11-inch or 11 × 17-inch sizes.

- An 11 × 17-inch format can be run anywhere, but you realize cost savings with a quick printer if you want more than a few dozen multipage copies. Presses that can handle large sheets of paper and extensive in-house facilities for trimming and binding make offset printing a cost-effective option for runs of several hundred copies, especially if you have eight pages (four trimmed sheets printed on both sides).

- A nonstandard format can be run by a quick printer or offset printer. Some quick printers will handle nonstandard formats but charge extra. Offset printing is generally your best option because of the more complex imposition and trimming required.

- Bleeds are best suited for offset printing. Commercial printers are most likely to have the necessary equipment and expertise to handle these trims.

NEWSLETTER SPEC SHEET

Margins _____ Top _____ Bottom
_____ Inside _____ Outside

Number of Columns _____

Spacing Between Columns _____

Nameplate (Typeface/fonts, Styles, Sizes, Leading) _____

Masthead (Typeface/fonts, Styles, Sizes, Leading) _____

Table of Contents (Typeface/fonts, Styles, Sizes, Leading) _____

Department Headings (Typeface/font, Style, Size, Leading) _____

Headlines (Typeface/font, Style, Size, Leading) _____

Subheads (Typeface/font, Style, Size, Leading) _____

Decks (Typeface/font, Style, Size, Leading) _____

Kickers (Typeface/font, Style, Size, Leading) _____

Body Copy (Typeface/font, Style, Size, Leading) _____

Captions (Typeface/font, Style, Size, Leading) _____

Header (Typeface/font, Style, Size, Leading) _____

Footer (Typeface/font, Style, Size, Leading) _____

Folio (Typeface/font, Style, Size, Leading) _____

Pull Quote (Typeface/font, Style, Size, Leading) _____

Jumpline (Typeface/font, Style, Size, Leading) _____

Color #1 _____ #2 _____

Photos (Kind & Quantity) B&W _____ Duotones _____ 4/C _____

Illustrations (Kind & Quantity) Line art _____ B&W _____ 4/C _____

Bleeds _____

Newsletter specification checklist

What Kind of Paper?

- A bright, white offset paper can be run anywhere.

- A bright, white text or bond paper can be run anywhere.

- A warm, white paper (yellow in tint) can be used with quick or offset printing.

- A colored paper can be used with quick or offset printing.

- Heavily textured papers, especially those with flocking or other unusual textures, should be used only with offset printing.

How Many Ink Colors?

- If you have only one ink color, black, your piece can be printed anywhere. However, you shouldn't use photocopying if you will have much reversed type or art or want areas of solid black. Subtle variations in grays will not reproduce well.

- If you have two or three colors, you can use a quick printer or offset printing. If one of those colors is a metallic or a fluorescent, make sure that your quick printer has worked with those inks before. If not, your best bet is offset printing.

- If you need four or more colors and can't afford to use match colors for them all, use offset printing. Process color is best done by offset printing.

What Kinds of Visuals?

- Simple line art can be run anywhere.

- Complex, detailed line art is best reproduced using offset printing. The plastic plates generally used for quick printing tend to deteriorate rapidly and will lose detail later in the run.

- Basic black-and-white halftones can be run anywhere. Many copy shops offer the option of making halftones, but it can get expensive.

- Black-and-white halftones that should be very high quality must be done by offset printing. Most quick printers use PMTs for halftone positives that yield only basic quality results. But don't pay

for more quality than you need. For an in-house newsletter that will be read and tossed out, basic quality is good enough.

- Full-color illustrations and photographs come out best with offset printing.

See pages 144-145 and 146-147 for an explanation of and guidelines for offset printing.

Handling the Elements of Newsletter Design

Typographic Design Options

Using the same typeface, in the same weight, at different sizes throughout your newsletter might be easy, but the resulting copy is too monotonous for most readers. It also makes the different types of information within your newsletter harder to identify. The typographic elements of your newsletter need to be unified, but they also need to be different enough from each other to provide some degree of visual interest and contrast.

- Pick a typeface or font and typestyle (bold, italic, roman or whatever) for each publication element, then stick with it throughout your newsletter. This type of unity helps your readers find their way around the publication. Don't change headline faces on page four just because it might be time for a change.

- Once you've determined what your text typeface will be, treat headlines and subheads with a bold version of the same typeface. Develop heads, captions, pull quotes and kickers with a very different version of the same typeface.

- Use a heavier variation of your text typeface on your nameplate; treat heads and subheads the same way but in a smaller type size. Use a contrasting typeface for headlines.

- Use all caps or small caps versions of your text typeface for column heads and nameplate, and a bold italic version of your text face for captions. Use a contrasting typeface for headlines, kickers and pull quotes.

- Use a sans serif font for heads and subheads, while using a serif font for text. You can also pick up the sans serif in bold for the captions and/or pull quotes.

- Choose a display face that works well at both large and small sizes and use it for the nameplate, heads and subheads. There are many period and otherwise unique display faces that will give your newsletter a distinctive look.

- Set off sidebars with a type change rather than a box, especially if you can't afford a second color. The switch from the text face to another face or style can be quite effective.

- Change alignment rather than typeface. Set your headlines and subheads centered or flush right while keeping your body copy flush left.

Ways to Add Graphic Accents

- Use provocative pull quotes prominently to break up large bodies of copy and grab the reader's attention.

- Print bold rules in a second color between the masthead and the rest of the page, to set off headlines from copy, or to separate sidebars and pull quotes from copy.

- Use screened-back black to create a gray tint or to screen back a tint of your second color behind sidebars, the masthead and other areas consistently set off from the rest of your copy. Tints can really punch up black-and-white illustrations or other visual elements behind the visual. Make sure the tint doesn't print *over* the visual, though.

- A series of rules that set off graphic quotes, column heads and so on can add interest. Run them vertically between columns of copy to visually separate narrow columns.

- Initial caps work well in place of subheads to visually break up large bodies of text. Make sure initial caps are consistent throughout and from one issue to the next.

- Add wide and bold borders to carry a

second color or thin and unobtrusive ones to delineate photos and sidebars.

- Reverse type out of black or a second color to set off logos and other symbols, type within a nameplate, a border, a pull quote, or any typographic situation not requiring more scrutiny than an "at-a-glance" treatment.

- Use clip art as spot illustrations or develop icons that run throughout to call attention to recurring topics or elements.

- Use a textured background or gradated tone behind sidebars, nameplate, pull quotes or table of contents to attract the reader's attention.

See pages 14-15 for more ways to set subheads off from text.

Ways to Add Visual Interest to a Nameplate

- Vary type weights to emphasize one or more words in a multiword nameplate, using heavier weights for primary words.

- Use outline type to emphasize one word in a multiword nameplate.

- Vary type sizes, emphasizing key words with large type and setting supporting words in smaller type.

- Set an acronym in large type with the words that each letter represents set in smaller type nearby for emphasis and clarity.

- Set it in all caps if you need to fit several long words on more than one line. You'll eliminate the extra leading that descenders would have required.

- Use small caps with an oversized initial cap for effect when you need to spread a short word across a wide space without losing legibility.

- Reverse type to emphasize primary words in a multiword nameplate or to add impact to short or single-word nameplates.

- Consider alternatives to the conventional "centered on the top" placement. Try an off-center alignment or run it vertically up the side of the newsletter.

- Add a pictorial element that's appropriate to the content and audience for your newsletter.

- Modify or distort the type—to add a sense of motion to a newsletter for bicyclists, for example.

- Use a texture in the nameplate or behind it.

Logo/Nameplate Guidelines

- Newsletter name.

- Name of organization, company or person publishing the newsletter.

- Dateline and volume number if appropriate.

- Some kind of graphic separation between the nameplate and the headlines and text on the rest of the front page.

- Company logo or other graphic symbol used consistently in its identification.

- A typeface or typographic treatment that can be repeated for other consistent elements of the newsletter.

- A second color, if possible, that can be used consistently with the other graphic elements in your overall design strategy.

Typical Newsletter Features

- Employee promotions, appointments and transfers

- New employees and retirements

- A message from the CEO or other corporate principal

- Letter from the editor

- Upcoming, current or recent events

- Personal news such as births and marriages—gossip

- Meeting reports

- Earnings reports

- Professional profiles, employee of the month

- Editorial or commentary, letters from readers

- Classifieds

- Industry news

Sample front page layouts

Prevent Photo Problems

- Crossover photos and headlines that jump the gutter should (if possible) be planned for center spreads where alignment isn't an issue.

- If the only photo available is a clipping that's already been screened, avoid re-screening, as a moire pattern may result. Shoot it at the same size and have it copy-dotted, where the halftone is reproduced as a line shot. The halftone dots are copied as line art.

- When running type over a photo, ensure its legibility by ghosting all or part of the photo. Because the tonal range is shortened, a fainter image results.

Handling Mug Shots

- Crop and size consistently. Avoid the flak that comes when one of your subjects claims that his "mug" wasn't featured as prominently as the next guy's.

- Vertical rectangular or square formats are safest to work with, particularly if you are working with a group of mug shots. Save more creative applications, such as running a rectangular mug shot horizontally, for special treatment of a columnist's photo.

- If you have a number of problem mug shots, you may be able to cover up the problem by putting each shot into a shape; for example, several photos of outstanding employees could be placed in star shapes.

- Never crop a photo so the person is viewed at a distance. Always crop and size so the face fills an area at least ¾ inch high.

- Crop in close to top of head and just below neck and shoulders, so that the subject's face falls within top two-thirds to three-quarters of picture area.

- Try to position mug shots so that subject is facing into the text, as opposed to glancing off the page.

- If you're stuck with a distracting background in a shot, run the photo as an outline halftone (the background is dropped out).

Chapter 11

If You Are Working on Ads

Concept Is Key to a Successful Ad

"The most successful ads I've seen communicate the advertising message on many different levels. All of the design components, the type, photography, etc., work together to support and enhance the ad's basic concept.

"Sometimes I've been asked to reformat existing ads by changing some of the graphic components, such as the layout and typography. I've found that redesigning someone else's ad is very difficult for me. I need to be immersed in an ad concept before I can bring it into play."

John Nagy is Associate Creative Director of Cincinnati-based Sive/ Young & Rubicam, a full-service advertising agency well known for its award-winning, innovative print ads.

Steps in Designing an Ad

❏ Identify the basic elements of the ad. Will there be a headline, photograph and copy? Will there be multiple illustrations, headlines and blocks of copy?

❏ Determine how prominent to make the most dominant element. (Keep in mind that giving equal emphasis to all items amounts to no emphasis.)

❏ Determine the hierarchy of elements. What will be emphasized the most in the ad: the art, the headline or the copy block?

❏ Plan space needs. How much space do you need for copy? Do you need to leave space for a coupon or a response form?

❏ Determine which publication(s) your ad will appear in so that similar-sized ads can do double duty (e.g., a full-page magazine ad that works in an 8×11-inch or $8\frac{1}{2} \times 11$-inch format).

❏ Decide if your ad will feature formal (symmetrical) or informal (asymmetrical) balance.

❏ Plan the ad's layout and how the reader's eyes will move through the ad.

❏ Position and size the hierarchy of elements. Give proper emphasis to the most dominant item and check the viewer's eye movement through the sequence of elements.

❏ Check the unity or "harmony" of the ad. Achieve harmony using similar shapes, sizes, texture, color and mood.

❏ Determine what else will unify the ad. Will it be borders, white space or a common axis?

❏ Match typeface to the mood of your ad and the image you want to project.

❏ Consider adding graphic elements. For example, borders can attract attention and set the ad off from surrounding text or ads. Enclose a coupon with a dashed line to encourage readers to cut it out.

❏ Select a typeface that works best in the allotted space and has the degree of emphasis you need for headlines and text.

❏ Choose visuals. Determine what kind of visual is appropriate for the ad. Should you feature people, actions or products? Illustration, photo or cartoon?

❏ Match type to the character of your art.

❏ If a variety of fractional formats (often called "adapts") will be used, make them visually consistent. Build your layouts from modular units of type and art that can be rearranged and used in a number of ad sizes.

When Designing an Ad, Remember:

• Make sure all the basic design elements are visually balanced.

• Give prominence to the most important elements. Surround these elements with white space to help emphasize them.

• Create visual "flow" among the design elements of the ad.

• Is there cohesiveness to the ad? Are design elements in harmony?

• Watch gutter jumps. On layouts that jump the gutter—that is, print on both pages of a two-page spread—break a headline between words, not letters. Position visuals so the gutter doesn't distort them.

• Place the company name, logo, address and phone number so they are easy to find. Typical placement is generally in the lower right-hand corner or centered at the bottom of the ad.

• Ensure that the ad is easily distinguishable from competitors' ads.

• Make a fractional ad ($\frac{1}{8}$, $\frac{1}{6}$, $\frac{1}{4}$, $\frac{1}{3}$, $\frac{1}{2}$, or $\frac{2}{3}$ of a page) stand out from surrounding copy and ads. Consider using reverses, borders and white space to set the ad off.

• Match the ad's "look" to its content. (A bold, masculine look won't attract many women to a perfume ad.)

• Be efficient. If you're working on a computer, remember to save fractional ads as templates for future layouts.

Publication Ad Requirements

Most publications list ad specifications on their rate card under mechanical requirements.

❏ Ad dimensions: Make sure your ad fits the dimensions of the standard sizes listed for the publication. If your ad is in proportion to one of the standard ad sizes, but larger than the exact dimensions, indicate at what percentage it should be shot and the size of the ad this percentage will yield.

❏ Bleed dimensions: Pay particular attention to this for a full-page bleed ad (or spread) where dimensions will generally exceed the publication's trim size by one-quarter to one-half inch.

❏ Color: Publications vary in what they offer. Although most magazines and major newspapers offer four-color process, check to be sure this is an option before designing a four-color ad. Second color availability will vary, as well. Some publications offer a choice of match colors or the option of a process color as a second color for your ad; others may only offer a preselected match color.

❏ Camera-ready art: The publication will supply camera services and will accept stats, veloxes or mechanicals for line art, along with cropped and sized photographs for halftone reproduction.

❏ Film: A line negative or combination of line and halftone film for black-and-white and two-color ads, or four-color separations are preferred.

❏ Proofs: Many publications require a proof if you're sending film, particularly for four-color ads. Find out if the publication requires this for black-and-white and/or color ads.

❏ Screen size: If the publication prefers film, or if that's what you would like to send, check their preferences for screen size. Generally, magazines prefer 133 to 150 line screens, whereas newspapers prefer 65 to 120 line screens.

❏ Right- or left-reading: This describes the film you supply to the publication. Right-reading, emulsion side down (which means the film's emulsion is on the underside) is what most publications prefer. Right-reading film shows you the ad as you read it in publication; left-reading shows you the ad backward. Be sure to alert your stripping house or service bureau to what your publication's specifications are when they prepare films for your ad.

❏ Reproduction: Whether the publication is printed by web or sheet-fed offset, the kind of paper it is run on affects the ad you design. Publications printed on high-gloss, top-quality paper use finer screens, which means you should pay more attention to detail than if your ad is printed on newsprint paper, which loses detail.

❏ Deadline: Many publications are very strict about enforcing this. If there is any chance that you may miss your deadline, call the publication ahead of time and alert them to your problem.

Newspaper Ad Sizes

Check the *Standard Rate and Data Service* for information on newspapers. *SRDS* is *the* comprehensive book of advertising, circulation and production information on all major U.S.-based dailies.

Newspapers are categorized alphabetically and by geographical area. Listings include contact information, ad sizes with dimensions, number of columns in the format and size of columns, and other mechanical requirements.

• Determine the number of columns in your chosen newspaper. Newspaper formats vary widely and can contain from four to nine columns.

• Find out the column width. Column widths range from $1^1/_{16}$ to $2^1/_4$ inches, with anywhere from $^1/_{16}$ to $^1/_4$ inch between columns. Check the *SRDS* listing or the newspaper's rate card to determine the best ad sizes and formats to work with.

Key Factors of a Good Ad

"First, good advertising clearly communicates a message to the consumer—a sense of the product or service's desirability, and it must be easily perceived or understood as such. Very often this can be accomplished, in part, by association through props, such as an expensive car, or an attractive model.

"It must also be memorable. Repetition of a look or design elements helps to accomplish this. Frequently a catchy slogan creates recall in the mind of the viewer, especially if it's been heard or seen many times before.

"Finally, a good ad must grab the viewer's attention. And in today's increasingly competitive visual environment, that's not an easy thing to do."

***Mike Quon** is principal of New York City-based Mike Quon Design Office, which counts American Express, AT&T and Coca-Cola among its many clients.*

Magazine Ad Sizes

- Use the *Standard Rate and Data Service* for magazines. It gives advertising, circulation and production information on most U.S.-based trade and consumer magazines and tabloids. Publications are alphabetically organized by interest.
- Know if a magazine is tabloid size. Larger "magazines" that are not perfect bound are classified as tabloids, such as *Rolling Stone* and *U&lc*. These publications are based on an 11×15-inch format, but can accommodate fractional ads between 4½ to 5 inches wide.
- Most U.S. magazines use an 8½×11-inch format. Final trim sizes can run anywhere from 8 to 8½ inches wide and from 10¾ to 11 inches long. Check a magazine's rate card or the *SRDS* listing to get the *exact* dimensions required for a certain ad size. Some magazines are in a 9×12-inch format (usually trimmed to 8⅞×11⅞ inches). These magazines usually accommodate fractional ad sizes that are common to magazines based on an 8½×11-inch format.

Typical Ad Formats and Their Sizes

These sizes, in inches, are based on the approximate 8½×11-inch format:

- Full Page: 7×10, 7×10⅜, 7¼×10
- Two Thirds: 4⅝×10, 4⅝×10⅜, 4⅝×9¾
- One Half Horizontal: 7×5, 7×4⅝, 7×4¾
- One Half Vertical: 3 5/16×10, 4¾×7, 4⅝×7⅜
- One Third Horizontal (or Square): 4½×4⅞, 4⅝×4¾, 4⅝×4⅞
- One Third Vertical: 2⅛×10, 2 3/16×9⅝, 2¼×9¾
- One Quarter Horizontal: 4⅝×3⅝, 4½×3½
- One Quarter Vertical: 3 5/16×4⅞, 3 5/16×5
- One Sixth Horizontal: 4⅝×2⅜, 4½×2 7/16
- One Sixth Vertical: 2⅛×4⅞, 2¼×4⅝

How to Calculate an Ad Size in Column Inches

Many publications sell ads by the column inch. The depth is determined by the number of inches purchased; for instance, a 6-inch ad will run 6 inches long and be one column wide. To determine the width of an ad with a horizontal emphasis, take the width of the number of columns your ad will be running and add the width of the space that falls between.

Transit Ad Sizes

Transit ads are shaped much like a two-page spread in a magazine ad and are printed on card stock. Don't overlook the opportunity to include a pad of coupons or order forms on an interior transit ad. Here are some common sizes:

- Interior: 14, 21, 28, 42 or 84 inches wide, by 11 inches deep.
- Exterior: 27, 36 or 44 inches wide, by 21 inches deep. A 12×2-foot ad is also available in some markets.

Coupons and Order Forms

- Make the tear-out easy for the reader. For example, place the coupon or order form along an edge, not in the center.
- Position the tear-out in bottom right-hand corner of the ad. Highest response occurs there.
- Use a border such as a dashed line to set it off from the rest of the ad.
- Make the order form easy to fill out.
- Never run the background in a color that interferes with readability.
- Add a code. To track the ad's response in different publications, assign a code to each publication and put the code on the coupon or order form.

Standard Layout Formats

Mondrian: This classic layout uses rectan-

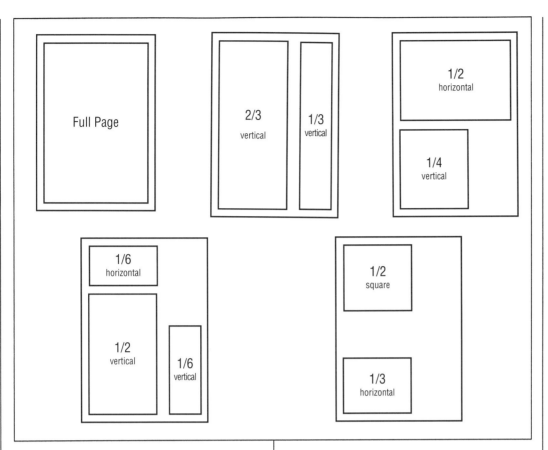

Typical magazine ad formats

gles of type or art, sometimes combined with lines or bars to separate elements. Proportion is the most critical design consideration, more so than eye movement or emphasis. The balance is almost always informal. Used more frequently in magazines than in newspapers.

Picture Window: Especially suited to magazines, this layout includes a generous display of art and tight editing of words. Pictures may bleed; headlines run below the picture and are centered on one line; and copy may run in two or three columns. The headline may overprint the art, which usually runs at the top of the ad.

Copy-heavy: This layout usually features a formal balance, since it is considered a more "serious" kind of layout. Headlines are centered and initial letters begin the copy, which runs in multiple columns. A secondary headline and subheads are common. Art is used if space permits. Copy-heavy ads contrast well in publications where the standard layout is Picture Window.

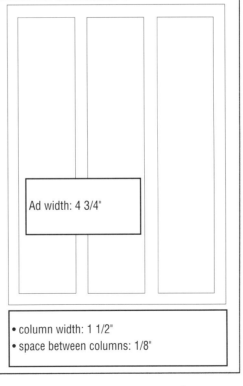

Calculating ad width in column inches

Frame: The Frame layout uses art, color, shape or texture to create a border or frame around the ad. It is especially useful for containing elements and preventing their association with other ads and is used most frequently in newspapers. The downside of this layout is the loss of precious, pricey ad space.

Circus: This type of advertising features disorder in the layout and serves to attract the reader and force her to spend more time with the ad. This layout uses reverse blocks, large type, starbursts, skewed type and other gimmicks to sell its product. The ad's contents usually feature many components. Unity is still an objective, as are proportion and contrast. Variety is achieved through size, shape and tonal changes. Retailers often rely on this ad style.

Multipanel: Also called an Omnibus layout, this style may resemble a comic-strip sequence. Illustrations and photos are used with accompanying copy usually running beneath the visual. Visuals are often of equal size and placed side by side.

Silhouette: Here, an ad features many elements composed to form an intriguing silhouette. In other words, the ad's overall design creates a unique shape. A designer should strive to produce an unusual shape, which can be "tested" by imagining the composing elements blacked out. Type and art are often superimposed to render a single shape. White space usually runs on the outside of the ad, as a border.

Big Type: Obviously, this layout features oversize and dominantly placed type, often single words or short phrases. Art, if there is any, is overpowered. Often upper- and lowercase letterforms are used for a more interesting effect. Letter spacing can be manipulated to change the ad's mood.

Guidelines for Good Newspaper Reproduction

The coarseness and high porosity of newsprint paper cause loss of details in visuals, loss of edge sharpness in headlines and mottling of solid areas of ink. Keep in mind the need to prioritize the ad's elements. As a result—and especially with small ads—you may have to sacrifice quality in reproduction of the less important elements. Every element can't be big.

- Size the art as large as possible so the details that do reproduce are readable.

- Maintain a reasonable text type size for readability. For an ad ¼-page or larger, run type no smaller than 9-point. For small ads—for example, 1 column × 4 inches—try to keep type around 8-point.

- Select a text typeface with the best reproduction possibility. Classic medium-weight serifs such as Century, and sans serifs such as Franklin Gothic, are less likely to have their open areas plugged up by overinking.

- Keep it clean. Make sure your mechanical is clear of any specks, smudges, or areas where hard edges of pasted-down type and other elements show up on film. Rub down borders or type firmly.

- Use high-contrast photography. This is particularly true if you're providing a halftone velox, which offers less contrast than a negative. Since grays tend to get lost in newspaper print, have halftones screened so the contrast is emphasized, with midtones reduced to the high or low end of the gray scale.

- Use a coarse-grained screen for halftone reproduction. Most newspapers prefer an 85-line screen, but a range of 65 to 120 is usually acceptable.

- Maintain high contrast in your layout. High-contrast photos, bold black headlines and wide borders or rules help create eye-catching contrast.

- Take care with reverses. Small text type such as a 6-point boldface or an 8-point regular type will become oversaturated with ink. The reversed letters will fill in and your ad copy will be illegible.

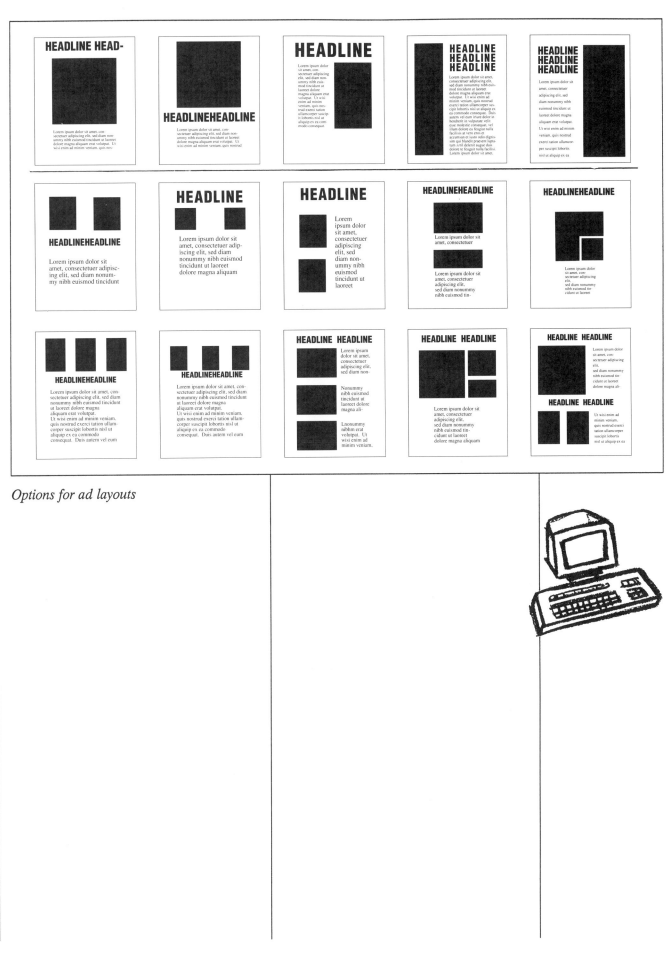

Options for ad layouts

Chapter 12

If You Are Working on Posters

Steps in Designing a Poster

Poster design offers an amazing degree of flexibility. Printing methods and paper and ink possibilities are practically limitless, depending on what the ultimate function of the poster will be. The key to designing a poster that communicates effectively is to get to the root of its functional goals and come up with a design strategy that meets them.

❏ Identify what the poster is advertising. Is it an event, product, service or group? What is the message or main feature of the issue?

❏ Find out where the poster will hang. Will it be posted on bulletin boards, in store windows, office cubicles, or on the walls of subway stations? Where a poster hangs determines at what distances it will be viewed and so how large to size elements on the poster. Check into size restrictions that may be imposed by bulletin board locations. Find out if local merchants will limit the size of the posters that go in their display windows.

❏ Ask how it will be distributed. If your poster will be sent out as a mail promotion, consider mailing requirements and postal rates, whether it will be sent in a tube or folded flat. All of these factors will affect the size and weight of the paper you print on.

❏ Provide incentives for hanging. If your poster is a mail promotion, it will do double duty as a marketing vehicle that will be seen and read by its recipient and, ideally, hung somewhere so others will see it. Think about an incentive for hanging it. Will the poster be so appealing that people will hang it to boost their morale or decorate a wall, or will including a calendar or other source of information give them more of an incentive for posting it?

❏ Assess its fine art potential. Posters promote, but they can also raise funds through fine art sales. If this is the case, you'll want to design accordingly and print on top-quality, archival stock.

❏ Determine who you want to respond to the poster. Whether the audience is rock star groupies or upscale professionals, your poster's message must be carried off in a way that makes it appealing to and/or noticed by the market it's pitching.

❏ Identify the budget and client priorities. These priorities, plus your own experience and design knowledge, will help allocate the budget in the most effective way.

❏ Determine the quantity needed. This knowledge will help you choose the most economical printing method. For example, a small number of posters may preclude offset printing and may be more cost effectively screen printed. You can even consider manual techniques for quantities of under one hundred, such as spray-painting with a stencil.

See pages 119-121 for information on postal service regulations and mailing costs and pages 18-35 and 110-111 for more information on paper.

When Designing a Poster, Remember:

• Design to get attention. Attention-arresting graphics—a photograph or illustration that evokes an emotional response from the viewer, even a clean typographical treatment of a clever statement—are often more likely to catch the eye than a pretty design.

• Think concept. A good concept carried off in a clean, well-thought out manner often makes the most attention-grabbing statement.

• Choose a message. Determine what the primary message is and what will best convey that message visually.

• Keep it simple. Choose one dominant element and a few key elements to supplement it, so the viewer won't get lost trying to find your message.

• Format a logical sequence. The sequence, from the most dominant to the least dominant, should run from top to bottom and from left to right.

Poster Design in a Nutshell
"Posters are the road signs of design. They should make sense in the rain and at 55 MPH."

Craig Frazier, *of San Francisco-based Frazier Design, has designed many award-winning posters. His work appears frequently in design journals and annuals.*

▶

- Think bold. Exaggerate to get noticed. Details and texture have to be bold to be seen and carried off. Use bold and ultrabold typefaces for headlines, high-contrast reproduction for photos, and bright colors for accents.

- Think big. Whether it's a relatively small poster or a colossal one, you're working on a different scale. When roughing and comping up a design, back up and view your concept at the distance from which it will most likely be viewed.

- Fudge details. Delicate, intricate borders and subtle textures are less likely to be appreciated at a distance. Because minute details aren't a factor, you can also cut corners and cost by using photocopied art and type as well as cruder printing techniques.

- Make it appropriate—to the message and those who are most likely to respond to it. A poster promoting a symphony performance is going to look very different from one promoting a mud-wrestling match at your local pub.

- Consider press size. The size of a press is determined by the largest paper size it can print, and the maximum area you can actually print is slightly smaller than that. It's wise to leave at least a quarter-inch border inside that maximum print area to avoid problems with trimming, especially when you're working with bleeds.

- Consider poster size. The size of your piece can also affect proofing costs. If your piece doesn't fit standard-sized proofing materials, custom-sized materials must be ordered. As with anything else custom ordered, this will add days and dollars to your schedule and budget.

Uses for Posters

- Announcement of performances, meetings and other special events
- Recruitment
- Fund-raising
- Announcement of a new product or service
- Promotion of existing product or service
- Public service message
- Calendar
- Self-promotion
- Fine artwork

Best Papers for Posters

Reproduction quality (particularly for four-color posters), size, durability and weight (if your poster will be mailed) are all considerations for selecting the paper.

Uncoated: These papers are available in standard sizes of 11×17, 17×22, 23×29 or 24×38, 22×34 or 23×35, and 34×44 or 35×45 inches. The heavier basis weights of text papers (40 to 100 lbs.) are preferred to bond for their durability; the heaviest basis weights also work best for larger posters. The high absorbency of uncoated paper makes it less suitable for four-color reproduction than coated papers. Crisp reproduction of four-color material may require an undercoat of opaque white to improve ink holdout. Two aesthetic advantages of uncoated paper are the color and texture choices. This paper is especially suited to situations in which a poster will be handled or viewed close up or when subtle textures require a close viewing distance.

Coated: The best four-color reproduction and the most vivid colors can be achieved on coated papers. The level of opacity and degree of brightness increases with the grade level and basis weight of the paper. Durability needs for large posters require a basis weight of 80 to 100 lbs., while 60 to 80 lbs. will suffice for smaller posters. Most coated lines are available in standard sheet sizes of 11×17, 17×22, 23×29 or 24×38, 22×34 or 23×35, and 34×44 or 35×45 inches. This is the paper of choice when you want to catch a viewer's attention at a distance. Coated papers come in a wider variety of standard sizes than do uncoated papers. And higher-grade coated papers come in more sizes than the lower grades.

Archival: Archival papers are made from 100 percent cotton. The low acidity of these cotton papers means that the paper will be less likely to disintegrate over time, and color will be less likely to fade. Archival paper is available in sizes and weights comparable to other text papers. Manufacturers of fine printing papers and art supply stores also sell 100 percent cotton for limited editions of silkscreened prints, but these papers are not suited to offset runs. If there's a chance your poster will be sold as a fine art print, check into archival grades as your paper choice.

Industrial: Don't overlook the possibility of screen-printing on industrial papers, such as kraft paper and corrugated cardboards. The high durability of corrugated cardboard and chipboard makes them appropriate for some applications. Posters printed on these papers can even be mailed as oversized "postcards" and will suffer a minimum of abuse. Industrial papers are not appropriate in situations where a poster must be affixed to a window or wall with tape. Kraft paper is about as durable as any text or coated paper, but lighter weight. The rough look of industrial paper makes it suitable for rugged imagery. It also contrasts nicely with glitzy metallic inks. For impact, nothing can compare with the surprise of seeing a poster, traditionally thought of as a fine arts vehicle, printed on industrial stock. Chipboard can be purchased from merchants in 50 lb. units, called bundles. The number of sheets per bundle depends on the size of the sheet. Single-walled corrugated comes in 250-foot lengths and is generally available in three standard widths.

See chapter 3 for more information on paper possibilities.

Efficient Trim Sizes for Posters

- Plan extra paper for bleeding color or image. The right trim size depends on whether or not you'll be bleeding color off any side (and possibly all four sides) of the poster. If so, allow an extra quarter inch of paper on the bleed edge.

- Determine your printer's press size. Check with him to determine the best trim for a bleed as well as what the final dimensions of your poster should be to make most efficient use of a particular sheet size.

- If your poster will be run on sheet-fed offset or screen printed, typical sheet sizes for text and coated papers are 23×29, 23×35, 25×38, 26×40 and 35×40 inches. Check with your paper rep to find out the exact sheet sizes available in your chosen paper.

Printing Methods for Posters

Sheet-fed Lithography: Offset lithography is your best choice for optimum reproduction quality of photographs and images in black and white and, especially, four-color process. It's also the most economical choice if your run is two hundred to three hundred pieces. Large presses can accommodate sheets of paper as large as 55×78 inches, and up to eight ink colors (or varnishes) at a time, but many printers work with 19×25- or 25×38-inch presses. If you're restricted to a specific printer for your poster, be sure to check the press size before specifying the size of your poster.

Web Lithography: If your run calls for more than 100,000 posters, and you're printing four colors, consider running your poster on a web press. Web rolls generally come in 26-inch widths, which would limit the size of your poster. Check this with your printer.

Silk-screen: This method is great for printing large, flat areas of color, where color purity, brightness and opacity are important. It's not the method of choice for optimum clarity on four-color process, where tight registration is required. It may be the most economical choice for smaller runs (generally one hundred to five hundred posters), depending on the number of colors involved. Do use silkscreening if you're printing on an industrial surface. This "hands-on" technique may also add value as an art print.

Chapter 13

If You Are Working on Packaging

Steps in Designing Packaging

❏ Determine what the marketing objectives will be. Make the packaging concept appealing to the targeted consumer group.

❏ Determine what the marketing environment will be. The packaging concept will depend on whether or not the product is shelf-competitive and whether the product will be sales assisted or will have to sell itself.

❏ Appeal to the consumer's need or desire for the product. Apparel packaging should make consumers want to wear the product, beverage packaging should make them want to drink it, and so on.

❏ Establish what is unique about the product. Package design should play up this aspect to prompt consumers' curiosity about the product and desire to try it.

❏ Size up the competition. If the product you're designing for is shelf-competitive, come up with a concept that will make your package stand out from the rest.

❏ Determine functional criteria for the product—weight, pourability, shipping and storage considerations, whether or not your package concept includes one container packaged within another.

❏ Determine what type of container(s) work best to fulfill these needs.

❏ Narrow the range of container possibilities, based on budget range and quantity needs.

❏ Determine type of printing, labeling, and other considerations in applying graphics to container(s).

When Designing Packaging, Remember:

• To fulfill functional requirements, your packaging concept must take into account the fragility of the product, its weight and weight distribution.

• Other functional and structural considerations to keep in mind include shelf stability, the right moisture barrier for the container, shipping protection, pourability and reclosability, and how well it will fit in a cupboard, refrigerator or freezer.

• Keep fillability in mind—how easily the container can be filled or packed with the product in an assembly-line situation.

• Promote brand identification and maintain visual consistency with other products within the same brand.

• When packaging involves a selection of similar items, such as different flavors or varieties of the same product, determine how to handle each item as a separate but consistent part of the brand series.

• When packaging involves establishing a hierarchy among a number of different items within a single brand, such as packaging for a designer line of clothing, design with priority of product visibility in mind.

• When you establish a brand's identity by selecting a dominant color for its packaging, you've got to get it right the first time. There's no turning back when consistent reinforcement of this image in the consumer's mind is all-important to a brand's success on the market.

How to Get a UPC Code

Universal Product Codes are those series of lines that are read by lasers at a retailer checkout counter. A UPC is a necessary item on any product packaging.

Contact the Universal Code Council, 8163 Old Yankee Rd., Suite J, Dayton OH 45458; (513)435-3870.

A free booklet available from the council outlines the assignment process for a code and the cost.

Color Use, Image and Association in Packaging

The right color for a packaging concept isn't necessarily the brightest one or the one that jumps off the shelf at you. Here are some considerations to keep in mind when selecting the right color for a packaging concept:

Packaging That's True to the Product

"Before we take on a packaging assignment, we have to feel good about the product. It's hard to design a package in good conscience for a substandard product that attempts to fool the consumer into believing they're purchasing something of quality.

"When we come up with a packaging concept we look for what's unique about the product and bring that out in the design. We try to prompt the consumer's curiosity about the product, so that they'll want to try it."

Joe Duffy *is founder and principal of Minneapolis-based Joe Duffy Design, known for its award-winning package design, including Ralph Lauren's Chaps line and Classico Pasta Sauces.*

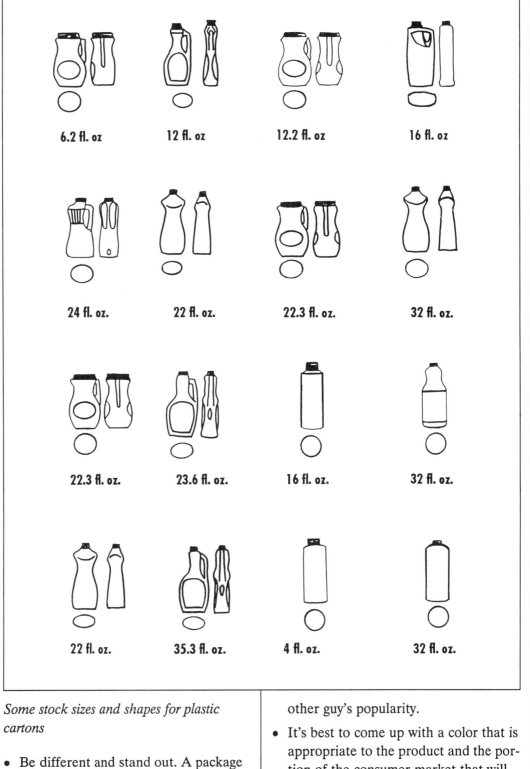

Some stock sizes and shapes for plastic cartons

- Be different and stand out. A package that's a different color than its competition can distinguish itself from competitive items on the shelf.

- Know when to imitate. In some cases, color association with a certain product can be so strong that it makes sense to use a similar color to cash in on the other guy's popularity.

- It's best to come up with a color that is appropriate to the product and the portion of the consumer market that will want it. It's almost unthinkable to consider packaging baby items in black. But then nobody would have thought that orange juice should be packaged in black until Minute Maid did it.

- Most packaging for perfume, makeup, cigarettes and alcohol rely on seven colors — brown, black, navy, gold, silver, white and red — to create expensive, elegant images.

- For a cool, sophisticated look combine black or blue with silver.

- For a look that's urbane and elegant, combine gold, brown and black.

- For a warm, sumptuous look, combine red and black, brown and gold, or white and gold.

- Pink packaging can be warm and accessible but tends to lack refinement.

- For an elegant package, use black and white or black and gold.

- If you are designing a product line using a two-color scheme, reverse the colors' relationship on some items for variety's sake.

Judge Your Packaging's On-Shelf Effectiveness

One of the best ways to judge how a package looks on-shelf is to prepare a computerized comp using a photoediting program and a 3-D modeling program. Scan a photo of a shelf filled with competing products, then create a new photo in your photoediting program that includes a series of your packaging comps as they would appear on-shelf in the store with their competition.

Packaging Containers and Materials

Folded Cartons: These are made of paper or cardboard that is scored, folded and glued to make a container. Carton stock can be coated, laminated and bonded with other materials to make it more rigid and improve its ability to resist moisture. Dies for custom cartons are fairly expensive, but many sizes and shapes are available as stock items. Carton styles consist of trays with hinged lids, such as perfume boxes, and tubes that open at either end, such as toothpaste boxes.

Set Up Boxes: These boxes are made of

heavier stock (nonbending paperboard), and are more rigid than folding cartons. The corners are usually reinforced with a paper tape, called stay paper.

Corrugated Cartons: Used for shipping and packaging, corrugated boxes are made of fluted paper sandwiched between a top and bottom sheet (called liners). Corrugated cartons are usually chosen for produce, dishes and other fragile products requiring the protection of this material's strength and durability.

Glass Bottles and Jars: Molten glass can be formed into containers by a number of processes. It can be blown into a shaped cavity (the most common method), pressed, or cast into a custom shape. Stock shapes and sizes are also available from glass container manufacturers. Graphics are applied to glass containers through screen printing or labeling.

Plastic Bottles and Jars: Plastic is used to produce bottles, jars, bottle caps and jar covers, egg cartons, bags and wrappers. It can be shaped into jars and bottles by injection molding, blow molding or thermoforming. Custom molds can cost as much as $30,000 and require months of lead time, but there are many stock container sizes and shapes. Plastic bags, pouches and wrappers are referred to as flexible packaging and are formed by extrusion molding.

Plastic and Metal Tubes: Tubes are used for the controlled application, through squeezing, of a liquid or viscous substance. They are made in metal and plastic. Metal tubes have the advantage of being easily emptied, but plastic tubes, because they suck back air, are more likely to keep graphics intact as the tube refills with air. Both are available as stock items in a variety of standard sizes.

Glass or Plastic Container Considerations

- Consider clarity and sparkle. Clear containers can be formed from plastic, but nothing can compare with the sparkle of glass.

- Consider moisture. Glass offers excel-

Packaging and the Environment

"The designer's role in packaging is taking on a broader scope than just projecting a point-of-sale message. Not only is the designer responsible for communicating the message the client wants to project, but there is more pressure to give consumers information they want. This demands more 'real estate' on the package, often leading to a larger box or surface area. This is good for the product (it gives it a larger shelf presence), it's good for the consumer (it offers a larger area for printing information about a product), but it's bad for the planet.

"Over-packaging, waste and paper use have become the topic of discussion for most graphic designers in the '90s. We hear about it at design conferences, we read about it in periodicals and we talk about it at lunch with our peers, but does the designer really care? What happens after lunch, or when the conference is over? Is it back to the drawing board to beautify more consumer waste?"

Rick Tharp *is founder and principal designer of the Los Gatos, California-based firm, Tharp Did It. His award-winning work includes package design for many West Coast wineries.*

▶

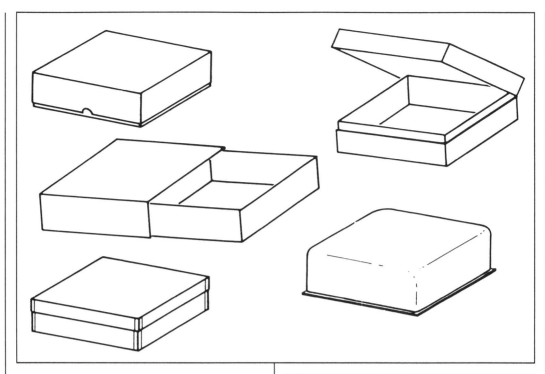

Set-up boxes

lent resistance against spoilage. Fragrances are kept intact and the taste of food remains unchanged for a long period of time.

- Consider moldability. Glass can be molded into a greater variety of shapes and sculptural effects than plastic.

- Consider fragility. The downside of glass, of course, is that it's more likely to break. This can make a difference in the container's filling line speed.

- Consider weight. Glass is heavier than plastic. This can make a difference in the shipping weight of the product and the container's filling line speed.

Printing Methods Commonly Used for Packaging

Printing on packaging materials usually requires printing on unusual shapes, surfaces and in *extremely large quantities*, which can only be done efficiently at very high speeds. Here are some common methods:

Flexography: This process uses plates of flexible rubber and thin, fast-drying, water-based or solvent inks on high-speed presses. Rolls of paper, foil and plastic are

More About Corrugated Cartons

Corrugated fluting is coded as A, B, C or E. A-fluting has the widest amount of spacing between ridges and absorbs shock better than B, C or E fluting. E-fluting has the narrowest amount of space between the ridges.

Because printing with offset lithography would crush the fluting on corrugated board, corrugated cartons are generally printed by flexography. However, ink registration with this method can be a problem. Designs that utilize four-color process or depend on butting two or more colors together should be avoided. Ways of getting around this problem include preprinting the liner sheet before it's fused with the fluting, and laminating a preprinted label to the carton prior to die-cutting and assembling the box.

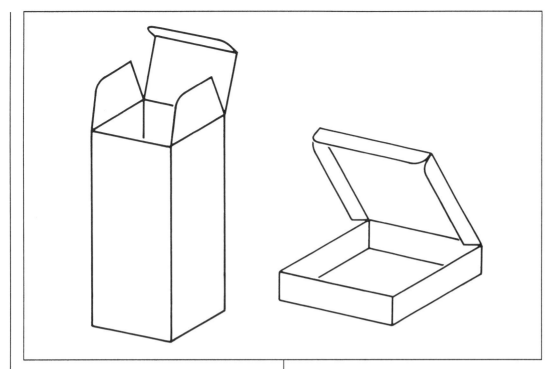

Folding cartons

fed into the flexography press to produce labels, wrappers, bags and gift wrap. Flexography is also used for printing on corrugated cardboard. Registration is not as tight as offset and ink coverage not as solid, but flexography's high speed enables printing impressions of a thousand feet per minute. Flexographic printers can often be found in the Yellow Pages under "Packaging."

Gravure: Gravure (or rotogravure) is another high-speed process where a direct impression is created from an image that has been etched into a metal plate. The gravure cylinder rotates in a fountain of ink, constantly filling these etched wells, and then transfers the image onto the paper as it passes through. Gravure is used for large runs of magazines and catalogs as well as packaging. It costs more than flexography and is more time-consuming, but the results, in terms of ink coverage and registration, are superior.

Ink-Jet Printing: Computer-directed ink droplets are used to form an image directly onto the paper surface. Some shops can print only one color, but others can handle four-color work where each nozzle controls

one of the four basic process colors (cyan, magenta, yellow and black) and is digitally controlled to spew out exactly the right amount necessary for an image. This method prints with incredible speed, because nothing mechanical strikes the paper. It's used for making proofs, billboards and direct mail pieces and is increasingly being used in packaging.

Screen Printing: This "print-on-anything" method of reproduction works on containers of any size and shape and on practically any type of surface material. Screen printers who handle this kind of work have special printing equipment; bottles or jars are mounted on a rotary device so their surface is spun against a squeegee. This method would be inappropriate for flat packaging materials such as cartons, which can be printed at high speeds in large runs using gravure and flexography.

For more information on screen printing, see chapter 17.

Chapter 14

Laws, Rules and Regulations

Laws, Rules and Regulations

Postal Regulations

Legal Issues

Copyright Guidelines

Registering a Trademark

More . . .

Postal Regulations

U.S. Classes of Mail

Express: This premium delivery service provides guaranteed overnight delivery for documents and packages weighing up to seventy pounds. Fixed costs are $9.95 for letters and packages weighing up to eight ounces and $13.95 for up to two pounds. Packages from three to seventy pounds are priced individually, with three pounds costing $15.95 and seventy pounds costing $91.60. You can get a free price chart from the post office. Pick-up service is $4.50.

Priority: This service, which guarantees, two-day delivery for packages and letters weighing under two pounds, costs $2.90 per piece. The Postal Service will also pick up your priority mail for $4.50.

First Class: This category of nonexpress mail receives the fastest delivery and costs the most of all regular mail. Rate for a standard-sized, one ounce letter is $.29.

Second Class: All newspapers, magazines and other periodicals qualify for second-class mailing and discounted rates. Rates are based on the amount of advertising within the publication and postal zones. An annual fee is $275.

Bulk: Bulk or third-class mail requires at least two hundred pieces or a group of items weighing fifty pounds or more to receive a discount. Pieces must be identical in weight, size and content and must be presorted by three- and five-digit zip codes and by state, and classified with postal stickers "D," "3" or "S." All pieces must be addressed to locations within the United States, must be mechanically produced, and must be promotional in nature. No personal messages, bills or statements. The annual bulk mailing fee is $75.

Fourth Class: This mailing class is often called book rate because publishers and distributors of books, magazines and other printed materials use it. It's slower than first class (sometimes taking as long as three weeks to deliver) but much cheaper than sending a weighty package via first class. Rate depends on total weight of package and the zone to which it is sent. There are three rate classes of fourth-class mail: book; bound and printed; and fourth class. Rates are cheapest for book and increase with bound and printed and fourth class. Delivery time depends on the zone but is always longer than first-class mail.

Business Reply: This type of mail lets you, the sender, pay for the recipient's response. You need a special permit and permit number. The annual fee of $75 covers the cost of your permit number, the bar code, Facing Identification Marks (FIM— vertical bar code used for mechanical sorting) and other information and artwork you need to print your business reply cards or envelopes. You will also pay $.40 for each response you receive, plus your original postage for the envelope or card. If you ▶

Business Reply Legend must appear above the address in all capital letters. Immediately below is "FIRST CLASS PERMIT NO.___" followed by name of issuing post office, also in capital letters. "Postage will be paid by addressee" is under legend.

FIM (Facing Identification Mark)

NO POSTAGE NECESSARY IF MAILED IN THE UNITED STATES

BUSINESS REPLY MAIL
FIRST CLASS MAIL   PERMIT NO. 17   CINCINNATI, OHIO
POSTAGE WILL BE PAID BY ADDRESSEE

HOW
PO BOX 12575
CINCINNATI OH 45212-9927

The space 5/8" from the bottom edge and 4-1/2" from the right edge of the mail piece is reserved for bar codes.

The Bar Code permits reliable mail sorting through automated bar code sorters instead of manual or mechanized methods. Area must be kept clear of all other printing.

Horizontal Bars facilitate rapid recognition of Business Reply Mail. Must be uniform in length and evenly spaced. Also must not extend below the delivery address line which contains the zip code.

Correctly designed business reply card

anticipate receiving at least six hundrd responses within a year, you can get a BRMAS each year for $185 and lower your costs significantly. Set up an account with your local post office when you apply for your permit or plan to pay your postal carrier when responses are delivered.

More About Bulk Mail

- Bulk-mail sizes for letters are 3½ to 5 inches high, 6⅛ to 11½ inches long; and for flats are 11½ to 15 inches long, 6⅛ to 12 inches wide, and ¼ to ¾ inch thick. Letters must also have a thickness of $7/1000$ and ¼ inch and a length-divided-by-height ratio ranging from 1.3 to 2.5. Rates for flats are about 20 percent more than for letters. (A flat is a piece of mail that exceeds the length and width of a letter.)

- Presort your mailing by zip code and state into bundles of ten or more pieces by five-digit zip code. After all mail is grouped by five-digit zip code, sub-divide each group by the first three digits of each zip code. Then subdivide these groups by state and put into tagged bags supplied by the post office. Your permit fee covers the bags, the stickers that you affix to the top of each bundle and any other postal supplies.

- Precancelled stamps can be purchased for bulk mailings, or you can print an indicia (cost is $75) with your permit number in the upper right-hand corner of your address panel.

More About Business Reply Postcards

To save yourself extra expense be aware of the following:

- A postcard between 3½ × 5 inches and 4¼ × 6 inches costs $.19; anything larger costs $.29. If your card is riding at the bottom of a 8½ × 11 or 8½ × 14-inch self-mailer, it's worth the extra cost to add an L-shaped perforation and keep the card within the lower-cost size.

- A response card must be printed on bristol board or card stock that has a basis

weight of 75 lbs. and a thickness of at least .007 inch but no more than .0095-inch.

Additional Postal Discounts

The Postal Service discounts rates if you use bar codes and Zip + 4 coding in your business mailings of 250 pieces or more.

- Zip + 4: To lower one ounce, first-class rate to $.275, include Zip + 4 coding on the address. Add the bar code and it drops to $.27.

- Zip + 4, Presorted, Bar Code: To lower one-ounce first-class to $.239, presort into the first three digits of the zip code and include Zip + 4 coding and bar code.

- Zip + 4, Bar Coding: Bulk mailing rates drop from $.198 to $.179 when Zip + 4 and bar coding are used. Do a five-digit sort and you pay $.146 per piece. Costs can be as low as $.081 per piece for a nonprofit association if you also do a five-digit sort.

Postal Standards for Mailing Pieces

Postal standards are revised constantly. Double check the following information to be sure your mailing piece complies with current regulations:

Size: All mailing pieces that qualify as letters or flats, ¼ inch thick or less, must be horizontally rectangular in shape and no smaller than 3½ × 5 inches.

Thickness: A mailing piece must be at least 9 points or .009 inch thick if it is more than 4¼ inches in height, or 6 inches in length, or if it exceeds these dimensions in both height and length. Pieces that don't exceed 4¼ inches in height and 6 inches in length must be at least 7 points or .007 inch thick.

Ratio of height to length: The standard ratio for height to length is between 1 to 1.3 and 1 to 2.5.

Address: Where you place the address establishes the length and height of mailing piece, with length being parallel to the address as it is read. To ensure proper handling, addresses should be typed in roman characters (no script), all caps, with no punctuation (except the hyphen in a Zip + 4 digit code); use two-letter codes for state designation.

Sealing Self-Mailers: Seal self-mailers with wafer seals, tabs, glue or cellophane tape, not staples or any clasp-type hardware that can damage processing equipment.

Sources of Postal Information

- The U.S. Postal Service publishes two manuals: *Domestic Mail Manual* (also called Publication 25) and *A Guide to Business Mail Preparation*. Additional literature includes pamphlets about Business Reply Mail and Third-Class Mail.

- Local postal line. Through a touch tone phone, you can access prerecorded messages on a wide number of topics.

- Many area post offices offer special courses, at no charge, on preparing bulk mail and presorting business mailings.

> **One Final Word**
> Take care to observe postal regulations. Pieces that don't meet the minimum size standards for a mailing piece won't be mailed. Letter mail that is nonstandard will be levied a surcharge to cover the expense of hand-sorting.

How to Get Indicia, FIM and Bar Codes

Indicia: To obtain an indicia, you must establish a trust account by making a small deposit with your local post office to cover the cost of your initial mailing needs. Your permit number and artwork specifications for an indicia are mailed to you when you establish this account. Your indicia shows that the postage has been paid and displays the permit holder's name or entry post office name and permit number; it's printed where a postage stamp would normally be affixed. The cost of maintaining an account is $75 per year. There is also a one-time charge for the permit number of $75. The account works much like a checking ac-

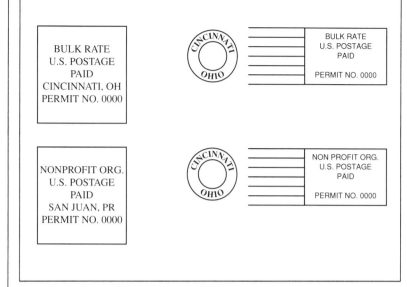

Examples of properly designed indicia/permit imprints

count: You must constantly replenish the funds to cover your mailing costs.

FIM and Bar Codes: FIM and bar codes are only supplied to postal customers printing business reply and courtesy reply (when your respondent affixes a stamp) postcards and envelopes. Artwork for these items and your permit number will automatically be mailed to you when you open a business reply account and pay your annual fee of $75. (For more information, see section on Business Reply Mail.) The artwork for courtesy reply mail is available at no charge from your local post office.

Legal Issues

Copyright Guidelines

- Pictorial, graphic and three-dimensional artwork can be copyrighted. Copy-

Correctly designed business reply envelope

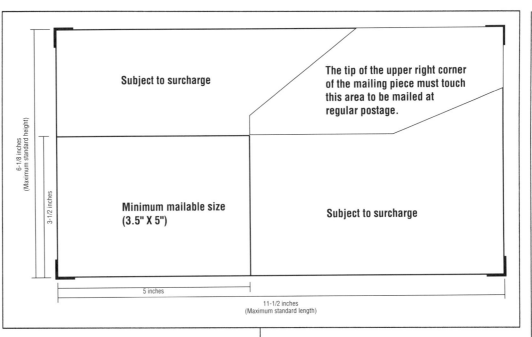

Template for checking for mailable size or surcharge

righted materials don't necessarily have to be registered with the copyright office. The moment you create a design, it is *your* copyrighted material.

- Discourage others from plagiarizing your work or otherwise profiting from it by including a copyright on your originals: © your name, year.

- You can register your work with the federal Copyright Office, Library of Congress, Washington DC 20559; (202)707-3000. They will furnish you with an application. Return the application with a twenty dollar filing fee, and in about sixteen weeks you will receive a certificate with a registration number for your copyrighted idea.

- If you sell a copyright to a client (such as for her logo) put the agreement *in writing*. Otherwise it's not official.

Handling Trademarks on Product Packaging

- A trademark indicates the origin of goods. Any word, symbol or combination of the two that is used by a manufacturer to distinguish its goods from the competition is considered a trademark.

- On product packaging you should show the symbol ™ juxtaposed to the product name or the logo in a prominent place. While it's not necessary to use the symbol every time, it's in your best interest to do so.

Registering a Trademark

- Save $600 to $1,000 in attorney's fees by registering a trademark yourself. Send your application; a copy of the mark; three typical uses for the mark on a product, label, tag, etc.; and a nonrefundable $210 filing fee to the Patent and Trademark Office, Washington DC 20231; (703)557-3158. If your application meets the requirements for filing, it will be assigned a serial number, and you will receive a filing receipt.

- After review and approval by the Examining Attorney, it will be published in the *Trademark Official Gazette*, a weekly publication of the Trademark Office. Objecting parties have thirty days to oppose the registration. If no opposition is filed, and the mark was published based upon its *actual use in commerce*, a registration for it will be issued.

- If the mark is published based on your *statement of intention*, a notice of allowance will be issued in three months. You then have six months from this date to either use the mark in commerce and submit a statement of use or request a six-month extension to file a statement of use.

- Call the Patent and Trademark Office at (703)557-3080 for forms, brochures and recorded information, or (703)557-7800 for more specific information.

Types of Infringements and Violations

People are often confused by the differences between copyright, trademark and trade dress infringements.

Copyright Infringement: Copyright law entitles a copyright owner to compensation for all derivative uses of his or her work. You're ripped off when someone takes your visual concept and renders it in a similar fashion—for example, using a different medium or different colors—but retains the basic concept and images involved. It's very difficult to take someone to court over this unless they are profiting at your expense. Consult a lawyer, and if you're truly being cheated, you may be able to sue. If you are confronted with an accusation and proof that the design concept you came up with for the city symphony concert was used to promote a similar event in a neighboring city the previous year, your reputation as an originator of unique concepts may be damaged, but legally you are not obligated to restore compensation to the originator of the concept.

Trademark Violation: A trademark violation occurs if a company's logo is used by a competitor as an identity or on a product. As a designer you are unlikely to be involved in decisions that violate trademark laws. The decision to profit on someone else's idea, by duplicating their product and affixing the originator's mark on it, is the manufacturer's. You could unknowingly create a logo that may be exactly like someone else's, but when that logo or mark is registered with the Patent and Trademark Office, the Trademark Examining Attorney will check to see whether that mark, or one very similar to it, is registered. If it is, the logo will not be approved.

When You Work for Others

Here are some things you should confirm with your client in writing—before beginning a job:

- Delivery Schedule—When the project (or stages in its development) is to be completed.

- Terms of Payment—When it is due (thirty days from invoice, etc.); service charges, interest on late payments, etc.; what client assumes if payment is defaulted; what expenses you expect to be reimbursed for.

- Payment of Outside Vendors—What expenses client will be billed directly for by outside vendors.

- Rights—If art is to be reproduced elsewhere.

- Cancellation—What you will be paid if the project is terminated.

- Revisions—That these will be billed separately.

- Return of Artwork—If necessary.

- Signature of Client—In acceptance of above terms.

What Constitutes an Employee

The IRS defines an employee as an individual you have control over as his or her employer. If you feel obliged to make a freelancer an employee, you are required as an employer to deduct social security tax, federal, state and local taxes, and unemployment taxes from wages paid to this individual. Individuals you hire are more likely to be considered employees than self-employed freelancers if you do the following:

- Contract with them for full-time work.

- Establish a continuing relationship with them of work performed at frequently recurring although irregular intervals.

- Pay with a regular check, for a consistent amount, over a period of time.

- Train them. (The IRS assumes that those you contract are already trained.)

- Integrate their services into your business.

- Establish set hours of work.
- Have them work on your premises.
- Pay for their business or travel expenses.

What Constitutes a Freelancer

If you want to retain your tax privileges as a self-employed freelancer you must comply with the following:

- Maintain your studio and equipment.
- Incur a normal business risk, in terms of possibly losing money on some of the projects you take on.

- Subcontract, or hire extra help, if necessary, in order to get a job done.
- Control how tasks will be completed and who will perform them.
- Advertise your services to the public.
- Have a contract or purchase order for the work you will be doing.
- Bill by the job, instead of receiving regular checks.
- Work for different individuals or firms.

Chapter 15

Presentation Techniques

For Better Portfolio Presentations:

- Show only your best work. It may be difficult to pare down what you have, but a dozen pieces are sufficient. Show varied work and include only the finest representative samples.

- Show your best work first. Whether you're making a personal presentation or mailing your portfolio, the first impression usually carries the most impact. Put your best work on the top of the stack or in the front of your book.

- Show a strong piece last. That and the first piece may be the only pieces a client remembers.

- Choose interchangeable pieces and a binding that makes it easy to rework your portfolio quickly. Interchangeable pieces let you customize your portfolio and show only what's most appropriate to your prospective client or employer's business.

- Customize your portfolio. When selecting pieces consider the needs of your prospective client. You'll waste both your time and your client's if you show newsletter samples when the client needs package design.

- Treat your portfolio as a design project. Make it look cohesive. To achieve unity for loose pieces, mount different-sized works on mat boards with the same outer dimensions. Use the same weight and color of mat board.

- Be neat and organized. The care and thought you put into your portfolio reflects the care and thought you would put into any project. Sloppy-looking samples, dog-eared matting, or poor organization gives the impression you don't care.

Comps

Basic Comping Tools and Techniques

"Comping" a project means to render a concept for presentation. You will need to take comps to a different level of completeness for different clients and projects.

There are several standard techniques used to realistically render broad and detailed areas of color, type, photos and illustrations:

Markers. Broad-nibbed and chisel-tipped markers render smooth areas of color that simulate printed ink. Their transparency lets black, inked or photocopied lines show through. Clear markers for blending are also available. Be aware that they contain a solvent that dissolves photocopier and laser print. Typical brands of markers include Design and Pantone.

Colored pencils. This medium renders a semitransparent color that goes down smoothly in areas requiring more control and detail. Use colored pencils for a crisp edge where markers would show a rough, uneven edge. To render a large color field, use a combination of marker and pencil to create smooth, even color and crisp, clean edges. Typical brands are Berol Prismacolor and Derwent Studio.

Marker sprayers. Markers are available that simulate airbrushing when attached to a can of compressed air. They are useful for blending colors and creating gradated tones and can also be used to add custom color to white transfer lettering.

Photocopies. Use a color copier to create realistic-looking four-color representations from slides, photos or illustrations, that match the size and cropping specifications of your layout. These can be adhered to the comp with spray adhesive. To simulate the look of black ink on colored paper, photocopy type and other graphic elements onto sheets of colored paper.

Colored paper and film. It's possible to purchase clear overlay film of solid colors and screen tints of colors, as well as solid colors on coated and uncoated papers. To simulate large areas of ink printed on coated or uncoated paper, use spray adhesive to adhere trimmed-to-size pieces of colored paper to a comp. Adhesive-backed film can be overlaid on photocopied and laser-printed areas to simulate background color behind printed black. Pantone makes films and papers that correspond to ink colors in the Pantone Matching System. Other brands of paper and film that don't necessarily correspond with PMS ink colors include Zipatone, Color-aid and Chroma-rama.

Transfer lettering. Rub-down letters come in black, white and basic colors as well as a variety of sizes to simulate type. You can also have transfers of logos and symbols custom made in specified colors.

Comping Products and Services

- Comping and Proof-making Services: Many such services exist locally and nationally. They produce rub-down transfers or will comp your artwork on the stock of your choice, boxes of all sizes, glasses and so on. Identicolor is a national comping and proof-making service that performs all the services mentioned above and works from shipped disk or mechanical or from artwork sent by modem. Call (800)346-8815.

- Color Tag: This heat and foil system developed by Letraset enables the user to iron plastic foil onto photocopied or laser-printed shapes. Available through Letraset USA, 40 Eisenhower Dr., Paramus NJ 07653.

- Design Film: This product lets the user output graphics from a laser printer onto a film in either clear matte and gloss finishes or opaque white. Self-adhesive backing affixes film to comp without glue. Manufactured by Chartpak. Call (800)628-1910.

- Desktop ColorFoils: This product uses heat from your copier or laser printer to adhere foil onto toner-produced images. Sixteen colors available. Call (800)272-7377.

- Paper Mills: Most paper mills or your local paper merchant will prepare comps of their papers, trimmed and folded into folders or bound into brochures to your size specs so you can determine how a piece will weigh and feel before you purchase paper for it.

Comping Tips and Shortcuts

Spray adhesive: To facilitate repositioning and help prevent trapped bubbles and dust beneath adhesive-backed film, remove the backing and adhere a piece of tracing paper to the back of the film. Apply this with spray adhesive as you would affix any sheet of paper.

Fake spot color: To create the effect of spot color, cut a piece from the backing on adhesive-backed film the approximate size of each color area. Position this portion of the film over the area where color is to be applied, burnish it down and trim to the exact shape you need for your comp.

Quick straight lines: When rendering lines in pencil or marker to represent lines of type in justified columns of text, use low-tack artist's tape to mask off the edges of the margins. Draw the lines, then remove the tape for neat, perfectly justified columns.

Lighter tints: Achieve a slightly lighter shade of a Color-aid, Chromarama or Pantone colored paper by adhering a piece of tracing paper to the top of the original sheet with spray adhesive.

Simulated varnish-finished or cast-coated stock: The frosted side of treated acetate has enough tooth or texture to take paint or an ink line quite nicely. Viewed from the opposite side, the effect is high-gloss and smooth—similar to UV-varnish finished or cast-coated stock. Paint or ink your image onto the frosted side, and once it has dried, mount it frosted side down onto a board or packaging comp with spray adhesive.

Quick blind embossing: To create the impression of a blind emboss (a colorless emboss) on heavy text stock, cut the embossed image out of heavy cardboard. Position it beneath the paper and burnish the area to emboss the image onto the paper.

Custom-colored lettering: Use a marker spray such as Letrajet to apply color to white transfer lettering before you apply them to the comp. Mix colors by respraying with a second or third color.

Make the Logo "Real" to the Client

"After a logo has been selected, it's important to show how the logo looks in various applications: the stationery kit, brochure system, report covers, newsletters, ads — even truck signage. Next, a choice of corporate colors are studied and presented. All of this helps to make the logo more 'real' to the client, and helps to build excitement."

Mike Quon is principal of New York City-based Mike Quon Design Office, which counts American Express, AT&T and Coca-Cola among its many clients.

Presentations

Things to Remember When Making a Presentation

Whether you're competing with other designers or are the sole designer presenting solutions to a client, keep the following in mind:

- Do your homework. Know the firm's products and services, its markets and competition in those markets. Be clear about your client's image and marketing objectives. Know the project's budget. (If you don't know the actual figure, estimate a range based on what you know about the project.)

- Use consistent size and format. If you're presenting thumbnails or other rough sketches, keep formats of different ideas for the same design problem consistent in size and format. For a brochure or other publication, work up all roughs or comps for page layouts at the same size. You don't want the client to favor one concept over another because it has been rendered differently.

- Be professional. Act the "businessperson," and dress for the role.

- Keep calm. No matter what happens, take a deep breath, relax and keep going. Never give an angry or abrupt response to something a client says or does. If your projector dies and another one isn't available, try to continue the presentation. Work around that part of the presentation while someone finds and brings another. Or draw pictures or create other, impromptu visuals to replace the slides.

- Sell yourself. Don't be overly aggressive, but show enthusiasm for what you've done and what you want to do for this client.

- Leave something behind. If you're showing your portfolio, leave a sample of your work or a self-promotion piece. If you're presenting some roughs and/or a proposal, have copies prepared for your client to keep.

Eight Keys to a Successful Presentation

1. Be prepared. Research the client and the market. Know who competitors are and what they're doing. Plan each stage of the presentation carefully.

2. Be knowledgeable. Demonstrate that you understand the client's problems and goals. Describe or reiterate what you know your client's marketing/image objectives to be.

3. Demonstrate the problems with prior, ineffective strategies. If appropriate, point out how the client's marketing or image objectives were not achieved with their previous design strategy.

4. Justify your ideas. Explain how your client's best interests can be served with the design strategy you've created. Focus on benefits and results.

5. Show visual examples. Explain exactly how your concept will help your client implement his or her goals.

6. Discuss the practical end of implementation. Explain how the design concept will be executed; include time frame and budget considerations.

7. Handle questions well. Respond to every question, even if you have to say, "I don't know the answer; I'll get back to you after this meeting." Think before you speak; rephrase the question as part of your response while you choose what to say if you need some time.

8. Describe the next steps. Close the meeting with a discussion of what the next step will be. Set a deadline, and make a commitment to a time when you will come through with the next stage in the design process, whether it be revisions on your initial concept or final films on an idea that was extremely well received!

Section 2

The Production Side

Chapter 16

Preparing for Production

What You Do and When You Do It

Production Checklist

- ❏ Copy obtained, specced for type house or prepared for in-house production.
- ❏ Typeset copy proofed by your firm as well as by client.
- ❏ Corrections made.
- ❏ Dummy completed.
- ❏ Printer is aware of job schedule and other specifications.
- ❏ Paper has been selected. Printer has contacted paper merchant to be sure adequate supply is on hand for the job.
- ❏ Other vendors (fulfillment houses, separators, bindery, etc.) have been contacted and are aware of job schedule and specifications.
- ❏ Corrections and client changes made.
- ❏ All photos and transparencies on hand.
- ❏ Photography scheduled for photos that are not furnished by client.
- ❏ Illustrator(s) selected, illustration(s) assigned.
- ❏ All illustrations, photos and transparencies cropped and sized for reproduction.
- ❏ Charts and other information graphics have been prepared and all other graphics (rules, borders, backgrounds, etc.) are camera-ready.
- ❏ All stats on hand.
- ❏ Mechanicals completed.
- ❏ Client approval obtained on all boards, proofs or pages of the mechanical.
- ❏ All corrections and client changes made to mechanicals.

Sample Production Schedules

The following production schedules serve as guidelines. Timing on any particular project will vary.

Three-Week Production Schedule for a Logo

This schedule is based on producing black-and-white line art and sketches of various logo uses.

Three Weeks Before Deadline

- ❏ Meet with client to get project brief.
- ❏ Develop design ideas.
- ❏ Make four to seven rough sketches of logo possibilities.
- ❏ Meet with client to discuss which designs to develop further.
- ❏ Begin refinements on client's choice of two designs.

Two Weeks Before Deadline

- ❏ Make rough sketches of designs applied to letterhead, business cards and other applications pertinent to client's needs.
- ❏ Meet with client to choose best design.
- ❏ Commission illustration, calligraphy or other service.

One Week Before Deadline

- ❏ Send out for typesetting of company name, or have service bureau output type for reproduction if separate from graphic elements.
- ❏ Have service bureau output any needed graphics if separate from logo or type.
- ❏ Make oversized mechanical of logo.
- ❏ Have final stats made for client: large-size original, reduced sizes for other logo applications.

Four-Week Production Schedule for Letterhead

This schedule is based on producing one thousand sheets of two-color letterhead, one thousand business cards and one thousand No. 10 envelopes. This schedule does not include time for designing a logo. If you are designing a logo as part of the letterhead project, add two weeks to the beginning of this schedule. If you have one or two other printed applications, such as business forms, add at least one week for design time and one to two weeks printing time.

Four Weeks Before Deadline

- ❏ Meet with client to get project brief.

▶

Make Your Service Bureau an Ally

"As a design studio producing electronic mechanicals, some of the most valuable production partners we have found have been our output vendors. Whether a fine commercial printer, a nationwide color house or a local service bureau, they have all become important assets in our efforts to efficiently produce high-quality work.

"We plan the job with them before any production begins, and sometimes before the actual designing of a concept has been started. In the case of some of the envelope-pushing work we've done for Radius, the headaches we avoid, and what we learn through working with our vendors yields a higher quality and often less expensive end product than we would have gotten had we just presented our files for output without any prior consultation."

Toni Hollander *is founder and principal of The Design Works, a Los Angeles-based design firm that has been recognized for its cutting-edge design work for Radius and other clients known for their high profile in the computer industry.*

❑ Pick up client's logo, address and any other information to go on letterhead.

❑ Develop design ideas.

❑ Make four to seven rough color sketches of letterhead, accompanying envelope and business card possibilities.

❑ Select paper samples.

Three Weeks Before Deadline

❑ Meet with client to choose the best letterhead design(s).

❑ Refine client's choice(s).

❑ Meet with client to choose one design to finalize.

Two Weeks Before Deadline

❑ Make necessary refinements to letterhead, business card, envelope and any other layouts.

❑ Send out for stats, typeset copy or other graphic elements.

❑ Prepare traditional or digital mechanicals.

❑ Proof all typeset copy.

❑ Obtain client approval.

One Week Before Deadline

❑ Give printer mechanicals and specs.

❑ Check and approve bluelines or color keys.

❑ Do press check.

❑ Approve samples.

❑ Follow up with client on whether job was received and is satisfactory.

Four-Month Production Schedule for a Restaurant Identity Program

This schedule is based on designing a logo, stationery, business cards and business forms, napkins, signage and a four-color, laminated menu. If you are producing a system that has only simple, printed applications in addition to a stationery system, you may want to follow the letterhead schedule above and add extra time for dealing with printing other items.

Sixteen Weeks Before Deadline

❑ Meet with client to get project brief; get copy of existing menu, if any, or sample, projected menu.

❑ Work up initial logo sketches.

❑ Work up production schedule.

Thirteen Weeks Before Deadline

❑ Finalize logo choice; get actual copy for menu, signage, business cards, forms and napkins.

❑ Produce initial roughs of menu, signage, business cards, forms and napkins.

Twelve Weeks Before Deadline

❑ Meet with client to choose design(s).

❑ Refine client's choice(s).

❑ Meet with client to choose one design to finalize.

Eleven Weeks Before Deadline

❑ Final identity system design approved by client.

❑ Finalize layout and copy on signage.

❑ Obtain client approval or signage copy and layout.

❑ Forward specs to sign fabricator.

Nine Weeks Before Deadline

❑ Finalize layout of business cards, forms and stationery.

❑ Obtain client approval of layout.

❑ Finalize printing bids.

Eight Weeks Before Deadline

❑ Typeset copy.

❑ Prepare mechanicals for business cards, forms and stationery.

❑ Obtain client approval of mechanicals.

❑ Deliver to printer.

❑ Finalize layout of menu.

❑ Obtain client approval of menu layout.

Seven Weeks Before Deadline

❑ Produce art and copy for napkins.

❑ Obtain client approval of napkin layout.

❑ Give specifications for napkins to supplier.

Six Weeks Before Deadline
Prepare artwork and/or mechanical for napkins.

❑ Obtain client approval of napkin artwork/mechanical.

❑ Proof stationery, business cards and business forms.

Five Weeks Before Deadline
❑ Conduct press check of stationery, business cards and business forms.

Four Weeks Before Deadline
❑ Have stationery and business materials printed, samples approved.

❑ Verify delivery and acceptance by client.

❑ Typeset copy; produce mechanical for menu.

❑ Obtain client approval on menu mechanical; send out for separations.

Three Weeks Before Deadline
❑ Deliver menu to printer.

Two Weeks Before Deadline
❑ Proof menu.

❑ Signs completed; installation begins.

One Week Before Deadline
❑ Laminated menus delivered to client.

❑ Napkins delivered to client.

Six-Week Production Schedule for a Brochure
This schedule is based on producing approximately ten thousand copies of a 12-page, 8½ × 11-inch, two-color brochure with an embossed cover. Art and copy are furnished by client. If client does not supply copy on disk allow time for keyboarding the copy.

Six Weeks Before Deadline
❑ Meet with client to get project brief.

❑ Obtain art and copy from client.

❑ Develop design ideas; select format, second color and paper.

❑ Prepare production schedule.

❑ Start layout roughs.

Five Weeks Before Deadline
❑ Produce comp.

❑ Obtain client approval of comp.

❑ Copy is typeset.

❑ Proofread galleys.

❑ Correct galleys.

❑ Send out for stats.

Four Weeks Before Deadline
❑ Crop, size and tag art.

❑ Paste up mechanicals or send page layout files for conversion.

❑ Obtain client approval of mechanicals.

Three Weeks Before Deadline
❑ Send cover mechanical to embossing service.

❑ Send remainder of job to printer.

Two Weeks Before Deadline
❑ Check and correct color proofs.

❑ Obtain client approval of proofs.

One Week Before Deadline
❑ Embossed covers are dropped off at printer or bindery.

❑ Brochures are assembled, bound, and delivered to client.

Eight-Week Production Schedule for a Catalog
This schedule is based on producing twenty-thousand copies of a sixteen-page, 8½ × 11-inch, four-color catalog with client-furnished product photos and copy. Printer and other vendors are local.

Eight Weeks Before Deadline
- ❑ Meet with client to get project brief.
- ❑ Obtain photos and copy from client.
- ❑ Develop design ideas and select paper.
- ❑ Produce rough layout.
- ❑ Determine production schedule.

Seven Weeks Before Deadline
- ❑ Produce comps.
- ❑ Make dummy to determine mailing costs.
- ❑ Obtain client's approval of comps; make client corrections.

Six Weeks Before Deadline (traditional mechanical)
- ❑ Prepare copy for typesetting.
- ❑ Send out copy for typesetting.
- ❑ Proofread and correct galleys.
- ❑ Crop and size photos and transparencies.
- ❑ Make "For Position Only" (FPO) prints.

Six Weeks Before Deadline (digital mechanical)
- ❑ Key-in copy if needed.
- ❑ Prepare final layout and flow in copy.
- ❑ Scan in photos.
- ❑ Position and size scans as FPO prints or for separation in layout.
- ❑ Proofread and correct copy in layout.

Five Weeks Before Deadline
- ❑ Paste-up traditional mechanicals or finalize digital mechanicals.
- ❑ Obtain client approval of mechanicals.

Four Weeks Before Deadline
- ❑ Send out mechanicals and transparencies for separations.
- ❑ Check and correct first set of color proofs.

Three Weeks Before Deadline
- ❑ Check second set of color proofs.
- ❑ Finalize separations.

Two Weeks Before Deadline
- ❑ Job goes on press.
- ❑ Do press check.

One Week Before Deadline
- ❑ Catalogs are bound and trimmed.
- ❑ Catalogs delivered to lettershop for addressing, presorting and mailing.

Three-Month Production Schedule for Annual Report

This schedule is based on printing approximately twenty thousand copies of a four-color, twenty-four-page annual report in 8½ × 11-inch format with saddle stitched binding. If you are working with out-of-town suppliers, add average transportation times to the schedule below. Designer hires and schedules photographers and copywriter and obtains all other services.

If you are working on a complex report or need many commissioned illustrations or photographs, add a margin of two weeks for design and/or for obtaining artwork. Allow ten working days for make-ready on dies for special cuts, foil stamping and simple embosses; allow even more time for sculptured embosses.

Twelve Weeks Before Deadline
- ❑ Meet with company officials and the writer to discuss concept, budget and schedule.
- ❑ Prepare initial production specifications (including paper) and get cost estimates from suppliers.

Eleven Weeks Before Deadline
- ❑ Work up concept, page distribution, cost estimate and schedule.
- ❑ Request draft of financial copy from client or copywriter with due date of three weeks.
- ❑ Select photographer(s)/illustrator(s).

Ten Weeks Before Deadline

❑ Present concept, page distribution, cost estimate and schedule to client.

❑ Obtain client approval of photographer(s)/illustrator(s).

❑ Request initial draft of text copy from client or copywriter with due date of two weeks.

❑ Assign photographer/illustrator and reserve appropriate blocks of time for their work and for art direction.

Nine Weeks Before Deadline

❑ Coordinate with client the subjects, locations and scheduling of photography (and illustration if needed).

❑ Review and revise budget estimate.

Eight Weeks Before Deadline

❑ Complete design concepts for charts, graphs and special pages.

❑ Photography begins.

❑ Review and approve outline and final copy; obtain approval of client.

❑ Obtain financial information.

Six Weeks Before Deadline

❑ Typeset financial information and copy and submit galleys to client for review.

❑ Send out for stats.

❑ Review photographs; schedule additional shots if necessary.

❑ Prepare finished dummy with art in place; review with client.

❑ Check type galleys for length; send to client for proofreading.

❑ If custom envelopes are needed for mailing the report, prepare and have mechanicals approved; send to printer.

Five Weeks Before Deadline

❑ Return revised galleys for final corrections.

❑ Submit all photographs to company and obtain approval for reproduction.

❑ Produce mechanicals; submit photocopies to company for approval.

Four Weeks Before Deadline

❑ Make final corrections to mechanicals and obtain client approval.

❑ Submit mechanicals, art and photography to separator/printer.

❑ Check envelope bluelines; arrange envelope delivery to lettershop.

Three Weeks Before Deadline

❑ Check and correct first-color proofs or bluelines.

❑ Let printer/binder know where specific quantities are to be shipped for bank, company divisions, mailing, and so on.

Two Weeks Before Deadline

❑ Check and correct second-color proofs or bluelines, if needed.

❑ Do press check when job goes on press.

❑ Give lettershop quantities and labels.

One Week Before Deadline

❑ Check advance copies before delivery.

Four-Week Production Schedule for a Newsletter

This is based on producing approximately ten thousand copies of a monthly, four-page, 8½ × 11-inch, two-color self-mailing newsletter with client-furnished photos and copy. This is not the first issue, so the format, grid, type design and so forth have already been established. Local printer and other vendors are used.

Four Weeks Before Deadline

❑ Produce thumbnails.

❑ Fit copy and estimate art sizes.

❑ Choose second color (if this varies with each issue) and spec tint.

❑ Review layout with client.

▶

Three Weeks Before Deadline (traditional mechanical)

❏ Send out copy for typesetting.

❏ Proofread galleys and send galleys to client for corrections.

❏ Review corrected galleys.

❏ Send out for halftones.

❏ Make sure printer or fulfillment house has address labels.

Three Weeks Before Deadline (digital mechanical)

❏ Keyboard copy, if needed.

❏ Pour copy into template.

❏ Scan in photos for FPO prints or reproduction as part of file.

❏ Position and size scans.

❏ Check and correct first proofs of layout.

❏ Make sure printer or fulfillment house has address labels.

Two Weeks Before Deadline

❏ Paste up traditional mechanicals or finalize digital mechanicals.

❏ Obtain client approval of mechanicals.

❏ Check and correct bluelines.

❏ Press run begins.

One Week Before Deadline

❏ Printed newsletters are folded and sealed.

❏ Sent to lettershop for mailing.

One-Week Production Schedule for a Newspaper Ad

This schedule is based on producing a simple, two-column, type-only ad for a local newspaper. Copy is supplied by the client.

❏ Meet with client to discuss project brief.

❏ Produce layout roughs; obtain client approval.

❏ Obtain copy from client; release for typesetting.

❏ Check and correct copy.

❏ Check second proof; release for camera-ready.

❏ Produce mechanical; obtain client approval.

❏ Send mechanical to newspaper.

Three-Week Production Schedule for a Magazine Ad

This schedule is for a one-shot, four-color ad in a local magazine.

Three Weeks Before Deadline

❏ Meet with client to get project brief.

❏ Obtain ad copy from client.

❏ Produce layout roughs; obtain client approval.

❏ Select illustrator or photographer; obtain client approval of choice.

❏ Assign photograpy or illustration.

Two Weeks Before Deadline

❏ Art direct photography or illustration.

❏ Release copy for typesetting.

❏ Proof and correct type.

❏ Proof corrected galley; release for camera-ready.

❏ Obtain client approval of photograph(s) or illustration(s).

❏ Produce traditional or digital mechanical.

One Week Before Deadline

❏ Size art.

❏ Send mechanical and artwork to separator.

❏ Check and correct color proofs.

❏ Send mechanical and films to magazine.

Four-Week Production Schedule for a Four-Color Poster

This schedule is based on printing approximately five thousand 22 × 34-inch posters with four-color process printing on a sheet-fed offset press with bleed. The printer is being paid for his services. If this were a trade of printing services for design services or a pro bono job for the printer, additional time should be allowed. The printer would fit a nonpaying project around paid work, and delays could occur.

Four Weeks Before Deadline

❏ Meet with client to discuss project brief.

❏ Agree on headline and type of visuals based on budget.

❏ Produce design roughs; obtain client approval.

❏ Obtain any needed copy from client.

❏ Select artist or photographer and obtain client approval.

❏ Schedule photography or illustration or start creating your own art.

Three Weeks Before Deadline

❏ Set type; proof and correct.

❏ Verify all schedule, location or ordering information with client.

❏ Size art.

❏ Prepare traditional or digital mechanical.

❏ Send mechanical to separator.

Two Weeks Before Deadline

❏ Check and correct first set of proofs.

❏ Check and correct additional sets of color proofs as needed.

❏ Obtain client approval of proofs.

One Week Before Deadline

❏ Job goes on press.

❏ Do press check.

❏ Posters delivered to client.

Mechanicals

Guidelines for Speccing Tints

If you are selecting only flat color for printing, choose the swatch you want from a color matching system, write down its number, and attach the swatch to the mechanical. If, however, you want to specify special colors or flat colors to be printed as process

colors, you will have to take a few additional steps:

❏ If you need to reproduce a match color with process inks, use the color specifier that comes with the system to get the correct proportions.

❏ If you are creating custom colors or converting match colors to process, verify that your printer can handle the proportions. Don't spec any percentage less than 5 percent, and try to make all percentages a multiple of five.

❏ Use two inks as often as possible when specifying a color, three only when necessary and four never.

❏ Compensate for dot gain, especially when printing on a web press, by specifying a slightly lighter value of the color than you actually want. Dot gain may cause a 50 percent dot to print as a 60 or 70 percent value. It's best to spec a tint of no more than 10 percent for any color that prints under type.

❏ Don't specify more than one solid (100 percent value) into a tint when you're printing on a web press. Uneven ink distribution can occur if there is too much ink in one area.

❏ To match a tint color to a portion of a four-color, printed photo, circle the color you want to match on the printed piece and give it to the separator.

Before the Mechanical Goes, Check:

❏ Artwork cropped, scaled and keyed to the mechanical.

❏ For Position Only (FPO) artwork prepared and in place.

❏ Guidelines for type and holding lines for art drawn on board.

❏ Cropmarks, folding lines and bleed lines drawn on board.

❏ Copy is in place.

❏ Overlays indicating placement of colors are attached.

❏ Project name and contact information are provided.

Production Management With the Computer
"We work on Macintoshes in my studio. All of them are connected to one another. We key into these computers the production schedules, printing specifications, supply lists and additional information. The Macintosh and System 7 have radically facilitated the production process by allowing everyone access to necessary information."

__Jennifer Morla__ is founder and principal of Morla Design, a San Francisco-based design studio. She has done work for clients such as Levi's, MTV, Fox Broadcasting, Cocolat and American President Lines.

▶

SERVICE BUREAU ORDER FORM

You can include this sheet or one like it with each job you send to the service bureau for output to make sure you've included all the information for your job.

Date: _____

From: _____ To: _____

_____ _____

_____ _____

Phone: _____ Phone: _____

Project Name/Description _____ Project # _____

Due Date (Date & Time): _____

PO #: _____

Rush Charges okay: ☐ Yes ☐ No

Submission Format: ☐ Floppy ☐ Modem ☐ Optical ☐ Tape ☐ Cartridge ☐ SCSI device ☐ Worm

Page Layout Program Used: _____ Version _____

Xpress Data Files Included ☐ Yes ☐ No

Font(s) Used in Document

Name: _____ Manufacturer: _____

Name: _____ Manufacturer: _____

Name: _____ Manufacturer: _____

Name: _____ Manufacturer: _____

File Name to Image: _____

Number of Pages: _____ Resolution _____ dpi _____

Output Size Excluding Trim Zone: _____

Type of Graphics File: ☐ TIFF ☐ PICT ☐ PICT2 ☐ EPSF ☐ Amiga ILF/ILBN

Type of Graphics File: ☐ TIFF ☐ PICT ☐ PICT2 ☐ EPSF ☐ Amiga ILF/ILBN

Type of Graphics File: ☐ TIFF ☐ PICT ☐ PICT2 ☐ EPSF ☐ Amiga ILF/ILBN

Type of Graphics File: ☐ TIFF ☐ PICT ☐ PICT2 ☐ EPSF ☐ Amiga ILF/ILBN

LineScreen: ☐ 85 ☐ 100 ☐ 110 ☐ 120 ☐ 133 ☐ 150 ☐ 175 ☐ 200

Sizing: ☐ Percent Given ☐ Stat Enclosed

Separations Required: ☐ Spot ☐ Screen Color ☐ Match Color(s) ☐ Process Colors

Proof Required: ☐ Matchprint ☐ Cromalin ☐ Color Keys ☐ Mac-driven Color Copier
☐ Other: _____

Special Instructions: _____

_____

❏ Special production directions such as reverses and dropouts are noted.

Special Considerations for Preparing an Electronic Mechanical

❏ Note all fonts on your order form or purchase order and list the manufacturer of each font.

❏ List the name and version number of all software programs used.

❏ List the page size, including bleed and trim sizes.

❏ Specify the line screen for output.

❏ Make sure all linked graphics are included on the same disk with the page layout file.

❏ Note film type needed for output: negative or positive, right-reading or wrong-reading, emulsion side up or down.

❏ Provide hard copy proof to serve as visual reference.

❏ Guard against blends and masks.

❏ Check that cropmarks and registration marks are included.

❏ Make sure the trapping was done properly.

❏ Specify type of proof required.

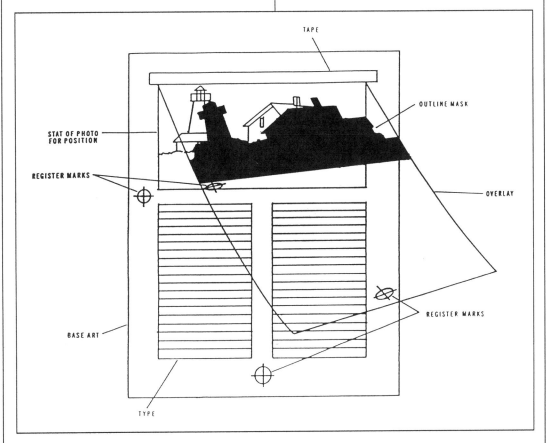

Parts of a traditional mechanical

Chapter 17

Working Effectively With Your Printer

Getting the Most for Your Money

Thirteen Ways to Save Money on Your Next Project

1. Try to get maximum usage from the sheet size your printer's press will accommodate.

2. Use your printer's house sheet whenever possible. This is usually paper that has been bought in bulk at a discounted price.

3. Get a two-color effect by printing a second color on only one side of a signature (called 2/1 printing). The effect will be color throughout your piece, without the cost of a full two-color job.

4. Avoid rush bids on out-of-the-ordinary requests. You'll fare better if your printer has had time to hear from all of the bidding vendors.

5. Catch errors as soon as possible. Keep in mind that making a change during production will increase costs tenfold with every step that takes you closer to the final product.

6. Limit the size of your mechanical to ½ inch beyond your trim size. If your printer prefers to gang your pages when making films, working with mechanicals that are close to trim size will enable the camera operator to do this.

7. Produce mechanicals on a one-page-per-board basis. This gives the printer the option of gang separating a larger number of boards than he could do with spreads. Check with your printer first.

8. Select the appropriate means of halftone reproduction for the job. Scanning in black-and-white photos for computer-generated halftone output is one possibility. If you're working with traditional mechanicals, creating to-size veloxes is another option. Some publications, such as magazines, require a high 133-line screen resolution.

9. A mechanical that isn't clean or accurate requires extra time for touching up the films and possibly for reshooting. Make sure all printable elements on your mechanical are in red or black. No other colors will reproduce as 100 percent black.

10. For publications such as newsletters where a second color is used from issue to issue, you may be able to save money by having a large quantity preprinted with just the colored elements. Then print each issue's information in black, and you'll have a low-cost, two-color piece.

11. Stick to four-color process colors, rather than match colors, when your budget calls for a four-color job.

12. Ask for overruns of book covers or dust jackets. They can be trimmed and promotional copy printed on the blank side.

13. Save money on paper by using a lower basis weight or a cheaper grade.

What to Do If Your Printer Screws Up

1. First, determine if you have a legitimate grievance. Printers' terms and conditions are usually fairly clear, and most printers go by an industry code of ethics called the Printing Trade Customs. You can get a copy of this code from your local chapter of the Printing Industries of America, or contact their national headquarters: 1730 N. Lynn St., Arlington VA 22209; (703)841-8100.

2. If you do have a legitimate gripe, decide whether or not your print shop is capable of reprinting the job. If the job was a total loss and you feel they've bitten off more than they could chew, take your job elsewhere, and point out to the original printer that you don't feel you should have to pay for a job that will have to be trashed.

3. If you're confident that your print shop has the potential to do the job right the second time around, point out what is specifically wrong with the job and insist that it be done again properly.

▶

4. If your printer balks at the idea of reprinting the job because the flaws are not substantial, compromise by paying for a portion of the reprint—for instance, paper and materials.

5. If your printer isn't amenable to any kind of settlement, have the disagreement arbitrated by an industry group such as Printing Industries of America.

Ganging
Gang Separating Transparencies or Prints

- Be sure that formats are the same. Separators can't gang transparencies and prints together.

- Try to keep prints or transparencies of similar subject matter and lighting together.

- Don't include any photos or transparencies with a definite color cast. If your separator makes a color correction based on one off-color item, it will affect the color of the other shots in the group.

- Spec the enlargements or reductions of ganged items for the same percentage.

Gang Printing Jobs

Similar print jobs, whether they belong to the same client or not, can be gang printed to save money.

- If your client needs a number of similar items for the coming year, try to get him to do them all on press at the same time.

- If your client can't crank out a year's worth of copy or whatever it takes to do a sizeable run, a savings might still be appreciated on a future two-color job. Run two colors on the current job and then have your printer not print the text color. When your client is ready to print text on the future job, run it on the sheets preprinted with the accent color for a one-color charge on a two-color job.

- Gang different identity materials that share a consistent look. Try to set them up so that all items are trimmed from the same sheet.

- Run two client's pieces in tandem, sharing paper and production costs. This is also a good way to give each client four-color printing for half price.

- Tack a small item, such as a business card, for yourself or another client on the trim from a client's project. Always get the primary client's okay first.

Technical Considerations for Gang Printing Jobs

- Use the same type of paper. Items on the same print run must print on the same type of stock, but not necessarily the same colored stock.

- Items on the same print run must share some ink colors but don't necessarily have to be designed with all these colors.

- Maximize the imposition. You can easily impose two jobs on the same sheet of paper.

- Separate four-color image areas on different projects. When impositioning two four-color jobs on a sheet of paper, position four-color image areas as far apart as possible to minimize the likelihood of their colors influencing one another.

- When impositioning large areas of color, butt bleeds of the same color together.

Printing Processes

Basic Printing Techniques

Sheet-Fed Offset Lithography: The most popular commercial printing method, offset lithography yields sharp images quickly and inexpensively. Metal plates are coated with an ink-receptive chemical that covers the image area. The image is then offset from the plate onto a rubber blanket, which is then offset from blanket to paper. Offset printing produces a sharp image because the rubber blanket conforms to the surface variations of the paper. Sheet-fed offset presses run individual sheets, varying in size from $8\frac{1}{2} \times 11$ inch to 55×78 inches. They can accommodate up to eight ink colors (or varnishes) at a time, depending on the size of the press, and are used for a wide variety of projects and quantity runs. Their limitation is that they cannot accommodate most industrial-grade or handmade papers.

Web Lithography: Offset presses that run paper on rolls are referred to as web presses. Web presses print more than one color on both sides of the paper with a single pass through the press. They come in sizes that accommodate rolls from 17 to 26-inches wide. These presses are frequently used for magazines and other publications where 26-inch wide rolls are folded and trimmed to create eight-page, 8½ × 11-inch booklets or signatures. Web presses generally print long runs more economically than sheet-fed presses do. However, there is no rule of thumb in determining where the most economical cutoff point is — it will always vary with each job.

Letterpress: The letterpress process involves literally hitting the paper with a photoengraved metal plate or metal type. The impact on the paper not only leaves an ink imprint, it leaves a debossed impression that imbeds the ink deep into the pulp fibers. The impression is particularly dramatic on soft handmade papers, but letterpress is also commonly used for printing on industrial stocks. The slower press speeds of letterpress make it less cost-effective for long runs as well as multicolor (particularly four-color process) but practical for short runs (one thousand pieces or less) of one or two colors. There are still quite a few print shops doing letterpress; many use it for simple commercial jobs, such as sequential ticket numbering. But there are quite a few shops capable of handling design-sensitive projects. Many also offer the wonderful antique typefaces that are original to this type of equipment. (For further information on letterpress see page 147.)

Silkscreen Printing: (Also called screen printing.) Ink is applied to a surface by drawing a squeegee across a silkscreen to which a stencil has been affixed. Ink is forced through the screen and onto the printing surface. The stencil is generally applied by making a photo silkscreen — a process where a negative of a halftone, black-and-white art or a mechanical is exposed with photo emulsion directly onto the silkscreen. When printing flat areas of color, one screen is used per color. However, multicolor, split-fountain effects can be achieved by blending colors on the screen as the squeegee is dragged across them. Inks generally take a while to dry, but can be UV-cured (dried with ultraviolet radiation) to a tough, high-gloss finish. Screen printed garments and other pieces are frequently run through a drier to facilitate handling. Screen printing can be used on all types of papers and on many surfaces that are not accommodated by offset lithography or letterpress, such as vinyl, fabric, plastic and metal. Because of this versatility, it's commonly used for signs and garment printing. Screen printing is frequently chosen for posters because inks generally provide denser, more brilliant color than offset inks. Because the process is more labor-intensive it's generally better suited to short runs (two thousand pieces or less).

Engraving: A printing method where a design is photoengraved, acid-etched or tooled by hand or machine onto a metal plate or die. The wells formed in the die are filled with ink. When the plate is forced into contact with the paper, the ink is lifted out of the plate, transferring a raised, glossy image to the front of the sheet, and creating a slight impression on the back. Although engraving uses inks other than litho inks, match colors can be easily achieved. Engraving inks also have high opacity and produce excellent metallic effects. More expensive than offset lithography or thermography, engraving conveys a sense of prestige and is frequently used for letterheads and other business materials, announcements and certificates. (For further information on engraving see pages 147-148.)

Thermography: A relatively inexpensive way to duplicate the look of engraving. A dull, glossy or semiglossy raised impression

▶

Ganging Four-Color for Separations

"When I worked as an art director for a magazine, we would gang our transparencies so that as many as possible could be shot for separations at the same percentage. You definitely need to keep color in mind and gang images with similar colors for the best result.

"Eventually, we also found out how the stripper mounted our ganged transparencies before they were shot. We cut our costs even further by mounting them ourselves on the same type of acetate they used."

Lori Siebert, *founder and principal of Cincinnati-based Siebert Design Associates, is a nationally recognized graphic designer and author of two books on design and layout.*

is achieved by heat-curing powder applied to wet ink on the paper. The height of the raised impression can be controlled by the amount of powder that is applied. Because spreading of color can be a factor, and cracking can sometimes occur when it is trimmed, thermography is generally limited to spot color applications. Thermography can be clear and duplicate the look of spot varnish in small areas, or create special effects, such as the clear, raised impression of rain drops. It's frequently used for invitations, letterheads and other business materials—particularly business cards. (For further information on thermography see page 148.)

Waterless Offset Printing: This process is also called dry offset or dry trap printing. It uses special silicone plates, thicker inks and temperature control systems. Waterless printing is more environmentally friendly than traditional offset printing and permits the reproduction of images at very high line screens, anywhere from 300- to 800-line screens. These fine screens are possible because waterless printing reportedly has a maximum dot gain of 8 percent in the midtone range, approximately 50 percent less than conventional offset. Inks are available in process and Pantone Matching System colors and are reputed to produce richer, more saturated colors than conventional inks.

However, there are some disadvantages to waterless offset. It is currently offered by only a handful of printers in the United States, so finding a printer can be difficult. Waterless offset generally adds about 10 percent to the cost of traditional offset printing. You'll also pay more for a separation with a 600 to 800 line screen than you would for a 133-line screen.

Guidelines for Offset Printing

- Designs printed on small presses should not have images within ⅜ inch of the leading edge of a sheet. This guarantees that you won't be missing part of an image where the gripper grabs the sheet.

- Presses can't print up to the edge of the sheet, so bleeds require the use of larger sized paper that is then trimmed to the desired size. Always tell your printer (and the paper buyer if the printer doesn't do this) that there will be bleeds so the right size paper is ordered.

- Web presses print long runs more economically than sheet-fed presses. Runs of more than 100,000 press sheets should be done on a web press. Below this level savings vary.

- Remember that only the most sophisticated web presses can deliver showcase quality printing. But most web presses can produce basic, good and premium quality work.

- Crossovers—elements that must line up across the gutter after the piece is folded, trimmed and bound—can be difficult and expensive to achieve. Avoid these whenever possible. Unless you can afford showcase printing, decide in advance how much misalignment you can accept. Let the printer know how much this is.

- You get what you pay for, but buy only the printing quality you need.

- Sheet-fed offset printing is generally more compatible with many on-line printing techniques used to embellish uncoated text and cover papers.

- Smoother-surfaced uncoated papers often perform better on a web press than do those that are deeply embossed or felt-marked.

- Halftones, duotones and color separations can lose detail and print darker with offset printing, especially on web presses, due to dot gain. Be sure that the film output for halftones, duotones and separations has been adjusted for dot gain.

- Finer screens are most affected by dot gain. If you are producing your own halftones on a desktop computer or ordering them from a vendor, spec the right screen for the paper and press.

- Don't be afraid to experiment; just because something has never been done, that doesn't mean you can't do it. Offset printing offers great creative freedom. You can print on many different papers and other materials.

- You can prevent ghosts (unwanted, faint images). Make sure areas of solid color are well distributed so the ink can build upon the rollers again. Balance halftones and other elements on a page so the ink pulls evenly. You can also plan an imposition pattern so that a page requiring heavy ink coverage runs next to one with a different pattern.

- Work-and-turn and work-and-tumble imposition is generally less expensive than sheetwise imposition. In the first two methods, one plate is used to print both sides of the sheet, while sheetwise imposition requires two plates—one for each side of the sheet. However, you can use different inks for each plate when printing with sheetwise imposition.

- Colors produced by process color printing can vary. Ink density, trapping and dot gain can all affect the results. Let your printer know from the outset where color matching is critical so time can be allowed in the schedule for extra rounds of proofing and corrections. If cost is a factor, try to keep all critical color in a few signatures or a few spreads so the rest of the job can move ahead.

Guidelines for Letterpress Printing

Letterpress printing can be used on many paper surfaces, such as handmade papers, chipboard and other industrial papers unsuitable for offset printing.

- Letterpress leaves the greatest impression on soft, absorbent papers. Its effect is totally lost on coated papers.

- This time-consuming process is ideal for short-run jobs in quantities under one thousand. Because of the extra time involved, rule out rush jobs.

- If using antique, hot-metal type, make sure copy will fit the exact area in which

it will appear. There's no second-guessing when you set copy with metal type.

- Letterpress runs one color on press at a time—an extremely time-consuming process for four-color process work where exact registration is required.

Guidelines for Silkscreen Printing

Silkscreen printing is ideal for bulky and/ or hard-to-print surfaces.

- Silkscreen is more time-consuming than offset, but ideal for short runs of two thousand or less.

- Consider silkscreen for pieces, such as posters, that are too large for offset.

- Silkscreen is well suited to pieces, such as posters and fabrics, that require even, brilliant color.

- Any type of artwork of any size can be used.

- Although halftones and color separations can be printed, they should be reproduced at a screen size no finer than an 85-line for smooth-surfaced paper and 55-line for textured paper or cloth.

- Make rules at least 2 points thick.

- Avoid extremely fine traps (where abutting colors overlap each other by less than $1/32$ inch). Paper can shrink during printing, making tight registration difficult to achieve.

- Because silkscreen inks are highly opaque, they overprint one another without bleeding through. Plan any overprinting carefully with the printer to be sure the results match your concept.

Guidelines for Engraving

- Don't plan on four-color process or trapping. The high opacity of engraving inks precludes this.

- Avoid applying large areas of color that can appear mottled or uneven. Instead, consider using a silhouette of your image or a screen tint.

- Discuss image needs with your printer. Image reproduction is as clear as with

Technical Tips for Printing With Pastel Colors

Pantone, Inc. recommends that printers keep the following considerations in mind when printing with pastel inks:

"Press maintenance is very important. You should know what was previously on the press before running a pastel job. New rollers may need to be installed, in order to avoid contaminating the light pastels with other colors.

"The press must be thoroughly cleaned. A three-step cleaning process of using solvent, opaque white, and then solvent is recommended. Opaque white ink works well as a cleaning agent because the inorganic particles in it will grind out the ink residue in the press from the previous job.

"A non-yellowing varnish is recommended for pastel inks to help prevent fading and yellowing of color. Normal quickset varnishes tend to cause yellowing of very pale colors."

Michael Garin *is senior vice president-R/D, manufacturing of Pantone, Inc., manufacturer of the Pantone Pastel Color Specifier and other color guides that are part of the Pantone Matching System and Pantone Process Color System.*

litho, but photographs and continuous-tone illustrations are etched and not reproduced as a series of halftone dots as they are with lithography. This fact may make engraving visuals cost prohibitive.

- Limit the size of the engraved area. Image area is limited to 5×8 inches, the plate size that most commercial engraving presses can accommodate. If the overall image is larger than 5×8 inches, try to divide it into smaller sections that can be engraved separately.

- Convert envelopes *after* they have been engraved to prevent the engraved impression from appearing on the back. Or you can print converted envelopes with flaps open to cover the deboss if the engraved area on the front is opposite and so hidden by the flap.

Guidelines for Thermography

- Use well-defined line art and 7-point type or larger. Avoid halftones and screen tints.

- Consider all your printing surface options. Coated or uncoated papers can be thermographed, but uncoated papers contrast nicely with the glossy surface of thermography. Thermography will also work on vinyl and polyester.

- Select a rigid stock with a minimum weight of 20 lb. Any cover weight will do. Avoid heavily textured papers that can trap powder in nonprinting areas.

- Stay away from large, solid areas of color that can blister.

- Use a die-cut to trim a thermography bleed. Guillotine trimming may crack the thermographed area.

- Don't print on paper that will be run through a laser printer or high-speed copier; the heat of these machines will melt the ink.

See the discussions of gravure, flexography and other printing techniques used mostly for packaging on pages 116-117.

Special Printing Effects

Foil Stamping: This is also called hot stamping, leaf stamping, pastelling, foil embossing or tint leaf embossing. A variety of high-gloss spot effects can be achieved relatively inexpensively. Foil stamping offers shimmery metallics and a variety of glossy colors. It also offers clean, solid color in situations where ink wouldn't work. Clear foil can even be used to simulate spot varnish, an option worth considering for uncoated stocks that absorb liquid varnishes. Dull, glossy and metallic colors, wood grains, marble, pearlescent and patterned effects are also available. (For further information on foil stamping, see the opposite page.)

Embossing/Debossing: These techniques offer a number of three-dimensional effects. You can use them with ink, with foil stamping, or "blind," that is, without color. You can emboss or deboss a visual, a logo or a company name. When combined with a printed image, the image must be inked before it is embossed or debossed. Using heat, pressure, a metal embossing die and a counter die, images can be stamped. Dies can be photomechanically produced for simple images, but when a highly detailed image is required, a craftsperson must hand-tool the metal die. There are three basic die types: Single-level, multilevel and sculptured. Single-level dies have only one level of depth and are the cheapest to produce. Multilevel dies involve more than one level of embossing. Sculptured dies are handmade and are cut into metal with grinders and chisels. Dies can also be beveled, round, flat or outlined. To produce a mechanical for an embossed or debossed image, you must provide black-and-white art for each level of a die. (This can require several acetate overlays on your base art if you are specifying a multilevel die.) Indicate on your mechanical the type (single, multileveled or sculptured) and slope of the image (beveled, round, flat or outlined). (For further information, see the opposite page.)

Varnishing: Varnishes are applied to a printed piece to protect any area from moisture, fingerprints and scuffing; to create a slick, glossy look; to enhance contrast and add dimension; and to produce rich, subtle visual effects. In addition to coating pieces that have already been printed, you can use varnish as an undercoat, to size uncoated paper and cause it to respond in a manner similar to coated papers. This can be especially useful when printing four-color process photos on uncoated stock.

Guidelines for Foil Stamping

- Use cover stock, 20 to 24 lb. writing paper, or 50 to 70 lb. uncoated text. Uncoated paper contrasts nicely with the smooth gloss of foil stamping. Coated papers are rarely foil stamped because of possible gas trapping between the foil and surface coating. Avoid heavily textured papers that can reveal a reverse impression on the opposite side.

- Create a foil-stamped comp of your idea. Foil stampers can provide samples of leaf or foil colors on your chosen stock. Companies that specialize in specialty stocks for your laser printer also carry foils that you can fuse to paper.

- Combine foil stamping with embossing to achieve a raised, glossy image.

- Test a foil-stamped comp as a safety measure. Foil-stamped paper generally will pass through a laser printer without puckering or bubbling.

- Don't place foil stamp/embossed art too close to the edge of a sheet to avoid wrinkling or puckering of the paper.

- Avoid papers that have been coated with varnish or inks with wax content.

- Avoid placing design elements too close together since foils tend to spread or fill in across narrow spaces.

- Avoid tight kerning and fine type, such as super condensed, because they are likely to fill with foil.

- Consider using foil tints. When pastelling or tinting (with foil) to achieve light

hues or subtle effects, choose a tint or pastel that is a close complement to the paper color for a two-tone look.

Guidelines for Embossing

- Use a rough-textured paper. Embossing tends to smooth out a paper's surface.

- Avoid printing type on the opposite side of your sheet, over the reversed, embossed image.

- Use a larger-than-usual type size and space type out to provide room for bevel-edged embossing.

- Recycle the die. After the expense of making the die, an emboss run costs about the same as a single-color press run.

- Provide the proper mechanical art. Halftones cannot be used as art for single-level embossing dies. For three-dimensional, sculptured dies, provide black-and-white art, a photograph or detailed rendering.

- Provide clear directions. For multilevel or sculptured dies, indicate the appropriate levels.

- Oversize the original art by $1/16$. The beveled or curved sides of the emboss cause the finished image to appear smaller than the original.

- Make rules at least 2 points.

- Avoid thin, tightly grouped lines, small type, and type with pointed serifs that may cause distortions in the paper.

- Consider what you're embossing. Designs should not be so high as to be crushed in duplicating, word processing or mailing equipment.

Types of Varnishes

Varnish is applied in two ways. Wet-trap varnishing is applied as the last color on the press, while the ink is still wet. This is your least expensive option because it does not require a separate press run. Dry-trap varnishing is applied as a separate run, after the ink has dried.

- Use a UV-cured finish for the most durable surface. Use it on magazine and brochure covers, pocket folders, packaging and other items that require a surface finish that can withstand frequent handling.

- Use an aqueous or water-based finish for product packaging. Printers who specialize in packaging and greeting cards have it; some other commercial printers do, too. Gloss and durability are close to UV finishes.

- Use a press-applied varnish to enjoy the greatest aesthetic effects. It is the least expensive — only slightly more expensive than conventional inks. A press-applied varnish doesn't require special equipment and can generally be applied within a single press run. It can be mixed with ink to further reduce cost as well as easily tinted with conventional inks. Choose between dull (to provide contrast against a glossy surface) or gloss (to contrast with dull surfaces). Don't choose this varnish as a means of protection.

- Don't overlook clear foil stamping as an alternative to spot varnishing, for providing a glossy coating over inks, or as an undercoat on uncoated papers.

Guidelines for Using Varnishes

- The varnish must be compatible with the press and drying method, the inks and paper.

- Coated papers yield the best varnish effects because of their smooth surfaces and excellent holdout.

- Don't request varnish to add gloss or dramatic effects to uncoated text or cover papers. Their rough surfaces and greater absorbency interfere.

- Use matte varnish, not gloss, for protection of dark colors, solids or high-density illustrations on uncoated stock. A spot matte varnish can be applied over photographs printed with process color to subtly change the contrast. A matte undercoat may improve ink holdout.

- Make sure you get a nonyellowing varnish for projects such as posters that will be exposed to light over a period of time.

- Varnish used on food packaging must be low odor and nontoxic.

- Specify imprintable varnish (waxfree varnish that can take impressions) if a varnished piece will be imprinted later. Also specify imprintability for folders if glue will later be applied to tabs or labels attached to the folders.

- When designing a catalog cover or other piece that will be handled extensively, either order the hardest dull varnish available or design the piece so varnished areas will get handled the least.

- Foil stamped over varnish may bubble.

- Varnish tends to deepen the color of the underlying ink. Check with your printer on the amount of change that will occur. You may need to spec lighter tints to get the colors you want.

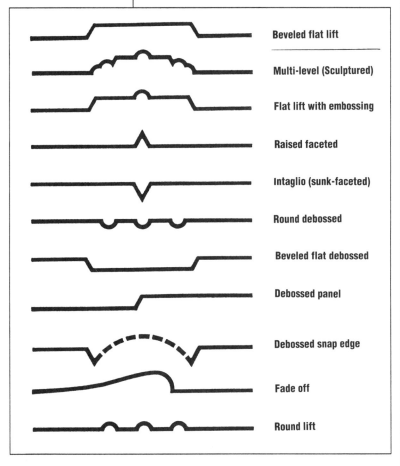

Beveled flat lift

Multi-level (Sculptured)

Flat lift with embossing

Raised faceted

Intaglio (sunk-faceted)

Round debossed

Beveled flat debossed

Debossed panel

Debossed snap edge

Fade off

Round lift

Embossing symbols

PAPERS FOR PRINTING PROCESSES

Most of the kinds of papers listed in the table are available as recycled papers also. Remember to check how any process and paper will perform when subjected to the high heat if the finished piece will be used for laser printing or photocopying.

Printing Process	Paper
Die Cutting	25%, 50%, 100% Cotton Bond/Writing papers Uncoated Text—Heavier weights are better Uncoated Cover—Heavier weights are better Coated Text—Heavier weights are better Coated Cover—Heavier weights are better
Laser Die Cutting	25%, 50%, 100% Cotton Bond/Writing papers Uncoated Text—Lighter weights are better Uncoated Cover—Lighter weights are better Coated Text—Lighter weight, matte or dull finish only Coated Cover—Matte or dull finish only
Embossing	Bond/Writing—24# preferred Uncoated Cover—Heavier weight, soft felt and textured stocks Uncoated Text—Heavier weight, soft felt and textured stocks Coated Text—Heavier weight, matte; high gloss or dull finish only when emboss is not extremely deep Coated Cover—Heavier weight, matte; high gloss or dull finish only when emboss is not extremely deep
Engraving	24#, 25%, 50%, 100% Cotton Bond/Writing, wove or laid finish Uncoated Text Uncoated Cover

Printing Process	Paper
Laser Engraving	Bond/Writing—20% and 24# Uncoated Text Uncoated Cover—No more than 110#
Foil Stamping	Bond/Writing Uncoated Text Uncoated Cover Coated Text—check with printer before using; gas trapping between foil and paper surface can be a problem Coated Cover—check with printer before using; gas trapping between foil and paper surface can be a problem.
Holograms	Mylar—2 ml thick with adhesive backing Foil stamping base—can then be applied to papers listed above
Letterpress	Bond/Writing Uncoated Text Uncoated Cover Coated Text Coated Cover Industrial Papers
Silk Screening/ Screen Printing	Bond/Writing Uncoated Text Uncoated Cover Coated Text Coated Cover Industrial Papers, such as Kraft and Chipboard
Thermography	Bond/Writing Coated Text Coated Cover Uncoated Text Coated Cover

- If it's important that the gloss level over a photo be uniform, a second hit of varnish may be needed to compensate for differences in ink coverage.

- If you can't afford to pay for an extra color but need a varnish, save a pass through the press by having the varnish mixed directly into the ink.

Printing on Industrial Papers

- Industrial surfaces can tear the blanket and damage other parts on an offset press. Check with your offset printer first when contemplating printing on an industrial stock, but be prepared to consider other printing alternatives such as letterpress or screen printing.

- Letterpress works great on chipboard and kraft paper but will crush the fluting of corrugated cardboard. Screen printing works well on industrial papers.

- Always request a drawdown when printing on industrial paper to test for ink opacity, color density and contrast as well as to check how the paper works for the project.

- Suggest that your printer try a varnish or a white undercoat to seal the sheet if there is trouble with color application.

- Foil stamping and embossing on industrial papers generally will not harm equipment. But because industrial papers are not assigned a basis weight or rated on their ability to take a finishing technique, it's hard to predetermine what the effect will be. It's best to try a test run first to determine if an industrial stock will perform as expected.

- When printing on industrial paper, especially items such as premade boxes creased or scored for folding, a break in the printed image can occur. If possible, try to plan breaks in your design to fit those creases.

- During screen printing, the printer may have to adjust pressure and/or ink viscosity because of irregularities in the paper.

- Screen-printed, UV-cured inks have a high-gloss finish that contrasts nicely with the rough surface of industrial stocks, but the high absorbancy of industrial stocks makes these inks difficult to work with and results can often be unpredictable. Most screen printers recommend printing with flat, solvent-based inks on industrial papers.

Printing on Recycled Papers

Recycled papers have come a long way toward matching the printability standards of virgin papers. Nevertheless, some possible problems to resolve with your printer include:

- Inconsistencies in the fibers and blemishes can cause mottled ink and other problems on press.

- Particles and other imperfections in the sheet can tear the blanket or ruin the dies on an offset press.

- The shorter fibers that make up recycled sheets can soak up ink like a blotter, causing appreciable dot gain on halftones and tints.

- Recycled sheets may not have the opacity, whiteness or brightness of virgin sheets.

- The shorter fibers in these sheets result in paper with less strength and rigidity.

Think Inks When Printing Transparent Inks

The transparency of standard offset inks—cyan, magenta, yellow and black—is what lets halftone dot patterns blend. Keep in mind these facts about inks:

- You can print one transparent ink over another to produce a third color, for the cost of a two-color job.

- You can specify any percentage of transparent ink to create a tint of that color.

- You can specify any percentage of color and combine it with one or more colors to create a new color.

- You can alter the transparent color by printing it on colored stock.

- You can enhance a color's value by applying two hits of the color—in other words, printing the color twice. You'll pay for an additional press pass, though.

Opaque Inks

Opaque pigments reflect light and are denser than transparent ink.

- If you are printing opaque ink onto pre-printed or colored stock, the heavy pigments help prevent the underlying color from showing through. However, these inks are not totally opaque; *very* dark-toned papers will influence their color.

- Opaque inks are your best choice when trying to achieve true color matches on colored papers.

- An undercoat of opaque white can achieve the effect of white, coated stock. But if you then overprint a photo, you may be surprised by the final effect. Whites in the photo may end up too stark because of the underprinting.

- You can combine opaque and transparent inks for many interesting effects.

Metallic Inks

Be prepared for metallics to print less predictably than other inks; the variables in their formula are harder to control than those of other inks.

- Use coarser screens to avoid plugging and globbing in halftones and tints.

- Overprint with varnish to protect against scuffing.

- Print on premium paper, a tightly woven surface offers best results.

- If true reflectivity is your goal, and you can't afford to print metallic inks on coated stock or with a varnish, consider foil stamping.

- Consider metallic silver on dark text and cover stocks for a more opaque underlay than you can get with opaque white.

Fluorescent Inks

These perky colors can be used alone or mixed with other inks to add sparkle to your design.

- Add fluorescent inks to conventional inks to create more brilliant colors.

- Substitute a transparent ink with a fluorescent to brighten a printed piece.

Vegetable-Based Inks

Soy-based inks and combination soy-, linseed- and corn-based inks (the vegetable additive replaces 20 to 25 percent of the petroleum) have come a long way in the past two years. Their on-press performance, color and level of gloss is now up to the standards of traditional 100 percent petroleum-based inks. Their major advantage over petroleum-based inks is that they clean up more easily and are more environmentally friendly. Common product names for these inks are Agritech and Envirotech.

Here are some considerations to keep in mind when contemplating the use of vegetable-based inks:

- Most colors, including fluorescents, are comparable to standard match colors, so standard matching systems can be used to spec colors for vegetable-based inks.

- Metallics are not available as vegetable-based inks.

- Halftones should be shot with a 10 to 15 percent reduction in dot size to compensate for some dot gain on press.

- Some printers are still reluctant to use vegetable-based inks, mostly because they represent a change.

Cost-Saving Printing Techniques
Split-Fountain Printing

This process involves dividing off one or more offset press ink fountains so they can print additional colors. Blending of these colors occurs on press, creating new colors that gradate between the original colors. The appearance of many colors is achieved for little more than the cost associated with printing the original number of colors.

Multicolor Effects on a Low Budget

"Overlaying two colors of ink in varying screen combinations can help create the impression of many colors with a two-color press run. If you add a split fountain to that, you'll come up with even more combinations. Using three to four colors at two stations on the press can produce the effect of a four-color job.

"When you choose to print a job with split fountains, there will always be some clean-up charges to prevent the colors from muddying up on press, but it's still a lot cheaper than a traditional four-color run."

Lori Siebert, *founder and principal of Cincinnati-based Siebert Design Associates, is a nationally recognized graphic designer and author of two books on design and layout.*

▶

Keep the following considerations in mind when contemplating a split-fountain run:

- It's most cost efficient to consider a split-fountain for jobs with a run between 5,000 and 100,000. Setup charges make a run of under 5,000 less cost efficient, and because split-fountain inks eventually run together and contaminate each other, a press washup is usually required on longer runs. Cleanup and setup charges are incurred, and you risk the possibility of variations in the blending after this is done.

- Consider using split fountains when trying to achieve a vignetted or airbrushed effect. It can be less expensive than commissioning an airbrush artist to do a piece of work that would have to be color separated and run in four colors.

- Don't forget to reserve a fountain for black or whatever your accent and/or text color(s) will be.

- Combine solid colors with a clear base for gradated effect that goes from heavy to light color saturation.

- When comping a split-fountain piece, use spray markers to simulate the effect of gradated and blended inks.

- Check with your printer to find out how many fountains can be used and broken down into splits to achieve desired blends.

- Because color blending occurs on press, duplicating the effect of a split fountain with a color key or other proof is virtually impossible. Prepare to be on hand for a press check to be sure you get the effect you're looking for.

Short-Run Options

Low-budget, short-run projects (under five thousand) that don't involve a lot of sophisticated graphics and inking can be handled by the following:

Photocopy centers: If your project is a simple, 8½ × 11- to 11 × 17-inch, text-heavy, black-and-white job, shops that use high-grade copiers are your best option. Halftone reproduction from veloxes is also possible, and collating is a cinch. Paper is always limited to whatever can run through a copier.

Quick-print shops: Go to a quick-print shop that uses a combination of copiers and small offset presses. They can do one- and two-color jobs and jobs requiring bleeds; they also offer better halftone reproduction than a photocopier. Although they can accommodate cover stocks and papers with a heavier basis weight, few are equipped to tackle coated papers.

Letterpress: For small runs of one thousand or less, letterpress can actually cost less than offset. It will definitely give you a rich look for less cost than other methods.

Screen printing: Handmade and industrial papers and other surfaces can be printed on with this method. The effect of several colors can be achieved by blending inks on the screen to simulate a split-fountain effect. Screen printing inks are more opaque, offering the option of dark and brightly colored papers and substrates.

Chapter 18

Special Production Considerations

Letterheads
Before and During Printing, Check:

❏ All information is accurate at the blueline stage. Avoid embarrassment and the expense of reprinting by checking and double-checking the accuracy of phone numbers, addresses and spelling.

❏ All type is there. Check this on the mechanical or film, the proofs, a press check and a sample of the finished piece. Type can easily get lost.

❏ The actual type is good quality and reproducing clearly. Check this at all stages, too.

❏ Type is not obscured by background colors. Paper color and texture can affect how dark a tint looks, so keep checking.

❏ All artwork is there. Check the mechanical to make sure that all visuals and graphics are clearly marked. Verify that you have included all artwork—stats, line art, halftones and so on—with the mechanical or that all graphics files are on the disk that's going to the service bureau. Get a proof from the service bureau before the piece goes to the printer; check it carefully and then use it to check the work on press.

❏ Background graphics or tints in the message area are not too dark for the typewritten message to be read.

❏ All colors are accurately reproduced and what you expected. Check both proofs and printed samples to be sure, especially if your design calls for a gradation with many steps or surprinting colors.

❏ Colors on each component of the stationery system match the others. While a perfect match isn't always possible, you want the pieces to appear part of a unified system. If all the components won't be printed at the same time or by the same printer, all later components should be matched to the piece that was printed first. This is critical if you are using a different stock for one or more components. If the budget and schedule allow it, ask the printer(s) for a drawdown of the ink on the actual stock before printing begins.

❏ Make sure that reversed rules and other graphics are not filling in from ink oversaturation with a resulting loss of detail. To achieve good coverage on uncoated stock printers often compensate for additional absorbency of the paper by overinking.

❏ Bleeds are properly trimmed. Check that you have clearly marked all bleeds on the mechanicals, and that you have allowed ⅛ to ¼ inch beyond the trim size for them. Ask to see trimmed samples before all the paper is cut.

❏ Special elements such as thermography, engraving, foil stamping and embossing are printing properly. Check proofs and printed samples for problems. If an element such as an embossed logo could be damaged by a run through the press, verify that all other processes are completed before that one is run.

❏ When doing a press check, hold paper up to the light to check for ruptures in the paper and pinholes. Make sure edges are crisp and square.

❏ If return address, BRM-related graphics or other copy is positioned close to the envelope edge, make sure at your press check that it isn't running off the edge.

❏ Return address area on envelope is not obscured by background colors, tints or graphics.

❏ The space below and on either side of the delivery address line should be clear of all nonaddress printing.

❏ Regulations for business reply envelopes are very stringent. Make sure that FIMs, indicia, horizontal bars and POSTNET bar codes fall *exactly* as they are positioned on your mechanical.

❏ If you're having the envelope converted, check that graphics and other items are printed exactly as they are positioned on the mechanical. Assure there will be no surprises when the envelope is finally trimmed and glued by trimming and folding a dummy from bluelines and again with press sheets at your press check, following the printed trim and fold guidelines.

For more information on the effects of printing colored inks, see pages 38-40.

Identity Systems

Before and During Printing, Check:

❏ Color consistency. Try to attend a press check for each item. Bring samples of all completed items in the system to ensure that the project on press matches all other components. If the client will handle the printing, supply type, paper and color specs, including color swatches in a manual that also specifies sizes, positioning and use of the various elements.

❏ All information is accurate at the blueline stage. Check with your client to be sure listings and other information are up-to-date.

❏ The type on every piece is correct. It's easy to assume that the type must be correct because you've copied every character from one layout file to the next. But mistakes happen.

❏ All artwork is there. Check each mechanical to make sure that all visuals and graphics are clearly marked. Verify that you have included all artwork with the mechanicals or that all graphics files are on the disks going to the service bureau. Get proofs from the service bureau before the piece goes to the printer; check it carefully and then use it to check the work on press.

❏ Logo usage and placement are consistent. Check each mechanical to make sure that no changes have occurred. This is critical if not all pieces are being printed at the same time. If any changes were made at late stages in the design process, make sure that every piece has been changed. If the client will handle the printing, supply stats of the logo in

a variety of sizes and include clear directions for acceptable usage.

❏ Printing is being done on the right materials. Changes in the type of paper or in the kind or quality of material used to make clothing can result in pieces that don't fit the overall look of the identity system. Color matching can also be adversely affected.

❏ Any special processes such as thermography, engraving, foil stamping and embossing are printing properly. Verify with the printer(s) before work starts that these processes will work with the surfaces and inks you have chosen.

How to Ensure That Colors Match Between Items

- When checking for color consistency, have other components of the identity system on hand. Check and compare items to project on press in daylight, fluorescent and incandescent lighting to be sure color is accurate.

- Compensate for color shifts when switching from printing corporate materials on one color or kind of stock to another.

- Make sure color is consistent when matching a number of different items—such as a plastic container or a logo on a letterhead that will also be applied to uniforms—by supplying everyone involved in color matching with swatches of the corporate color in typical applications.

- Use an ink and color system specially designed for color matching different materials. Minneapolis-based Colorcurve Systems, Inc., is one company that specializes in achieving color matches for cross industrial purposes. (For more information call or write Colorcurve Systems, Inc., 123 N. Third St., Minneapolis MN 55401; (612)338-0833.)

- Because screen-printing inks are not mixed according to a swatch and matching system as offset inks are, screen

▶

printers are accustomed to following a client's direction in mixing pigments. Let your printer know that you want to be on hand to ensure that the color match is accurate.

When You Need an Envelope Conversion

You should have envelopes converted—printed flat, then folded and glued—if your design involves any of the following:

- Your print area runs across the fold or seam of the envelope.

- A foil-stamped or embossed image is being used.

- Four-color process is involved.

- You want to print a solid color or tint on the inside of the envelope.

- You want a bleed along the short edges of the envelope.

Brochures

What to Check for Before and During Printing

☐ Watch for flaws in negatives, impurities such as dust, pinholes in film on proofs and on printed samples. These will show up as black specks.

☐ Be sure color is true to what was specced. Check this on color keys or chromalins and then during the press check. Also check that elements picked up from other sources are stripped in where specified.

☐ Omissions of type, isolated graphic elements. These items are often overlooked or inadvertently masked out, particularly if they're set away from long passages of text. Pay particular attention to folios that are frequently missed when a job is stripped up. If this is a revision make sure that all copy has been changed.

☐ Areas of isolated type are overprinted or reversed out properly. Colored type that overprints an image can also be particularly hard to spot on a blueline. When proofing, compare blueline with

mechanical to be sure all items are included. Check a sample before the brochure is delivered to the client.

☐ Pay special attention to covers and pages that carry addresses, phone numbers and other contact information to be sure that all of this information is accurate at the blueline stage.

☐ All information on pricing or spec lists must be correct and legible. A mistake here could be quite expensive for the client. Give careful attention to the financial sections of annual reports, especially if you had to rekeyboard these, if several rounds of changes were made, or if the copy needed a lot of work during typesetting.

☐ Crossovers that jump the gutter are properly aligned. Rule edges of images, background color and baseline of headline type to be sure they line up on the mechanical. Although you should check alignment of these elements on the proof, crossovers require precision stripping, printing and folding and must, therefore, be checked at each step.

☐ Proper registration of four-color separations. Check with a loupe to be sure edges are clean and dots from one color don't overhang. Compare proofs with original photographs and transparencies to be sure color is true to the original. Make sure images are not fuzzy, color balance is correct, and edges of screen tints and solid colors are clean and sharp.

☐ Color on press is true to proofs. Be especially wary of neutrals where a 5 percent shift in color can turn maroon into brown or gray into tan.

☐ Type that overprints images is legible. Pay particular attention to areas where colored type has been specced to be sure it contrasts enough with surrounding four-color areas. Check areas where images have been ghosted behind type to be sure that type stands out prominently.

☐ All visuals are positioned as indicated,

particularly when dealing with similar product items or mug shots. Double-check all FPO stats or prints and verify that each is correctly labeled on the mechanical and the art tag.

❑ Reverses printed with process inks are in register. Registration that is off by a hairline can cause some fill of color in a character or cause one color to hang over the edge of the letters in a word. Oversaturating the press can also contribute to thinning of letterforms.

❑ Images within a photo that run as an outline with the background "knocked out" are included in their entirety. All four process colors have been masked beyond the image edge.

❑ Posterizations, mezzotints and other photo treatments that are made when photos are converted to film achieve the desired effect. Have color keys or chromalins made of duotones, tritones and quadratones.

❑ No streaks or ghosts appear on press sheets. Check for changes in color density. Check for hickeys. A hickey that appears consistently in a run may indicate the need for a new blanket or plate.

❑ Check imposition of pages, that folios and other consistent graphics are correctly placed by folding and comparing with mechanical.

❑ Check allowance for gutters, especially on a piece that will be saddle stitched. Allowances should be made for wider gutters on outer pages, narrower gutters on innermost pages. Have your printer make up a blueline dummy to ensure that allowances have been made for this.

❑ Make sure guidelines such as trim marks, folding and scoring lines and die-cutting indications are included when bluelines are produced. If possible, have your printer make up a blueline dummy to be sure these guidelines are accurately placed.

❑ If your printer hasn't supplied you with a trimmed dummy, use a ruler to draw trim and fold lines, following printed guidelines.

Special Problems With Folding Coated Papers

To avoid cracks when folding:

- Plan the fold so it is in the direction of the paper's grain. Also run the paper on press *grain long* (with the grain of the paper parallel to the width of the press cylinder) to ensure less cracking when scoring and folding.

- Score the fold. Letterpress scoring is particularly effective in guarding against cracks on cast-coated papers.

- Use one-sided coating if possible.

Special Considerations With Coated Papers

- Trim with coated side up to protect against cracks.

- Enhance the high-gloss look of cast-coated papers with gloss or semigloss transparent inks.

- Protect against scuffing and fingerprints by using varnish to protect areas with heavy ink coverage.

- Run a dull varnish on the areas where text will appear if you want to use a high-gloss stock for photo reproduction but want to reduce the resulting glare.

- Some coated stocks may not work well for perfect binding. They may be too slick for the glue to adhere well. Check with your binder before speccing a slick, glossy stock for a publication such as a catalog that will get a lot of use.

Special Folding and Binding Considerations

- Ensure that a barrel-folded brochure folds within itself properly.

- Unbalanced folds are the most difficult for the binder to execute properly.

- Any piece with more than five folds may be impossible for your binder to fold properly. If your design is this complex,

▶

consult your binder before going any further.

- The paper weights a binder can easily fold usually range from 50 to 80 lb.; anything heavier or lighter will cost extra.

- Beware of the creep. When a press sheet is folded into signatures, especially with saddle stitching, the inside pages creep away from the spine and stick out beyond the edges of the other pages. Using thick paper or inserting too many signatures can cause creep, as can making margins too narrow or using bleeds on inner pages. Make a paper dummy out of the same stock with the same number of pages and work out the margins, especially the gutter.

Newsletters

What to Check for Before and During Printing

❏ The right paper has been used. You should have specced a sheet that is opaque enough for good type and photo reproduction but lightweight enough to avoid excessive mailing costs.

❏ All type is included. Check mechanicals, proofs and press sheets to be sure nothing has been masked off when the job was stripped or it may be trimmed off at the completion of the job. Pay particular attention to folios and isolated areas of type.

❏ Type is legible and reproducing clearly. Check at the blueline stage. If type appears fuzzy, check the negatives. Check the plate if films aren't being used.

❏ Date and issue number are correct.

❏ The mailing permit, return address and other mailing information are correct.

❏ Be sure all visuals are included with job and are identified and coded with their position on the mechanicals. If you're working with computer files, get a proof from the service bureau before the job is sent to the printer.

❏ Color is correct. Have your printer make a color key to indicate where color will

be on a two-color job or have him indicate on bluelines where the second color will appear.

❏ Halftones and line art meet your standards for reproduction quality.

❏ All visuals are in the right places; all sidebars and pull quotes are properly positioned.

For an explanation of and guidelines for offset printing, see pages 144-147. Newsletter design is covered in chapter 10, pages 87-100.

Folding, Binding and Trimming Considerations

- Indicia and return address must be properly placed on mailing panel when a self-mailing newsletter is folded. Manually trim and fold blueline dummy and press sheets to be sure all graphic items, trim and fold guidelines are positioned properly.

- Check to be sure bleeds fall at least ⅛ inch beyond trim lines. Make sure type positioned close to the page edge, particularly folios, falls no closer than ⅜ inch from edge.

- When folding coated paper that has been printed with large areas of solid color, score on opposite side of fold to avoid cracking.

- Basis weight and thickness of paper have some bearing on how many pages can be folded; generally thicknesses of more than twelve pages will start to present a problem.

Ads

Before Sending Ads to Publisher, Check:

❏ All type is clear and legible. Copy is accurate, no typos or misspellings.

❏ Ad dimensions are accurate and in accordance with dimensions specified on rate card.

❏ Copy falls within "live area" dimensions of ad. If ad is a bleed, bleed areas meet bleed dimension requirements.

❏ Coupon instructions are clear and accurate. If supplying films, check to be sure all information is included on coupon after films have been shot.

❑ Two-page spreads requiring crossovers of visuals and graphics are aligned.

❑ Cropmarks coincide with dimension requirements.

❑ Copy of insertion order is included to verify schedule.

❑ All items are clearly labeled with your firm's name and address, contact information and where to return originals.

Designing ads is covered in chapter 11, pages 101-107.

To Ensure Good Photo Reproduction:

• Follow the publication's screening requirements.

• If the publisher will be shooting the halftone for your ad, include more than one exposure of your photo so that the experts can select the best one.

• Try to supply a photo with less contrast for newspaper use.

• Request prepress proofs of a color ad. To check color, get a Chromalin (DuPont) or a Matchprint (3M) proof. For a less accurate color proof you can request a color key. Check the layout of elements in your ad but not the color accuracy with a thermal print.

Packaging

Before and During Printing, Check:

❑ All type is clear and legible. Check small type on mechanicals. Make sure patent information, content information, net weight, etc. are accurate and readable.

❑ All type is included. Check proofs to be sure a number or a line of small type hasn't been inadvertently masked off.

❑ Trademark and registered trademark symbols have been included. Check that they are on the mechanical. Make sure they appear on proofs and films.

❑ Color is accurately depicted on packaging for paints, fabric dyes, cosmetics and other products where accuracy is critical.

❑ UPC code is legible and correctly placed on mechanicals, proofs and on press checks. Keyline a window around it on your mechanical if the rest of the container or labels will be on a color field, and spec this area for no color. Check color proofs and on press to make sure it appears on a white ground and hasn't been reversed or overprinted on a color.

❑ Reversed and overprinted type is legible.

❑ Trim guidelines are correct. Make sure trim guidelines for labels are in accordance with label dimensions and borders are even. Check trim for boxes by making a photocopy of mechanical, trimming, folding and assembling a dummy. Make sure trim lines are included on proofs and press copies. Cut up a printed sample if possible; otherwise, measure it.

❑ Fold guidelines are correct. Make a dummy and check to be sure graphics are centered between the panels on a box. Be sure fold guidelines are included on proofs and press sheets. Fold a printed sample if possible; otherwise, measure it.

❑ Die-cuts are positioned correctly. Make sure areas to be die-cut are clearly indicated on the mechanical. This is especially important when producing custom labels for a container. Check proofs and press sheets as well as mechanical to be sure die-cuts are where they are supposed to be.

❑ Color hasn't been specced for areas that will be glued. Glue doesn't adhere well to inked surfaces.

❑ Broad areas of color are durable. Use coated paper and have packaging laminated to prevent cracks and rub-offs. Get a printed sample of a box before it's folded and try to ruin the color.

Special Production Considerations

• Check for color consistency on labels, wrappers, bags and boxes. Make sure it's consistent on proofs and, if possible, on press checks. It's especially important to be sure components match when more than one type of package is used for a product.

- Check for accurate color in plastic containers. Compare to color chips or other plastic containers used for packaging.

- Make sure product depictions are correct, color accurate and true to actual product. Check this on transparency, color proofs and press checks. Don't take a chance on depicting a product inaccurately and having it construed as consumer fraud.

- Check for proper four-color registration, flaws in negatives and other imperfections on four-color proofs. Use a loupe to be sure films are accurate and of superior quality. Try to ensure that color registration is consistent with that of films on press run, but be aware that it's hard to maintain on long runs, particularly with flexography, where registration tends to be less exact in general.

Chapter 19

Proofing

Staying Efficient With Technology
"We started working on Macintoshes quite awhile ago, and with the Macintosh it's been two years since we've shown the art boards for an annual report to a client. We go straight to film. We have a Techtronics color printer and we show the client a color proof of every page that we've generated on this printer. Just before we go to press we show them a [Linotronic] L-300 proof—it's like a blueline, and that's what the client signs off on."

Mike Zender *is founder and principal of Zender Associates, an award-winning, Cincinnati-based design studio.*

How to Mark-Up a Proof

- If you lack technical knowledge, state the result you want, not how to achieve it.

- Be specific. It's not enough to say "Re-proof—see original." Instead, say, "Make blue darker—see original."

- Be concise. Specify only what is wrong and use as few words as possible.

- Circle the problem area but don't cover the actual problem.

- Keep comments well spaced; draw lines from circled area to the comment.

- If corrections are serious, extreme or extensive, request a second proof.

What to Look for on Bluelines

- ❏ Sharpness. Check—with a magnifying glass, if necessary—to be sure that all areas of detail are crisp.

- ❏ Spots, marks, flaws, flecks and scratches. If they aren't on your mechanical, they indicate flaws in the negatives.

- ❏ Broken screens. Check for disruption of dot pattern, white specks.

- ❏ Position. Check visuals are where you indicated they should be.

- ❏ Cropping and scaling. Be sure that all visuals are the right sizes and that they are positioned properly within the holding lines.

- ❏ Flopping and flipping. Check that no photos or illustrations are reversed from left to right or turned upside down.

- ❏ Type. Be sure there are no white specks in the type, that no type is missing, and that type color doesn't change dramatically. Check for correct placement of copy.

- ❏ Impurities. Check for pinholes in the film, keyline marks that should have been omitted, and obvious dust on the film.

- ❏ Borders. Be sure color and position are correct.

- ❏ Folding/Scoring/Trims. Check for

proper placement, consistent with your mechanical, particularly when paginating a document.

- ❏ Unwanted additions.

- ❏ Sign off. The job won't go ahead without your written approval. Remember to mark "okay as is" if you have no changes, "okay with changes marked" or "make changes and submit second proof" to make clear what must happen.

Color Proofs

Types of Proofs and How They Differ
The type of proof you see will depend on the type of piece you're printing and the number of colors being used.

Blueline (or Dylux): Method of proofing one- or two-color films, where color representation isn't necessary. Used for checking position of elements, pagination, nicks in photography and type and so forth.

Velox (or KIND): Photographic print made from a negative to check halftone quality. Offers more clarity than a blueline but is usually more expensive. Usually used exclusively for judging sharpness of detail and overall quality of halftone films, rather than for checking type, pagination, etc.

High-End Color Inkjet Printer: Digital color printers, made primarily by Iris Graphics and Stork Bedford B.V. and available at some service bureaus, that produce accurate color reproduction from computer files. Can print proofs on paper used for a project. Because these proofs do not show color layers or halftone dots, they can't be used to check trapping or moires.

Direct Digital Color Proof: A fairly new technology that accepts Scitex, Hell or Crosfield files (not PostScript) and outputs them on paper with results similar to those obtained from an integral proof. A DDCP system cannot accurately reflect what the final film of halftones will look like because the mechanism that produces halftone dots is not the same as that of an imagesetter. This method is comparatively expensive and not widely offered, but proofs can be obtained quickly because no film is made.

Overlay Proof: Although there are several brands, these are often called Color-Keys after the 3M product; others are DuPont Croma Check and Enco. The oldest method of color proofing uses films (one for each color) overlaid in registration on white paper to show two to four colors. Color is not as accurate as in an integral proof. The many layers of film tend to make most colors look darker. Halftone dots are visible, so trapping and moires can be checked.

Integral Proof: These proofs are often known by their brand names: DuPont Chromalin, 3M Matchprint, Fuji ColorArt, Hoechst Pressmatch, Agfaproof and Kodak Signature. Common color-proofing alternative to the color key where layers of film are fused together into one final print. Allows for proofing on all black-and-white details (positioning, type, etc.) as well as judgments on four-color representation. A few of these systems will let you print the integral proof on the desired paper. Generally more expensive than an overlay proof.

Press Proofs: Proof run with the same paper, inks and plates to be used in the final printing on the actual press (most expensive type of proof) or on a similar one (less expensive). Although the results on a similar press won't be an exact match, the cost savings are generally the better trade-off. A progressive is a press proof showing each color of a job separately or several colors in combination. Press proofing is still the only way to proof work with metallic or other specialty inks or when effects with varnish, overlapping screens and finish are being tried. Press proofing is expensive and takes a great deal of time.

What to Look for on Color Proofs

❑ Omissions. Also make sure that nothing blocks the corners of the images.

❑ Additions. Check that nothing is there that shouldn't be.

❑ Spots and scratches. Specks and other marks in black, magenta, yellow or cyan can represent flaws in the negatives. Watch out for hickeys (a light halo around a dark blot).

❑ Registration. Check for fuzzy areas or a shadowy effect. If you think you've spotted a problem, check the registration mark. If it's correct, you'll see only black; if it's out of register, one or more other colors will show next to the black.

❑ Ghosts or streaks.

❑ Colors butting up against each other accurately. A gap of white paper may indicate a trapping problem or that the film was not properly fitted together.

❑ Check color bar. This will show if too much or too little of a color has been used.

❑ Color accuracy. Compare the original art with the proof using a lightbox or in a viewing booth equipped with 5,000K bulbs.

❑ Neutral areas. Check grays to be sure they're free from green, blue or reddish casts.

❑ Broken screens. In four-color photos, broken screens appear as areas where either magenta, cyan, black or yellow is missing.

❑ Background tints. Check for consistency throughout a project. Illustrations or photos appearing on these same pages can throw the tint off if the art requires a different amount of inking. Sometimes you will have to choose between a perfect match for the background tint and good reproduction of the art.

❑ Tints. Check all tints for moire or mottling. Check process ink tints against a tint chart. Check process colors and solids against tint chart, swatch book or approved proof.

❑ Trim and bleed. Check that trim marks are positioned accurately and that the bleed allowance is correct.

❑ Sharpness. Check—with a magnifying glass, if necessary—to be sure that all areas of detail are crisp.

▶

Computers and Proofing Responsibility

"Computers make designers lazy. They make clients lazy too. People today look at a laser-printed comp and assume the copy must be correct— someone must have *looked at the copy, right? But many designers just shrug their shoulders and claim it isn't their problem. They feel the client is responsible for all copy.*

"Just a few years ago you would have sent copy out for typesetting. A good type shop would not only produce beautiful type, they would catch grammar and spelling errors as well. Computers have forced designers to take on the responsibility of producing good type, yet some designers still refuse to take this responsibility seriously. It's essential that designers accept this responsibility and charge their client extra for these services. Those who don't are hurting the entire industry."

Michael J. Sullivan *is founder, president and artistic director of Imprimatur Design Systems, in Cambridge, Massachusetts, a full-range design firm that specializes in integrated media management. He frequently writes for graphic arts and information technology publications.*

❑ Position. Check that visuals are where you indicated they should be.

❑ Flopping and flipping. Check that no photos or illustrations are reversed or turned upside down.

❑ Size. Check that all visuals are the right sizes; you or someone at the prepress service may have made a scaling error.

❑ Type. Be sure there are no white specks in the type, that no type is missing, and that type color doesn't change dramatically.

❑ Impurities. Check for pinholes in the film, keyline marks that should have been omitted, and dust on the film.

❑ Borders. Be sure color and position are correct.

❑ Folding/Scoring/Gutter. Check for proper placement, consistent with your mechanical, particularly when paginating a document.

❑ Overall size. Check that the whole piece is the right size and that the live area within the trim marks is sized correctly.

❑ Sign off. The job won't go ahead without your written approval.

Typical Color Proof Corrections

• Too much contrast.

• Too little contrast.

• Loss of detail.

• Detail too hard.

• Detail too soft.

• Too much cyan.

• Too much magenta.

• Too much yellow.

• Too little cyan.

• Too little magenta.

• Too little yellow.

• Tint too dark. Lighten.

• Tint too light. Darken.

• Tint uneven.

• Type/art/color out of register.

• This area too (red/yellow/blue).

• Art crooked/flopped/upside down.

• Art on wrong page. Move to page *xx*.

What to Look for at a Press Check

❑ Special effects. Check that these are printing as you envisioned them.

❑ Varnish. Check whether this needs to be adjusted.

❑ Metallic ink. Check that the amount of sheen is acceptable.

❑ Effect of an ink color on colored paper. Check that this works the way you thought it would.

❑ Previous corrections. Make sure that all requested changes and corrections have been made.

❑ Paper. Check that the job is being printed on the right paper.

❑ Ink density. Check that colors are even and consistent.

❑ Registration. Make sure that changes in the paper during printing or how it is running through the press haven't affected registration.

❑ Color in critical areas. You should have caught and corrected problems in color reproduction during proofing, but dot gain, ink density and paper color can affect the job once it's on press.

Chapter 20

Wrapping Up the Job

Great Design Communicates

"Designers must be concerned first and foremost with communication. Those who follow the style/look/fashion path will find people treating them like home decorators — expensive luxuries that only the rich can afford. Likewise, those who overly concern themselves with production issues will become design factories with 'bang 'em out' for their motto. Only those designers whose concern is to maximize communication through the most appropriate vehicle will prosper in the years to come.

"Electronic tools can be a great ally in this endeavor, but the siren call of technology has been embraced by far too many who don't realize the consequences to themselves or to their industry."

Michael J. Sullivan *is founder, president and artistic director of Imprimatur Design Systems, in Cambridge, Massachusetts, a full-range design firm that specializes in integrated media management. He frequently writes for graphic arts and information technology publications.*

Review the Project at Its Completion

Was Your Overall Design Concept . . .

- Effective in getting the client's message across?

- Successful in soliciting the kind of response the client was looking for?

- The right format and size for communicating its message?

- Appropriate to the client's image?

- Appropriate to the message?

- Appropriate to its audience?

- In visual harmony with the client's other communication materials (if applicable)?

- Able to be produced effectively within the client's budget?

- Appropriate to the chosen method of reproduction?

Did Production Go Smoothly?

- Was the job completed on time? If not, where did production fall behind schedule?

- If the job fell behind schedule, was it because not enough time was allowed for a portion of the job?

- Was the job completed within budget? If not, where were the additional expenses incurred?

- Were there any surprises, such as a bill from a supplier that was considerably more than their estimate?

- Was the amount of time you spent on the job in keeping with what was charged to the client?

- Was computer-generated work compatible with vendors' and client's systems?

- Were there typographical errors? If so, were they the responsibility of the typesetter, proofreader or client?

- Were the typefaces appropriate to the column width and the amount of copy involved in the piece?

- Did the paper hold up to the reproduction demands of the job? Was texture appropriate? Did halftones have good clarity? Did embosses and/or die-cuts turn out well?

- Was the paper appropriate for the mailing weight, bulk and durability of the piece?

- Did photos, transparencies and illustrations reproduce as expected? If not, was there a problem with the originals or the films?

- Were illustrations and photography appropriate to the project's message and budget? Were they cropped and scaled in a way that made the most of them?

- Were illustrations and photographs positioned, sized and cropped as indicated? Were any images flopped?

- Were there any on-press errors? If color was uneven or reverses fuzzy, was it the fault of the pressman or the choice of paper? Was a blemish the result of a hickey or did somebody miss a problem in the films when checking proofs?

- Were inks opaque enough to achieve the desired effect on colored paper?

- Were there errors in the way the job was impositioned, trimmed or bound? Why did the misunderstanding occur? Was the mechanical inaccurate or instructions unclear?

- Were there other finishing errors, such as improper folds, ink cracks at fold lines, poor varnish application and so on?

How Did It Go With the Client?
Concept

- Was the client "in synch" with your concept from the very beginning, or did you struggle to develop a design strategy that you could both agree upon?

- Was the client quality or cost oriented?

- Was there a clear understanding at the outset of the project as to what you and your client expected from each other?

- Did the client supply you with all the

marketing materials you needed when you needed them and in a form that you could use?

- If you did your own research, what did you do well? What could you have done better?

- Did you communicate the reasoning behind your design decisions clearly?

- Did you show your client what this design solution could do in terms of improved sales, image or other relevant benefit?

- Should you have shown additional materials when presenting the concept so the client could better understand it? What would those have been?

- Did you keep meetings to a reasonable length? If not, what caused them to be so long? Could these problems have been avoided?

- What went especially well on this project? How could you do more of this in the future when working with this client?

Working Relationship

- Did the client come through with copy, photography and other items she agreed to furnish you in a timely manner?

- Did the client give you the quality of materials you needed to deliver an acceptable finished job?

- Did you clearly explain what you needed from the client and when? And did she understand what you wanted or just think she understood?

- Did you carefully proof all materials before they went to the client?

- Were client revisions extensive? If so, were they unreasonable? Was this a control issue or did the client fail to make it clear what you should do? How could you manage this situation better the next time?

- Did the client feel comfortable with work done by any illustrator, photographer, copywriter or editor who also did work on the job?

- Did the client stick to your agreed-upon schedule for making revisions and approving mechanicals and proofs?

- Was the client accessible when questions came up or approval was needed during the design and production of her project?

- In general, were there few disagreements or many?

- Were you pleased with the final product? If not, what went wrong?

- Was the client pleased? If not, why?

- Were invoices sent to the client paid on time and without challenge?

After the Job Has Been Completed and Delivered, Remember to Do the Following:

- ❏ Retrieve originals, mechanicals and other job-related items furnished to your service bureau, separator or printer.

- ❏ Carefully review all job materials to be sure nothing is missing.

- ❏ Return all client-furnished materials to the client or wherever client directs you to return them.

- ❏ Obtain extra printed samples of project for your files.

- ❏ Obtain copies of invoices for services your client has agreed to pay and make sure your vendors know your client's billing address for same.

- ❏ Place all copies of job-related items in appropriate job jacket.

- ❏ Remove all job files and mechanicals from the active work area and store them in a safe place.

- ❏ Invoice the client for your time and services.

- ❏ Write the client a thank-you letter (even if it was an unpleasant job) and ask what, if anything, could have made the job go more smoothly. You may learn something, even if you never want to work with that client again.

Glossary

Brightness. Measure of how much light is reflected off a printing paper.

Burn. In printing, to expose a plate or blueline to light. In photography, to add exposure to a specific area of a print.

Butt (aka Kiss). To join two elements edge to edge.

Chalking (aka Powdering). Condition in which the pigment in the ink does not adhere correctly to the printing surface, causing the ink to dust or chalk off. Caused by rapid absorption of the binding medium into improperly cured paper.

Color bars. Strip of colors printed on the edge of four-color process proofs to check registration of all colors and to evaluate ink density.

Color break. In multicolor printing, the point where one ink color stops and another begins.

Color separation (aka Separation). Separating art into the four process colors (yellow, magenta, cyan, black). These are screened to make four halftone negatives that are used to make a printing plate for each color.

Comb binding. Binding a publication by inserting the teeth of a flexible plastic center strip (comb) through holes in a stack of paper.

Converter. A business that makes boxes, displays and so on by combining printed sheets with other materials, such as industrial papers and pressboard.

Copy-dotting (aka Dot-for-dot reproduction). Photographic reproduction of halftones as line copy.

Crossover (aka Gutter bleed). When an image carries over from one page of a bound publication across the gutter to the opposite page.

Deboss. To produce a sunken image in the surface of paper by means of a die striking above the paper into a counter die below the paper.

Die. Sharp metal rules mounted on a letterpress used for die-cutting, or a metal block used for embossing, debossing or foil stamping.

Die-cutting. Using a sharp metal rule (die) to cut irregular shapes in paper.

Dot-for-dot reproduction. See Copy-dotting.

Dot gain (aka Dot spread). When dots print slightly larger on paper than they are on the negatives or plate, causing darker tones and colors in reproduction.

Double bump. To print two layers of ink for a single image.

Double burn. To expose two or more film images onto a single film to create a composite image.

Drawdown. A smear of ink deposited on paper by a smooth blade; used to evaluate color and density of the ink on a specific paper stock.

Dropout halftone. A halftone with no dots in the highlight areas, only the white of the paper.

Emboss. To produce a raised image on the surface of paper by means of a die striking from beneath the paper into a counter die above the paper.

Emulsion side. The dull, matte, emulsion-coated side of photographic film.

Engraving. Printing method using a metal plate (die) with an image carved into it.

Felt side. The top side of a sheet of paper, as opposed to the underside, or wire side.

Flat color. In printing, any color other than a process color.

Flat tint halftone (aka Fake duotone). A black halftone printed over a flat tint of a second color.

Flexography. Letterpress printing process using wraparound rubber or plastic plates and fast-drying inks; widely used in the packaging industry.

Fluorescent ink. Inks with fluorescent characteristics that result in a brilliant, glowing effect.

Foil stamping. Letterpress printing method using a die and thin metallic or pigmented film.

Fountain. Reservoir for ink or water on a printing press.

Gang printing (aka Gang run). A cost-saving run that prints any number of different jobs or multiple copies of the same job on one sheet of paper.

Gather (aka Collate). To assemble individual pages or signatures into the proper sequence for binding.

Ghosted halftone. See Screened-back halftone.

Ghosting. A condition in which a faint repeat of a printed image appears where it was not intended, usually above or below the actual image.

Grain. The direction in which the fibers are aligned in paper.

Gripper edge. The leading edge of a sheet of paper clamped by metal grippers as it is pulled through the printing press.

Gripper margin. The necessary amount of space that must be allowed on the paper's edge to keep the grippers from damaging the printed image.

Halftone. To reproduce continuous-tone copy (e.g., photographs) by photographing it through a fine screen to convert the image into a series of dots.

Halftone dot (dot). Units in a halftone that by their various sizes recreate a continuous-tone image.

Halftone screen. A fine-line photographic film screen used to convert continuous-tone copy into halftone dots for reproduction.

Head trim. A standard amount of space (usually ⅛ inch) at the tops of pages that is trimmed off.

Hickey. A halo-shaped imperfection on a printed piece caused by dust, dirt or any other particles in the ink or on the plate or the offset blanket.

Imposition. Arrangement of pages in a mechanical so that they will appear in proper sequence when folded, trimmed and bound.

Imprint. To print additional copy, usually a name and address, on a previously printed sheet.

Ink holdout (aka Holdout). Characteristic of paper that keeps the ink on the surface instead of being absorbed into the paper, causing the ink to lose luster and definition.

In-line. Any operation tied to the printing process, such as folding, trimming, embossing, gluing, etc.

Jogging. To straighten or align the edges of a stack of paper by vibration.

Knock out. See Mask out.

Line art. See Line copy.

Line conversion. Process of eliminating the middle tones from continuous-tone copy to convert it to line copy.

Line copy. Black-and-white copy with no gradation of tones.

Lines per inch (lpi). The number of lines or rows of dots in a screen, and therefore in a halftone, screen tint or separation.

Mask out (aka Knock out). To cover selected art or copy to protect it from being exposed to light.

Mezzotint. A random-dot patterned halftone produced to imitate the "burred" effect of fine art mezzotint etching.

Moire. Undesirable patterns in printed halftones caused by improperly aligned screens.

Mottling. Uneven or spotty impressions caused by too much pressure or unsuitable paper or ink; especially noticeable in large printed solids.

Multilith. A lithography press used for small jobs such as envelopes, cards and letterheads.

One-up, two-up, etc. Printing one (two, three, etc.) impression(s) at a time in a single job.

Outlined halftone. See Silhouette halftone.

Overprint. See Surprint.

Overrun. Sheets printed in excess of the quantity specified.

Perfect binding. Binding method in which the pages are glued together and trimmed to produce a flat-edged spine.

Photostat (aka Stat). A positive print transferred directly to paper with a photstat machine; used in mechanical to indicate size, cropping and position of continuous-tone copy.

Pinholes. Tiny holes in the emulsion of a photographic negative that must be opaqued before platemaking.

PMT—Photomechanical transfer (aka Diffusion transfer). Kodak trade name for a process used to make positive paper prints of line copy and halftones.

Press proof. A proof made on the actual production press with the paper and ink specified for the job; used to show exactly how the form will look when printed.

Press sheet. One sheet as it comes off the press.

Register. In printing, the correct positioning of one film or printing plate over another so that both give the effect of a single image.

Saddle stitching. Binding a publication with staples through the folding line in the center.

Score. Creasing paper or board so that it will fold more easily.

Screen density. Percentage of ink that is allowed to print through a specific screen.

Screen ruling. Number of rows or lines of dots per inch in a screen for a tint or halftone.

Screen tint (aka Tint). To reduce the ink density of a solid color by screening to simulate shading or a lighter color.

Screened-back halftone (aka Ghosted halftone). A halftone that has been screened to produce a very faint image.

Self-cover. The same paper stock is used on the cover as on the inside pages.

Side stitching. Binding a publication by stapling it through the spine from front to back.

Silhouette halftone (aka Outlined halftone). A halftone in which the background has been removed in order to outline or silhouette the image.

Slurring. A distortion of the printed image caused by halftone dots that appear elongated or smeared because of a drag or slipping in printing.

Split fountain. A printing technique in which two or more colors can be printed at the same time by dividing the ink fountain on the press.

Stock (aka Substrate). Any surface (usually paper) used to receive a printed image.

Stripping (aka Film assembly). Assembling negatives (type, art and other design elements) into position to prepare to make printing plates.

Surprint (aka Overprint). Printing one color over another; or to combine images from two different negatives by superimposing a second negative onto an already exposed first negative.

Thermography. Printing method that simulates engraving by combining resinous powder with a wet image and adding heat, resulting in raised images.

Trapping. The ability to print wet ink over already printed ink.

Typographic color. Relative lightness or darkness of typographic elements on a page, with darkest elements achieving most prominence and lightest achieving the least.

Wire side. The underside, or wrong side, of paper as opposed to the felt, or right side, of the paper.

Work and tumble. A printing technique that prints both sides of a shot with one plate. The sheet is printed on one side, then flipped from front to back to print the backside. Two different gripper edges are used.

Work and turn. A printing technique that prints both sides of a shot with one plate. The sheet is printed on one side, turned over from left to right to print the backside. The same gripper edge is used for both sides.

Index

List Title Index